ALEXANDER MACLAREN'S S[...]

By Alexander MacLaren

ISBN: 9781520500867

January 2017

Alexander MacLaren's Ephesians Commentary Contents

FOREWORD

Alexander MacLaren (1826-1910) was a Scottish Baptist Pastor in England. Born in Glasgow he grew up in Edinburgh while his father worked in Australia. It was during this time that MacLaren took Christ as his Saviour and underwent baptism sometime between the ages of 11 and 13. It was this change in his life that led him to train for ministry in the Baptist Church.

MacLaren devoted himself to his studies and particularly came under the influence of Dr. David Davies who was renowned Hebrew scholar. This interest developed into a passion for MacLaren and he threw himself into the study of both Greek and Hebrew. His reading was not just confined to his studies as he read widely in English literature.

His ministry began in Portland Chapel in Southampton where he worked for 12 years. It was here that his ability as a preacher became known. His reputation spread far and wide with many churches seeking to take him for their own minister. Eventually MacLaren received and accepted a call from Union Chapel in Manchester. This was his second and final pastorate where he served up until his retirement in 1903.

Such was MacLaren's stature amongst the Baptist churches that he served twice as the president of the Baptist Union of Great Britain.

Martyn Lloyd-Jones described Alexander MacLaren as having a golden hammer in relation to his ability to divide and split the passage. One tap from the hammer and it appeared that passage simply fell apart to the right portions.

As you read these messages allow the work of a master expositor enrich your soul as he opens God's word to you.

EPHESIANS 1

EPHESIANS CHAPTER 1 CONTENTS

SAINTS AND FAITHFUL

Ephesians 1:1.

That is Paul's way of describing a church. There were plenty of very imperfect Christians in the community at Ephesus and in the other Asiatic churches to which this letter went. As we know, there were heretics amongst them, and many others to whom the designation of 'holy' seemed inapplicable. But Paul classes them all under one category, and describes the whole body of believing people by these two words, which must always go together if either of them is truly applied, 'saints' and 'faithful.'

Now I think that from this simple designation we may gather two or three very obvious indeed, and very familiar and old-fashioned, but also very important, thoughts.

I. A Christian is a saint.

We are accustomed to confine the word to persons who tower above their brethren in holiness and manifest godliness and devoutness. The New Testament never does anything like that. Some people fancy that nobody can be a saint unless he wears a special uniform of certain conventional sanctities. The New Testament does not take that point of view at all, but regards all true believers in Jesus Christ as being, therein and thereby, saints.

Now, what does it mean by that? The word at bottom simply signifies separation. Whatever is told off from a mass for a specific purpose would be called, if it were a thing, 'holy.' But there is one special kind of separation which makes a person a saint, and that is separation to God, for His uses, in obedience to His commandment, that He may employ the man as He will. So in the Old Testament the designation 'holy' was applied quite as much to the high priest's mitre or to the sacrificial vessels of the Temple as it was to the people who used them. It did not

6

imply originally, and in the first place, moral qualities at all, but simply that this person or that thing belonged to God. But then you cannot belong to God unless you are like Him. There can be no consecration to God except the heart is being purified. So the ordinary meaning of holiness, as moral purity and cleanness from sin, necessarily comes from the original meaning, separation and devotion to the service of God.

Thus we get the whole significance of Christian holiness. We are to belong to God, and to know that we do belong to Him. We are to be separated from the mass of people and things that have no consciousness of ownership and do not yield themselves up to Him for His use. But we cannot belong to Him, and be devoted to His service, unless we are being made day by day pure in heart, and like Him to whom we say that we belong. A human being can only be God's by the surrender of heart and will, and through the continual appropriation into his own character and life, of righteousness and purity like that which belongs to God. Holiness is God's stamp upon a man, His 'mark,' by which He says-This man belongs to Me. As you write your name in a book, so God writes His name on His property, and the name that He writes is the likeness of His own character.

Note, again, that in God's church there is no aristocracy of sanctity, nor does the name of saint belong only to those who live high above the ordinary tumults of life and the secularities of daily duty. You may be as true a saint in a factory-ay! and a far truer one-than in a hermitage. You do not need to cultivate a mediaeval or Roman Catholic type of ascetic piety in order to be called saints. You do not need to be amongst the select few to whom it is given here upon earth, but not given without their own effort, to rise to the highest summits of holy conformity with the divine will. But down amongst all the troubles and difficulties and engrossing occupations of our secular work, you may be living saintly lives; for the one condition of being holy is that we should know whose we are and whom we serve, and we can carry the consciousness of belonging to Him into every corner of the poorest, most crowded, and most distracted life, recognising His presence and seeking to do His will.

The saint is the man who says, 'O Lord, truly I am Thy servant; Thou hast loosed my bonds.' Because He has loosed my bonds, the bonds that held me to my sins, He has therein fastened me with far more stringent bonds of love to the sweet and free service of His redeeming love. All His children are His saints.

The Old Testament ritual had one sacrifice which carried this truth in it. It is the first prescribed in the Book of Leviticus, the ceremonial book-namely, the burnt offering. Its especial meaning was this, that the whole man is to be laid upon God's altar and there consumed in the fire of a divine love. It began with expiation, as all sacrifices must, and on the footing of expiation there followed the transformation, by the fire of God, from gross earthliness into vapour and odour which went up in wreaths of fragrance acceptable to God. So we are to be laid upon the divine altar. So, because we have been accepted in the Beloved, and have received the atonement for our sins through His great sacrifice, we are to be consecrated to His service and, touched by the fire which He sends down, we are to be changed into a sweet odour acceptable to Him as were 'the saints which are in Ephesus.'

II. Further, Christian men are saints because they are believers.

'The saints' and 'the faithful' are not two sets of people, but one. The Apostle starts, as it were, on the surface, and goes down; takes off the uppermost layer and lets us see what is below it; begins with the flowers or the fruit, and then carries us to the root. The saints are saints because they are first of all faithful. 'Faithful' here, of course, does not mean, as it usually does in our ordinary language, 'true' and 'trusty,' 'reliable' and 'keeping our word,' but it means simply 'believing'; having faith, not in the sense of fidelity, but in the sense of trust.

So, then, here is Paul's notion-and it is not only Paul's notion, it is God's truth-that the only way by which a man ever comes to realise that he belongs to God, and to yield himself in glad surrender to His uses, and so to become pure and holy like Him whom He loves and aspires to, is by humble faith in Jesus Christ. If you want to talk in theological terminology, sanctification follows upon faith. It is when we believe and trust in Jesus Christ that all the great motives begin to tell upon life and heart, which deliver us from our selfishness, which bind us to God, which make it a joy to do anything for His service, which kindle in our hearts the flame of fructifying and consecrating and transforming love. Faith, the simple reliance of a desperate and therefore trusting heart upon Jesus Christ for all that it needs, is the foundation of the loftiest elevation and attainment of the Christian character. We begin down there that we may set the shining topstone of 'Holiness to the Lord' upon the heaven-pointing summit of our lives.

Note how here Paul sets forth the object of our faith and the blessedness of it. I do not think I am forcing too much meaning into his words when I ask you to notice with what distinct emphasis and intentional fulness he employs the double name of our Lord here to describe the object upon which our faith fixes, 'Faithful in Christ Jesus.' We must lay hold of the Manhood, and we must lay hold of the office. We must rest our soul's salvation on Him as our brother, Jesus who was incarnate in sinful flesh for us; and we must also rest it on Him as God's anointed, who came in human flesh to fulfil the divine loving-kindness and purposes, and in that flesh to die. A faith in a Jesus who was not a Christ would not sanctify; a faith in a Christ who is not Jesus would be impalpable and impotent. We must take the two together, believing and feeling that we lay hold upon a loving Man, 'bone of our bone and flesh of our flesh'; and also upon Him who in His very humanity is the Messenger and Angel of God's covenant; the Christ for whom the way has been being prepared from the beginning, and who has come to fulfil all the purposes of the divine heart.

And notice, too, how there is suggested here also, the blessedness of that faith, inasmuch as it is a faith in Christ. The New Testament speaks in diverse ways about the relation between the believing soul and Jesus Christ. It sometimes speaks of faith as being towards Him, and that suggests the going out of a hand that, as it were, stretches towards what it would lay hold of. It sometimes speaks of faith as being on Him, which suggests the idea of a building on its foundation, or a hand leaning on a support. And it sometimes speaks, as here, of faith being 'in Him,' which suggests the folded wings of the dove that has found its nest, the repose of faith, the quiet rest in the Lord, and 'waiting patiently for Him.' Such trust so directed is the one condition of such tranquillity. Then, again, note a Christian is all that he is because he is 'in Christ.' That phrase 'in Him' is in some sense the keynote of this Epistle to the Ephesians. If you will look over the letter, and pick out all the connections in which the expression 'in Him' occurs, I think you will be astonished to see how rich and full are its uses, and how manifold the blessings of which it is the condition. But the use which Paul makes of it here is just this-everything in our Christian life depends upon our being rooted and grafted in Jesus. Dear brethren, the main weakness, I believe, of what is called Evangelical Christianity has been that it has not always kept true to the proportionate prominence which the New Testament gives to the two thoughts, 'Christ for us,' and 'Christ in us.' For one sermon that you have heard which has dwelt earnestly and believingly on the thought of the indwelling Christ and the Christian indwelling in Him, you have heard a hundred about the Sacrifice on the Cross for sins, and the great atonement that was made by it. Those of you, who have listened to me from Sunday to Sunday, know that I am not to be charged with minimising or neglecting that truth, but I want to lay upon all your hearts this earnest conviction, that a gospel which throws into enormous prominence 'Christ for us,' and into very small prominence 'Christ in us,' is lame of one foot, is lopsided, untrue to the symmetry and proportion of the Gospel as it is revealed in the New Testament, and will never avail for the nourishment and maturity of Christian souls. 'Christ for us' by all means, and for evermore, but 'Christ in us,' or else He will not be 'for us.'

III. Lastly, a Christian may be a saint, and a believer, and in Christ Jesus, though he is in Ephesus.

Many of you know that probably the words 'in Ephesus' are no part of the original text of this epistle, which was apparently a circular letter, in which the designation of the various churches to which it was sent was left blank, to be filled in with the name of each little community to which

Paul's messenger from Rome carried it. The copy from which our text was taken had probably been delivered at Ephesus; and, at any rate, one of the copies would go there. What was Ephesus? Satan's very headquarters and seat in Asia Minor, a focus of idolatry, superstition, wealth, luxury springing from commerce, and moral corruption. 'Great is Diana of the Ephesians.' The books of Ephesus were a synonym for magical books. Many of us know how rotten to the core the society of that great city was. And there, on the dunghill, was this little garden of fragrant and flowering plants. They were 'saints in Christ Jesus,' though they were 'saints in Ephesus.'

Never mind about surroundings. It is possible for us to keep ourselves in the love of God, and in the fellowship of His Son wherever we are, and whatever may lie around us. You and I have too to live in a big, wicked city, and to work out our religion in a society honeycombed with corruption, because of commerce and other influences. Do not let us forget that these people whom Paul called 'saints' and 'faithful' had a harder fight to wage than we have, with less to hearten and strengthen them in it. Only remember if the 'saints in Ephesus' are to be 'in Christ,' they need to keep themselves very straight up. The carbonic acid gas is heavy and goes down to the bottom of the cave, and if a man will walk bolt upright, he will keep his nostrils above it; but if he stoops, he will get down into it. Walk straight up, with your head erect, looking to the Master, and your respiratory organs will be above the poison. If we are to be in Christ when we are in Ephesus, we need to keep ourselves separate and faithful, and to keep ourselves in Christ. If the diver comes out of the diving-bell he is drowned. If he keeps inside its crystal walls he may be on the bottom of the ocean, but he is dry and safe. Keep in the fortress by loyal faith, by humble realisation of His presence, by continual effort, and 'nothing shall by any means harm you,' but 'your lives shall be holy, being hid with Christ in God.'

ALL SPIRITUAL BLESSINGS

Ephesians 1:3

It is very characteristic of Paul's impetuous fervour and exuberant faith that he begins this letter with a doxology, and plunges at once into the very heart of his theme. Colder natures reach such heights by slow degrees. He gains them at a bound, or rather, he dwells there always. Put a pen into his hand, and it is like tapping a blast furnace; and out rushes a fiery stream at white heat. But there is a great deal more than fervour in the words. In the rush of his thoughts there is depth and method. We come slowly after, and try by analysing and meditation to recover some of the fervour and the fire of such utterances as this.

Notice that buoyant, joyous, emphatic reiteration: 'Blessed,' 'blest,' 'blessings.' That is more than the fascination exercised over a man's mind by a word; it covers very deep thoughts and goes very far into the centre of the Christian life. God blesses us by gifts; we bless Him by words. The aim of His act of blessing is to evoke in our hearts the love that praises. We receive first, and then, moved by His mercies, we give. Our highest response to His most precious gifts is that we shall 'take the cup of salvation, and call upon the name of the Lord,' and in the depth of thankful and recipient hearts shall say, 'Blessed be God who hath blessed us.'

Now I think that I shall best bring out the deep meaning of these words if I simply follow them as they lie before us. I do not wish to say anything about our echo in blessing God. I wish to speak about the original sweet sound, His blessing to us.

I. And I note, first of all, the character and the extent of these blessings which are the constituents of the Christian life.

'All spiritual blessings,' says the Apostle. Now, I am not going to weary you with mere exegetical remarks, but I do want to lay stress upon this, that, when the Apostle speaks about 'spiritual blessings,' he does not merely use that word 'spiritual' as defining the region in us in which the blessings are given, though that is also implied; but rather as pointing to the medium by which they are conferred. That is to say, he calls them 'spiritual,' not because they are, unlike material and outward blessings, gifts for the inner man, the true self, but because they are imparted to the waiting spirit by that Divine Spirit who communicates to men all the most precious things of God. They are 'spiritual' because the Holy Spirit is the medium of communication by which they reach men's spirits.

And I may just pause for one moment-and it shall only be for a moment-to point out to you how in-woven into the very texture of the writer's thoughts, and all the more emphatic because quite incidental, and needing to be looked for to be found, is here the evidence of his believing that the name of God was God the Father, Son, and Holy Spirit. For it is the Father who is the Giver, the Son who is the Reservoir, the Spirit who is the Communicator, of these spiritual gifts. And I do not think that any man could have written these words of my text, the main purpose of which is altogether different to setting forth the mystery of the divine nature, unless he had believed in God the Father, Son, and Holy Ghost.

But, apart altogether from that, let me remind you in one sentence of how the gifts which thus come to men by that Divine Spirit derive their characteristic quality from their very medium of communication. There are many other blessings for which we have to say, 'Blessed be God'; for all the gifts that come from 'the Father of Lights' are light, and everything that the Fountain of sweetness bestows upon mankind is sweet, but earthly blessings are but the shadow of blessing. They remain without us, and they pass. And if they were all for which we had to praise God, our praises had need to be often checked by sobs and tears, and often very doubtful and questioning. If there were none other but such, and if this poor life were all, then I do not think it would be true that it is

'better to have loved and lost,

Than never to have loved at all.'

It is but a quavering voice of praise, with many a sob between, that goes up to bless God for anything but spiritual blessings. Though it is true that all which comes from the Father of Lights is light, the sorrows and troubles that He sends have the light terribly muffled in darkness, and it needs strong faith and insight to pierce through the cloud to see the gleam of anything bright beneath. But when we turn to this other region, and think of what comes to every poor, tremulous, human heart, that likes to take it through that Divine Spirit-the forgiveness of sins, the rectification of errors, the purification of lusts and passions, the gleams of hope on the future, and the access with confidence into the standing and place of children; oh, then surely we can say, 'Blessed be God for spiritual blessings.'

But if the word which defines may thus seem to limit, the other word which accompanies it sweeps away every limit; for it calls upon us to bless God for all spiritual blessings. That is to say, there is no gap in His gift. It is rounded and complete and perfect. Whatever a man's needs may require, whatever his hopes can dream, whatever his wishes can stretch out towards, it is all here, compacted and complete. The spiritual gifts are encyclopaediacal and all-sufficient. They are not segments, but completed circles. When God gives He gives amply.

II. So much, then, for the first point; now, in the second place, note the one divine act by which all these blessings have been bestowed.

'Blessed be God who has given'; or, still more definitely, pointing to some one specific moment and deed in which the benefaction was completed, 'Blessed be God who gave.'

When? Well, ideally in the depths of His own eternal mind the gift was complete or ever the recipients were created to receive it, and historically the gift was complete in the act of redemption when He spared not His Own Son, but gave Him up unto the death for us all. A man may destine an estate for the benefit of some community which for

14

generations long may continue to enjoy its benefits, but the gift is complete when he signs the deed that makes it over. Humphrey Chetham gave the boys in his school to-day their education when, centuries ago, he assigned his property to that beneficent purpose. So, away back in the mists of Eternity the gift was completed, and the signature was put to the deed when Jesus Christ was born, and the seal was added when Jesus Christ died. 'Blessed be God who hath given.'

So, then, we may not only draw the conclusion which the Apostle drew, 'how shall He not with Him also freely give us all things?' but we can draw an even grander one, 'Has He not with Him also freely given us all things?' And we possess them all to-day if our hearts are resting on Jesus Christ. The limit of the gift is only in ourselves. All has been given, but the question remains how much has been taken.

Oh, Christian men and women, there is nothing that we require more than to have what we have, to possess what is ours, to make our own what has been bestowed. You sometimes hear of some beggar, or private soldier, or farm labourer, who has come all at once into an estate that was his, years before he knew anything about it. There is such a boundless wealth belonging by right, and by the Giver's gift, to every Christian soul; and yet, here are we, many of us, like the paupers who sometimes turn up in workhouses, all in rags, and with deposit-receipts for L200 or L300 stitched into the rags, that they get no good out of. Here are we, with all that wealth, paupers still. Be sure that you have what you have. Do you remember the exhortation to a valiant effort in one of the stories in the Old Testament-'Know ye that Ramoth-gilead is ours, and we take it not?' And that is exactly what is true about hosts of professing Christians who have not, in any real sense, the possession of what God has given them. It is well to ask, for our desires are the measures of our capacities. It is well to ask, but we very often ask when what is wanted is not that we should get more, but that we should utilise what we have. And we make mistakes therein, as if God needed to be besought to give, when all the while it is we who need to be stirred up to grasp and keep the things that are freely given to us of God.

III. In the next place, notice the one place where all these blessings are kept.

'Blessed be God who has blessed us with all spiritual blessings in heavenly places.' 'In heavenly places.' Now that does not merely define the region of origin, the locality where they originated or whence they come. It does do that, but it does a great deal more. It does not merely tell us, as we often are disposed to think that it does, that 'every good and every perfect gift is from above, and cometh down'-though that is perfectly true, but it means much rather that in order to get the gift we must go up. They are in the heavenly places, and they cannot live anywhere else. They have been sticking shrubs in tubs outside our public buildings this last week. How long will they keep their leaves and their freshness? How soon will they need to be shifted and taken back again to the sweeter air, where they can flourish? God's spiritual gifts cannot grow in smoke and dirt and a polluted atmosphere. And if a professing Christian man lives his life on the low levels he will have very few of the heavenly gifts coming down to him there. And that is the reason-the reason above all others-why, with such a large provision made for all possible necessities and longings of all sorts, people who call themselves Christians go up and down the world feeble and poor, and with little enjoyment of their religion, and having verified scarcely anything of the great promises which God has given them.

Brother, according to the old word with which the Mass used to begin, 'Sursum corda'-up with your hearts! The blessings are in the heavens, and if we want them we must go where they are. It is not enough to drink sparing draughts from the stream as it flows through the plain. Travel up to the headwaters, where the great pure fountain is, that gushes out abundant and inexhaustible. The gifts are heavenly, and there they abide, and thither we must mount if we would possess them.

Now that this understanding of the words is correct I think is clearly shown by a verse in the next chapter, where we find the very same phrase employed. In this connection the Apostle says that 'God hath raised us up together in heavenly places in Christ Jesus.' That is to say, the true ideal of the Christian life is that, even here and now, it is a life of such intimate union and incorporation with Jesus Christ as that where He is we are, and that even whilst we tabernacle upon earth and move about amongst its illusions and changing scenes, in the depth of our true being we may be fixed, and sit at rest with Christ where He is.

Do not dismiss that as mere pulpit rhetoric. Do not say that it is mystical and incomprehensible, and cannot be reduced into practice amidst the distractions of daily life. Brethren, it is not so! Jesus Christ Himself said about Himself that He came down from heaven, and that though He did, even whilst He wore the likeness of the flesh, and was one of us, He was 'the Son of Man which is in Heaven,' when He lay in the manger, when He worked at the carpenter's bench in Nazareth, when He walked with weary feet those blessed acres, when He hung, for our advantage, on the bitter Cross. And that was no incommunicable property of His mysterious nature, but it was the typical example of what it is possible for manhood to be. And you and I, if we are to possess in any measure corresponding with the gift of Christ the spiritual blessing which God bestows, must have our lives 'hid with Christ in God,' and sit together with Him in the heavenly places.

IV. Lastly, note the one Person in whom all spiritual blessings are enshrined.

'In the heavenly places in Christ Jesus.' You cannot separate between Him and His gifts, neither in the way of getting Him without them, nor in the way of getting them without Him. They are Himself, and in the deepest analysis all spiritual blessings are reducible to one-viz. that the Spirit of Jesus Christ Himself shall dwell with us.

Now, that union by which it is possible for poor, empty, sinful creatures to be filled with His fulness, animated with His life, strengthened with His omnipotence, and sanctified by His indwelling-that union is the very kernel of this Epistle to the Ephesians.

I dare say I have often drawn your attention to the singular emphasis and repetition with which that phrase 'in Christ' occurs throughout the letter. Just take the two or three instances of it that I gather as I speak. In this first chapter we read, 'the faithful in Jesus Christ.' Then comes our text, 'blessings in heavenly places in Christ.' Then, in the very next verse, we read, 'chosen us in Him.' Then, a verse or two after, we have 'accepted in the Beloved,' which is immediately followed by, 'in whom we have redemption through His blood.' Then, again, 'that He might gather together in one all things in Christ, in whom also we have obtained the inheritance.' I need not make other quotations, but throughout the letter every blessing that can gladden or sanctify the human spirit is regarded by the Apostle as being stored and shrined in Jesus Christ: inseparable from Him, and therefore to be found by us only in union with Him.

And that is the point of all which I want to say-viz. that, inasmuch as all spiritual blessings that a soul can need are hived in Him in whom is all sweetness, the way, and the only way, to get them is that we, too, should pass into Him and dwell in Jesus Christ. It is His own teaching: 'I am the Vine, ye are the branches. Abide in Me. Separate from Me ye can do nothing,' and get nothing, and are nothing.

Oh, brethren! it is well that all our treasures should be in one place. It is better that they should all be in One Person. And if only we will lay our poor emptiness by the side of His fulness there will pass over from that infinite abundance and sufficiency everything that we can require.

We abide in Him by faith, by meditation, by love, by submission, by practical obedience, and, if we are wise, the effort of our lives will be to keep close to that Lord. As long as we keep touch with Him we have all and abound. Break the connection by wandering away, in thought and desire, by indulgence in sin, by letting earthly passions surge in and separate us from Him-break the connection by rebellion, by making ourselves our own ends and lords, and it is like switching off the electricity. Everything falls dead. You cannot have Christ's blessing unless you take Christ.

And so, dear brethren, 'abide in Me and I in you.' There is nothing else that will make us blessed; there is nothing else that will meet all the circumference of our necessities; there is nothing else that will quiet our hearts, will sanctify our understandings. Christ is yours if 'ye are Christ's.' 'Of His fulness have all we received,' for it all became ours when we became His, and Christian growth on earth and heaven is but the unfolding of the folded graces that are contained in Him. We possess the whole Christ, but eternity is needed to disclose all the unsearchable riches of our inheritance in Him.

ACCORDING TO (PART 1)

Ephesians 1:5; Ephesians 1:7.

That phrase, 'according to,' is one of the key-words of this profound epistle, which occurs over and over again, like a refrain. I reckon twelve instances of it in three chapters of the letter, and they all introduce one or other of the two thoughts which appear in the two fragments that I have taken for my text. They either point out how the great blessings of Christ's mission have underlying them the divine purpose, or they point out how the process of the Christian life in the individual has for its source and measure the abundances, the wealth of the grace and the power of God. So in both aspects the facts of earth are traced up to, and declared to be, the outcome of the heavenly depths, and that gives solemnity, grandeur, elevation, to this epistle all its own. We are carried, as it were, away up into the recesses of the mountains of God, and we look down upon the unruffled, mysterious, deep lake, from which come the rivers that water all the plains beneath.

Now of these two types of reference to the divine will and the divine wealth, I should like to gather together the instances, as they occur in this letter, in so far as I can, in the course of a sermon, touching them, it must be, very imperfectly. But I fear that it is impossible to deal with both the phases of this 'according to,' in one discourse. So I confine myself to that which is suggested by the first of our two texts, in the hope that some other day we may be able to overtake the other. So then, we have set before us here the Christian thought of the divine will which underlies, and therefore is manifest by, the work of Jesus Christ, in its whole sweep and breadth. And I just take up the various instances in which this expression occurs in a great variety of forms, but all retaining substantially the same meaning.

I. Note that that divine will which underlies and is operative in, and therefore is certified to us by the whole work of Jesus Christ, in its facts and its consequences, is a 'good pleasure.'

Now there are few thoughts which the history of the world has shown to be more productive of iron and steel in the human character than that of the sovereign will of God. That made Islam, and is the secret of its power to-day, amidst its many corruptions. Because these wild desert tribes were all stiffened, or I might say inflamed, by that profound conviction, the sovereign will of God, they came down like a hammer upon that corrupt so-called Christian Church, and swept it off the face of the earth, as it deserved to be swept. And the same thought of the sovereign will, of which we are but instruments-pawns on its chessboard-made the grand seventeenth century Puritanism in England, and its sister type of men and of religion in Holland. For this is a historically proved thesis, that there is nothing which so contributes to the formation, and valuation of, and the readiness to die for, civil liberty, as the firm grasp of that thought of the divine sovereignty. Just because a man realises that the will of God is supreme over all the earth, he rebels against all forms of human despotism.

But with all the good that is in that great thought-and the Christianity of this day sorely wants the strength that might be given it by the exhibition of that steel medicine-it wants another, 'the good pleasure of His will.' And that word, 'good pleasure,' does not express, as I think, in Paul's usage of it, the simple notion of sovereignty, but always the notion of a benevolent sovereignty. It is 'the good pleasure'-as it is put in another place by the same Apostle-'of His goodness.' And that thought, let in upon the solemnity and severity of the other one, is all that it needs in order to make the man who grasps it not only a hero in conflict, and a patient martyr in endurance, but a child in his Father's house, rejoicing in the love of his Father everywhere and always.

Paul would have us believe that if we will take the work of Jesus Christ in the facts of His life, and its results upon humanity, as our horn-book and lesson, we shall draw from that some conceptions of the great thing that underlies it, 'the good pleasure of His will.' We stand in front of this complex universe, and some of us say: 'Law'; and some of us say: 'A Lawgiver behind the law; a Person at the heart of all things'; but unless we can say: 'And in the heart of the Person a will, which is the expression of a steadfast, omnipotent love,' then the world seems to me to be a place of unsolvable riddles and a torture-house. There goes the great steam-roller along the road. Everybody can see that it crushes down, and makes its own path. Who drives it? The steam in the boiler, or is there a hand on the lever? And what drives the hand? Christianity answers, and answers with unfaltering lip, rising clear above contradictions apparent and difficulties real, 'The good pleasure of His will,' and there men can rest.

Then there is another step. Another form in which this 'according to' appears in this letter is, if we adopt the rendering, which I am disposed to do in the present case, of the Authorised Version rather than of the Revised, 'according to His good pleasure ... which He hath purposed in Himself.' The Revised Version says, 'Which He hath purposed in Him,' and that is a perfectly possible rendering. But to me the old one is not only more eloquent, but more in accordance with the connection. So I venture to accept it without further ado-'His good pleasure which He hath purposed in Himself.'

That brings us into the presence of that same great thought, which in another aspect is expressed in saying 'His name is Jehovah,' and in yet another aspect is expressed in saying 'God is love,' viz. the thought which sounds familiar, but which has in it depths of strength and illumination and joy, if we rightly ponder it, that, to use human words, the motive of the divine action is all found within the divine nature.

We love one another because we discern, or think we discern, lovable qualities in the being on whom our love falls. God loves because He is God. That great artesian fountain wells up from the depths, by its own sweet impulse, and pours itself out; and 'the good pleasure of His goodness' has no other explanation than that it is His nature and property to be merciful. And so, dear brethren, we get clean past what has sometimes been the misapprehension of good people, and has oftener been the caricatured representation of Evangelical truth which its enemies have put forth-that God was made to love and pity by reason of the sacrifice of the Son, whereas the very opposite is the case. God loves, therefore He sent His Son, 'that whosoever believeth in Him should not perish but have everlasting life,' and the notion of the Cross of Christ as changing the divine heart is as far away from Evangelical truth as it is from the natural conceptions that men form of the divine nature. We shake hands with our so-called antagonists and say, 'Yes! we believe as much as you do that God does not love us because Christ died, but we believe what perhaps you do not, that Christ died because God loves us, and would save us.' 'The good pleasure which He hath purposed in Himself.'

Then, still further, there is another aspect of this same divine will brought out in other parts of this letter, of which this is a specimen, 'Having made known unto us the mystery of His will, according to His good pleasure which He hath purposed in Himself, that in the dispensation of the fulness of the times He might gather together in one all things in Christ,' which, being turned into more modern phraseology, is just this-that the great aim of that divine sovereign will, self-originated, full of loving-kindness to the world, is to manifest to all men what God is, that all men may know Him for what He is, and thereby be drawn back again, and grouped in peaceful unity round His Son, Jesus Christ. That is the intention which is deepest in the divine heart, the desire which God has most for every one of us. And when the Old Testament tells us that the great motive of the divine action is for 'My own Name's sake,' that expression might be so regarded as to disclose an ugly despot, who only wants to be reverenced by abject and submissive subjects. But what it really means is this, that the divine love which hovers over its poor, prodigal children because it is love, and, therefore, lovingly delights in a loving recognition and response, desires most of all that all the wanderers should see the light, and that every soul of man should be able to whisper, with loving heart, the name, 'Abba! Father!' Is not that an uplifting thought as being the dominant motive which puts in action the whole of the divine activity? God created in order that He might fling His light upon creatures, who should thereby be glad. And God has redeemed in order that in Jesus Christ we might see Him, and, seeing Him, be at rest, and begin to grow like Him. This is the aim, 'That they might know Thee, the only true God ... whom to know is eternal life.' And so self-communication and self-revelation is the very central mystery of the will.

But that is not all. Another of the forms in which this phrase occurs tells us that that great purpose, the eternal purpose which He purposed in Christ Jesus our Lord, was that, 'Now unto the principalities and powers in heavenly places might be known' by the Church 'the manifold wisdom of God.' And so we get another thought, that that whole work of redemption, operated by the Incarnation, and culminating in the Crucifixion and Resurrection and Ascension of Jesus Christ, stands as being the means by which other orders of creatures, besides ourselves, learn to know 'the manifold wisdom of God.' According to the grand old saying, at Creation the 'morning stars sang together for joy.' All spiritual creatures, be they 'higher' or 'lower,' can only know God by the observation of His acts.

"Twas great to speak a world from nought,
'Tis greater to redeem,'

and the same angelic lips that sang these praises on the morning of Creation have learnt a new song that they sing; 'Glory and honour and dominion and power be unto the Lamb that was slain.'

Thus to principalities and powers, a diviner height in the loftiness, and a diviner depth in the condescension, and a diviner tenderness in the love, and a diviner energy in the power, of the redeeming God have been made known, and this is the thought of His eternal purpose. And that brings me to another point which is involved in the words that I have just quoted, which stand in connection with those that I have previously referred to. The phrase 'eternal purpose' literally rendered is, 'the purpose of the ages,' and that, no doubt, may mean 'eternal' in the sense of running on through all the ages; or it may mean, perhaps, that which we usually attach to the word 'eternal,' viz. unbeginning and unending. I take the former meaning as the more probable one, that the Apostle contemplates that great will of God which culminates in Jesus

Christ, as coming solemnly sweeping through all the epochs of time from the beginning. In a deeper sense than the poet meant it, 'Through the ages an increasing purpose runs,' and that binds the epochs of humanity together-'the purpose of God in Christ Jesus.' The philosophy of history lies there, and it is a true instinct that makes the cradle at Bethlehem the pivot around which the world's chronology revolves. For the deepest thing about all the ages on the further side of it is that they are 'Before Christ,' and the formative fact for all the ages after it is that they are Anno Domini.

And now the last thing that is suggested by yet another of these eloquent expressions is deduced from another part of the same phrase. The purpose of the ages is described as that which 'He purposed in Christ Jesus our Lord.' Now the word 'purposed' literally is 'made.' And it may be a question whether 'purposed' or 'accomplished' is the special meaning to be attached to the general word 'made.' Either is legitimate. I take it that what the Apostle means here is that the purpose of God, which we have thus seen as sovereign, self-originated, having for its great aim the communication to all His creatures of the knowledge of Himself, and running through the ages, and binding them into a unity, reaches its entire accomplishment in the Cradle, and the Cross, and the Throne of Jesus Christ our Lord.

He fulfils the divine intention. There is that one life, and in that life alone of humanity you have a character which is in entire sympathy with the divine mind, which is in full possession of the divine truth, which never diverges or deviates by a hair's-breadth from the divine will, which is the complete and perfect exponent to man of the divine heart and character; and that Christ is the fulfilment of all that God desired in the depths of eternity, and the abysses of His being. Did He will that men should know Him? Christ has declared Him. Did He will that men should be drawn back to Him? Christ lifted on the Cross draws all men unto Him. Was it 'according to the good pleasure of His goodness' that we men should attain to the adoption of sons? By that Son we too became sons. Was it the purpose of His will that we should obtain an 'inheritance'? We obtain it in Jesus Christ, 'being heirs of God, and joint-heirs with Christ.' All that

God willed to do is done. And when we look, on the one hand, up to that infinite purpose, and on the other, to the Cross, we hear from the dying lips, 'It is finished!' The purpose of the ages is accomplished in Christ Jesus.

Is it accomplished with you? I have been speaking about the divine counsel which is a 'good pleasure,' which runs through the whole history of mankind. But it is a divine purpose that you can thwart as far as you are concerned. 'How often would I have gathered ... and ye would not,' and your 'would not' neutralises His 'would.' Do not stand in the way of the steam-roller. You cannot stop it, but it can crush you. Do not have Him say about you, 'In vain have I smitten, in vain have I loved.' Bow, accept, recognise that all God's armoury is brought to bear upon each of us in that great Cross and Passion, in that great Incarnation and human life. And I beseech you, in your hearts, let the will of God be done even as for a world it has been done by the sacrifice of Calvary.

ACCORDING TO (PART 2)

Ephesians 1:7.

We have seen, in a previous sermon, that a characteristic note of this letter is the frequent occurrence of that phrase 'according to.' I also then pointed out that it was employed in two different directions. One class of passages, with which I then tried to deal, used it to compare the divine purpose in our salvation with the historical process of the salvation. The type of that class of reference is found in a verse just before my text, 'according to the good pleasure of His will.' There is a second class of passages to which our text belongs, where the comparison is not between the purpose and its realisation, but between the stores of the divine riches and the experiences of the Christian life. The one set of passages suggests the ground of our salvation in the deep purpose of God; the other suggests the measure of the power which is working out that salvation.

The instances of this second use of the phrase, besides the one in my text, 'according to the riches of His grace,' are such as these: 'According to the riches of His glory'; 'According to the power that worketh in us'; 'According to the measure of the gift of Christ'; 'According to the energy of the might of His power, which He wrought in Christ when He raised Him from the dead.'

Now it is clear that all these are varying forms of the same thing. They vary in form, they are identical in substance. What a Jew calls a 'cubit' an Englishman calls a 'foot,' but the result is pretty nearly the same. Shillings, marks, francs, are various standards; they all come to substantially the same result. These varying measures of the divine gift which is at work in man's salvation, have this in common, that they all run out into God's immeasurable, unlimited power, boundless wealth. And so, if we gather them together, and try to focus them in a few words, they may help to widen our conceptions of what we ought to expect from

God, to bow us in contrition as to the small use that we have made of it, and to open our desires wide, that they may be filled.

I only aspire, then, to deal with these four forms which I have already suggested.

I. The measure of our possible attainments is the whole wealth of God.

'According to the riches of His grace.' Another angle at which the same thought is viewed appears in another part of the letter, where we have this variation in the expression, 'According to the riches of His glory.' 'Grace' and 'Glory' are generally opposed antithetically; in this epistle they are united, for in the verse before my text I:read: 'To the praise of the glory of His grace.' So the first thought is, the whole wealth of God is available for every Christian soul.

Now it seems to me that there are very few things that the popular Christianity of this day needs more than a furnishing up of the familiar old Christian terminology, which has largely lost the freshness and the power that it once had. They tell us that these incandescent burners, that we are using nowadays, are very much more bright when they are first fixed than after the mantle gets a little worn. So it is with the terminology of Christianity. It needs to be re-stated, not in such a way as to take the pith out of it, which is what a great deal of the modern craze for re-statement means, but in such a way as to brighten it up again, and to invest it with something of the 'celestial light' with which it was 'apparelled' when it first came. Now that word 'grace,' I have no doubt, sounds to you hard, theological, remote. But what does it mean? It gathers into one burning point the whole of the rays of that conception of God, with which it is the glory of Christianity to have flooded and drenched the world. It tells us that at the heart of the universe there is a heart; that God is Love, that that love is the motive-spring of His activity, that it comes and bends over the lowliest with a smile of amity on its lips, with healing and help in its hands, with forgiveness for all sins against itself, with boundless wealth for the poorest, and that the wealth of His self-communicating love is the measure of the wealth that each of us may possess.

God gives 'according to the riches of His grace.' You do not expect a millionaire to give half-a-crown to a subscription fund; and God gives royally, divinely, measuring His bestowments by the abundance of His treasures, and handing over with an open palm large gifts of coined money, because there are infinite chests of uncirculated bullion in the deep storehouses. 'How great is Thy goodness which Thou hast manifested before the sons of men for them that fear Thee. How much greater is Thy goodness which Thou hast laid up in store.' But whilst He gives all, the question comes to be: What do I receive? The measure of His gift is His measureless grace; the measure of my reception is my-alas! easily-measured faith. What about the unearned increment? What about the unrealised wealth? Too many of us are like some man who has a great estate in another land. He knows nothing about it, and is living in grimy poverty in a back street. For you have all God's riches waiting for you, and 'the potentiality of wealth beyond the dreams of avarice' at your beck and call, and yet you are but poorly realising your possible riches. Alas, that when we might have so much we do have so little. 'According to the riches of His grace' He gives. But another 'according to' comes in. 'According to thy faith be it unto thee.' So we have to take these two measures together, and the working limit of our possession of God's riches comes out of the combination of them both.

Let me remind you, before I pass on, of what I have already suggested is but another phase of this same thought, Paul says in this epistle that God gives not only 'according to the riches of His grace,' but 'according to the riches of His glory,' and that the latter expression is substantially identical with the former, is plain from the combination of the two in an earlier verse of this chapter: 'To the praise of the glory of His grace.' Thus we come to the blessed thought that the glory of God is essentially the revelation of that stooping, pitying, pardoning, enriching love. Not in the physical attributes, not in the characteristics of the divine nature which part Him off from men, and make Him remote, both from their conceptions and their affections, but in the love that bends to them is the true glory of God. All these other things are but the fringes; the centre of glory is the Love, which is the mightiest and the divinest thing in the Might Divine. The sunshine is far stronger than the lightning, and there is more force developed in the rain than in an earthquake. That truth is what Christianity has made the common possession of the world. It has thereby broken the chains of dread; it has bridged over the infinite distance. It has given us a God that can love and be loved, can stoop and can lift, can pardon and can purify. 'According to the good pleasure of His goodness,'-there is the foundation of our salvation. 'According to the riches of His grace,'-there is the measure of our salvation.

II. We have another form of the same measure in another set of verses which speak of the present working of God's power.

The Apostle speaks in regard to his own apostolic commission of its being given 'according to the working of His power'; and he speaks of all Christian men as receiving gifts 'according to the power that worketh in us.' So there we have a standard that comes, as it were, a little closer to ourselves. We do not need to travel up into the dim abysses above, or think of the sanctities and the secrecies of that divine heart in the light which is inaccessible, but we have the measure in ourselves.

The standards of length are kept at Greenwich, the standards of capacity are kept in the Tower; but there are local standards distributed throughout the land to which men may go and have their measures corrected. And so besides all these lofty thoughts about the grace and the glory which measures His gift, we can turn within, if we are Christian people, and say, 'According to the power that worketh in us.'

Ah, brethren! there are few things that we want more than to revive and deepen the conviction that in every Christian man, by virtue of his faith, and in proportion to his faith, there is in operation an actual, superhuman, divine power moulding his nature, guiding, quickening, ennobling, lifting, confirming, and hallowing and shaping him into conformity with Jesus Christ. I would that we all believed not as a dogma, but realised as a personal experience, that irrefragable truth,

'Know ye not that the Spirit of Christ dwelleth in you, except ye be reprobate?' The life of self is evil; the life of Christ in self is good, and only good. And if you are Christian men, and in the proportion, as I have said, in which you are living by faith, you have working in your spirits the very Spirit of Christ Himself.

And that power is the measure of your possibilities. Obviously 'the power that worketh in us' is able to do a great deal more than it is doing in any of us. And so with deep significance the Apostle, side by side with his adducing of this power as being the measure of our possible attainments, speaks about God as being 'able to do for us, exceeding abundantly above all that we can ask or think.' 'The power that works in us' transcends in its possibilities our present experience, it transcends our conceptions, it transcends our desires. It is able to do everything; it actually does-well, you know what it does in you. And the responsibility of hampering and hindering that power from working out its only adequately corresponding results lies at our own doors. 'A rushing, mighty wind'-yes; and in myself a scarcely perceptible breathing, and often a dead calm, stagnant as in the latitudes on either side of the Equator, where, for long, dreary days, no freshening motion in the atmosphere is perceptible. 'A fire?'-yes; then why is my grate full of grey, cold ashes, and one little spark in the corner? 'A fountain springing into everlasting life?'-yes; then why in my basin is there so much scum and ooze, mud and defilement, and so little of the flashing and brilliant water? 'The power that works in us' is sorely hindered by the weakness in which it works.

III. In the third place another form of this measure is stated by the Apostle, 'According to the measure of the gift of Christ.'

That means, of course, the gift which Christ bestows. It is substantially the same idea as I have just been dealing with, only looked at from rather a different point of view. Therefore, I need not dwell upon its parallelism with what has just been occupying our attention, but rather ask you simply to consider one point in reference to it, and that is that, side by side with the reference to the gift of Christ as being the measure of our possible attainments, the Apostle enlarges on the Infinite variety of the shapes which that one gift takes in different people. 'He gave some apostles, some prophets,' etc.; one man receiving according to this fashion, and another according to that, and to each of us the distribution is made 'according to the measure of the gift of Christ.' That is to say, it takes us all, the collective goodness and beauty of the whole community of saints, to approximate to the fulness of that gift, and all are needed in their different types and forms of excellence, sanctity and beauty, in order to set forth, even imperfectly, the richness and the manifoldness of His great gift. And so 'we all come'-there is a multiplicity-'unto the perfect man, the measure of the stature of the fulness of Christ'-there is a unity in which the multiplicity inheres.

So try to get a little more of some different type of excellence than that to which you are naturally inclined. Seek, and consciously endeavour, to appropriate into your character uncongenial excellences, and be very charitable in your judgments of the different types of Christian conformity to Christ our Lord. The crystals that are set round a light do not quarrel with each other as to whether green, or yellow, or blue, or red, or violet is the true colour to reflect. We need all the seven prismatic tints to make the perfect white light. The gift of Christ is many-sided; try not to be one-sided in your reception of it.

IV. And now the last form of this measure is 'according to the energy of the might of His power, which He wrought in Christ when He raised Him from the dead.'

When we gazed upon the riches of God's grace, they were high above us, when we looked upon 'the power that worketh in us,' we saw it working amidst many hindrances and hamperings, but here there is presented to us in a concrete example, close beside us, of what God can make of a man when the man is wholly pliable to His will, and the recipient of His influences. And so there stands before us the guarantee and the pattern of immortal life, the Christ whose Manhood died and lives, who is clothed with a spiritual body, who wields royal authority in the Kingdom of the Most High. And that is the measure of what God can do with me, and wishes to do with me, if I will let Him. Christ is my pattern, and the measure of my own possibilities.

To be with Him, where and what He is, is the only adequate result of the power that works in us, and of the process that is already begun in us, if we are Christian people. You are sometimes-there is one eminent example of it in that great Medicean Chapel at Florence-a statue exquisitely finished in all its limbs, but one part left in the rough. That is the best that Christian people come to here. Shall it always be so? Do not the very imperfections prophesy completion, and is it not certain that the half-finished torso will be carried to the upper workshop, and be there disengaged from the dead marble and made to stand out in perfect beauty and fullest completeness? Christ is the object of our hopes, and no hopes of the Christian life are adequate to the power that works in us, or to the progress already made, which do not see in the 'energy of the might of the power' which wrought in Christ, the example and the guarantee of the exceeding greatness of 'His power which is to usward.'

And now, one last word. Besides all these passages which have been occupying us, there is another use of this same phrase in this letter which presents a very solemn and grim contrast. I can do no better with it than simply read it: 'Ye were dead in trespasses and sins; wherein in time past ye walked according to the course of this world, according to the prince of the power of the air, the spirit that now worketh'-mark the allusion to the other words that we have been referring to-'in the children of disobedience.' So there you have the alternative, either 'dead in trespasses and sins,' whilst living the physical and the intellectual life, or partaking of the life of Him 'who was dead, and is alive for ever more'; either 'walking according to the course of this world,' which is 'disobedience' and 'wrath,' or walking 'according to the power that worketh in us'; either 'putting on,' or rather continuing to wear, 'the old man which is corrupt according to the lusts which deceive,' or 'putting on the new man, which according to God is created in righteousness and holiness and truth.' The choice is before us. May God help us to choose aright!

GOD'S INHERITANCE AND OURS

Ephesians 1:11

A dewdrop twinkles into green and gold as the sunlight falls on it. A diamond flashes many colours as its facets catch the light. So, in this context, the Apostle seems to be haunted with that thought of 'inheriting' and 'inheritance,' and he recurs to it several times, but sets it at different angles, and it flashes back different beauties of radiance. For the words, which I have wrenched from their context in the first of these two verses, are more accurately rendered, as in the Revised Version, in 'whom also we were made,' not 'have obtained'-'an inheritance.' Whose inheritance? God's! The Christian community is God's possession. Then, in my second text, we have the converse thought-'the earnest of our inheritance.' What is the Christian's possession? The same God whose possession is the Christian. So, then, there is a deep and a wonderful relation between the believing soul and God, and however different must be the two sides of that relation, the resemblance is greater than the difference. Surely that is the deepest, most blessed, and most strength-giving conception of the Christian life. Other notions of it lay stress, and that rightly, upon certain correspondence between us and God. My faith corresponds to His faithfulness and veracity. My obedience corresponds to His authority. My weakness lays hold on His strength. My emptiness is replenished by His fulness. But here we rise above the region of correspondences into that of similarity. In these other aspects the convexity fits the concavity; in this aspect the two hemispheres go together and make the complete globe. We possess God, and God possesses us, and it is the same set of facts which are set forth in the two thoughts, 'We were made an inheritance, ... the earnest of our inheritance.'

I. Now, then, let me ask you to look first at this mutual possession.

We possess God; God possesses us. What does that mean? Well, it means plainly and chiefly this, a mutual love. For we all know-and many of us thankfully can bear witness to the truth of it in our earthly relationships,-that the one way by which a human spirit can possess a spirit is by the sweet mutual love which abolishes 'mine' and 'thine,' and all but abolishes 'me' and 'thee.' And so God sets little store by the ownership which depends on divinity and creation, though, of course, that relation brings with it a duty. As the old psalm has it, 'It is He that hath made us, and we are His'; still, such a relationship as this, based upon the connection that subsists between the Maker and the work of His hands, is so purely external, and harsh, and superficial, that God does not reckon it to be a possession at all.

You perhaps remember how, in the great word which underlies all these New Testament conceptions of God's ownership of His people, viz. the charter that constituted Israel into a nation, He said, 'Ye shall be unto Me a people for a possession above all nations, for all the earth is Mine.' And yet, though that ownership and mastership extended over everything that His hands had made, He-if I might so say-contemned it, and relegated it to a secondary position, and told the people that His heart hungered for something deeper, more real, more vital than such a possession, and that therefore, just because all the earth was His, and that was not enough to satisfy His heart, He took them and made them a peculiar treasure above all nations. We have, then, to think of that great Divine Love which possesses us when He loves us, and when we love Him.

But remember that of this sweet commerce and reverberation of love which constitutes possession, the origination must be in His heart. 'We love Him because He first loved us.' The mirrors are set all round the great hall, but their surfaces are cold and lifeless until the great candelabrum in the centre is lit, and then, from every polished sheet there flashes back an echoing, answering light, and they repeat and repeat, until you scarce can tell which is the original and which is the reflection. But quench the centre-light, and the daughter-radiances vanish into darkness. The love on either side is on one side spontaneous and underived, and on the other side is secondary and evoked, but it is love on both sides. His possession of us is, as it were, the upper side, and our possession of Him is, as it were, the underside of the one golden bond. It matters not whether you look at the stream with your face to its source or with your face to its mouth, the silvery plain is the same; and the deepest tie that knits men to God is the same as the tie that knits God to men. There is mutual possession because there is mutual love.

Then again, in this same thought of mutual possession there lies a mutual surrender. For to give is the life-breath of all true love, and there is nothing which the loving heart more desires than to be able to pour itself out-much rather than any subordinate gifts-on its object. But that, if it is one-sided, is misery, and only when it is reciprocal, is it blessed. God gives Himself to us, as we know, most chiefly in that unspeakable gift of His Son, and we possess Him by virtue of His self-communication which depends upon His love. And then we possess Him, and He possesses us, not less by the answering surrender of ourselves, which is the expression of our love. No love subsists if it is only recipient; no love subsists if it is only communicated. Exports and imports must both be realised in this sweet commerce, and we enrich ourselves far more by what we give to the Beloved than by what we keep for ourselves.

The last, the hardest thing to surrender, is our own wills. To give them up by constraint is slavery that degrades. To give them up because we love is a sacrifice which sanctifies, even in the lowest reaches of daily life. And the love that knits us to God is not invested with all its blessed possession of Him, until it has surrendered its will, and said, 'Not as I will, but as Thou wilt.' The traveller in the old fable gathered his cloak around him all the more closely, and held it the more tightly, because of the tempest that blew, but when the warm sunbeams fell he dropped it. He that would coerce my will, stiffens it into rebellion; but when a beloved one says, 'Though I might be much bold to enjoin thee, yet for love's sake I rather beseech,' then yielding is blessedness, and the giving ourselves away is the finding of God and ourselves.

I need not touch, in more than a word, upon another aspect of this mutual possession, brought into view lovingly in many parts of Scripture, and that is that there is in it not only mutual love and mutual surrender, but mutual indwelling, 'He that dwelleth in love dwelleth in God, and God in him.' Jesus Christ has said the same thing to us, 'I am the Vine, ye are the branches. He that abideth in Me bringeth forth much fruit.' We dwell in God, possessing Him; He dwells in us, possessing us. We dwell in God, being possessed by Him. He dwells in us, being possessed by us. And He moves in the heart that loves, as the Master walking through His house, as the divinity is present in the temple, and as the soul permeates the body, and is sight in the eye and colour in the cheek, and force in the arm, and deftness in the finger, and swiftness in the foot. So the indwelling God breathes through all the capacities, and all the desires, and all the needs of the soul which He inhabits, and makes them all blessed. The very same set of facts-the presence of a divine life in the life of the believing spirit-may either be looked at from the lower end, and then they are that I possess God, and find in Him the nutriment and the stimulus for all my being, or may be looked at from the upper end, that He possesses me and finds in me capacities and a nature the emptiness of which He fills, and organs which He uses. In both cases mutual love, mutual surrender, mutual inhabitation, make up God's possession of me and my possession of God.

II. And now let me point you in a very few words to some of the plain, practical issues of this mutual possession.

God's possession of us demands our consecration. 'Ye are not your own, ye are bought with a price,' therefore, to live for self is to fly in the face of the very purpose of Christ's mission and of God's communication of Himself to us. There are slaves who run away from their masters and 'deny the Lord that bought them.' We do that whenever, being God's slaves, we set up anything else than His will as our law, or anything else than His glory as the aim of our lives. To live for self is to die, to die to self is to live. And the solemn obligations of that most blessed possession by God of us are as solemn as the possession is blessed, and can only be discharged when we turn to Him, and yield the whole control of our nature to His merciful hand, believing that He has not only the right to dispose of us, but that His disposition of us will always coincide with our sanest conceptions of good, and our wisest desires for happiness. Yield yourselves to God, for He has yielded Himself to you, and in the yielding we realise our largest and most blessed possession. It is a good bargain to give myself and to get God.

God's possession of us not only demands consecration, but it ensures safety. Remember that great word, 'No man is able to pluck them out of My Father's hand.' God is not a careless owner who leaves His treasures to be blown by every wind, or filched by every petty robber. He is not like the king of some decrepit monarchy, slices of whose territory his neighbours are for ever paring off and annexing. What God has God preserves. 'He is able to keep that which I have committed unto Him against that day.' 'They are Mine, saith the Lord, My jewels in the day which I make.' But our security depends on our consecration. 'No man is able to pluck them out of My Father's hand.' No! But you can wriggle yourself out of your Father's hand, if you will. And the security avails only so long as you realise that you belong to God, and are living not for yourself.

Possessing God we are rich. There is nothing that is truly our wealth which remains outside of us, and can be separated from us. 'Shrouds have no pockets,' says the Spanish proverb. 'His glory shall not descend after him,' says the grim psalm. But if God possesses me He is not going to let His treasures be lost in the grave. And if I possess Him then I shall pass through death as a beam of light does through some denser medium-a little refracted indeed, but not broken up; and I shall carry with me all my wealth to begin another world with. And that is more than you can do with the money that you make here. If you have God, you have the capital to commence a new condition of things beyond the grave.

And so that mutual possession is the real pledge of immortal life, for nothing can be more incredible than that a soul which has risen to have God for its very own, and has bowed itself to accept God's ownership of it, can be affected by such a transient and physical incident as what we call death. We rise to the assurance of immortality because we have an inheritance which is God Himself. And in that inexhaustible Inheritance there lies the guarantee that we shall live while He lives, because He lives, and until we have incorporated into our lives all the majesty and the purity and the wisdom and the power that belong to us because they are God's.

But we have to notice the two words that lie at the beginning of our first text-'In whom we were made an inheritance.' That opens up the whole question of the means by which this mutual possession becomes possible for us men. Jesus Christ has died. That breaks the bondage under which the whole world is held. For the true slavery which interferes with the free service and the full possession of God is the slavery of self and sin. Jesus Christ has died. 'If the Son make you free ye shall be free indeed.' That great sacrifice not only 'breaks the power of cancelled sin,' but it also moves the heart, in the measure in which we truly accept it, to the love and the surrender which make the mutual possession of which we have been speaking. And so it is in Him that we become an Inheritance, that God comes to His rights in regard to each of us. And it is in Him that we, trusting the Son, have the inheritance for ours, and 'are heirs with God, and joint heirs with Christ.' So, dear friends, if we would 'be meet for the inheritance of the saints in light,' we must unite ourselves to that Lord by faith, and through Him and faith in Him, we shall receive 'the remission of sins and inheritance among all them that are sanctified.'

THE EARNEST AND THE INHERITANCE

Ephesians 1:14

I have dealt with a portion of this verse in conjunction with the fragment of another in this chapter. I tried to show you how much the idea of the mutual possession of God by the believing soul, and of the believing soul by God, was present to the Apostle's thoughts in this context. These two ideas are brought into close juxtaposition in the verse before us, for, as you will see if you use the Revised Version, the latter clause is there rightly paraphrased by the addition of a supplement, and reads 'until the redemption of God's own possession.' So that in the first clause we have 'our inheritance,' and in the second we have 'God's possession.' This double idea, however, has appended to it in this verse some very striking and important thoughts. The possession of both sides is regarded as incomplete, for what we have is the 'earnest' of the 'inheritance,' and 'God's own possession' has yet to be 'redeemed,' in the fullest sense of that word, at some point in the future. An 'earnest' is a fraction of an inheritance, or of a sum hereafter to be paid, and is the guarantee and pledge that the whole shall one day be handed over to the man who has received the foretaste of it in the 'earnest.' The soldier's shilling, the ploughman's 'arles,' the clod of earth and tuft of grass which, in some forms of transfer, were handed over to the purchaser, were all the guarantee that the rest was going to come. So the great future is sealed to us by the small present and the experiences of the Christian life to-day, imperfect, fragmentary, defective as they are, are the best prophecy and the most glorious pledge of that great to-morrow. The same law of continuity which, in application to our characters, and our work, and our daily life, makes 'to-morrow as this day, and much more abundant,' in its application to the future life makes the life here its parent, and the life yonder the prolongation and the raising to its highest power, of what is the main though often impeded tendency and direction of the present. The earnest of the 'inheritance' is the pledge until the full redemption of 'God's own possession.' I wish,

40

then, to draw attention to these additional thoughts which are here attached to the main idea with which we were dealing in the last sermon.

I. And I ask you to look with me, first, at the incompleteness of the present possession.

I tried to show in my last sermon how those great thoughts of God's having us, and our having God, rested upon the three ideas of mutual love, mutual communication, and mutual indwelling. On His side the love, the impartation, the indwelling, are all perfect. On our side they are incomplete, broken, defective; and, therefore, the incompleteness on our side hinders both God's possession of us, and our possession of Him; so that we have but the 'earnest' and not the 'inheritance.' That is to say, the ownership may be perfect in idea, but in realisation it is imperfect.

And then, if we turn to the word in the other clause, 'the redemption of the purchased possession,' that suggests the incompleteness with which God as yet owns us. For though the initial act of redeeming is complete, yet redemption is a process, and not an act. And we 'are having' it, as the Apostle says in another place very emphatically, in continual and growing experience. The estate has been acquired, but has not yet been fully subdued. For there are tribes in the jungles and in the hills who still hold out against the reign of Him who has won it for Himself. And so seeing that the redemption in its fulness is relegated to some point in the future, towards which we are progressively approximating, and seeing that the best that can be said about the Christian experience here is that we have an 'earnest of the inheritance,' we must recognise the incompleteness to-day of our possession of God, and of God's possession of us.

That is a matter of experience. We know that only too well. 'I have God'- have I? I have a drop at the bottom of a too often unsteadily held and spilling cup, and the great ocean rolls unfathomable and boundless at my feet. How partial, how fragmentary, how clouded with doubts and blank ignorance, how intermittent, and, alas! rare, is our knowledge of Him. We sometimes go down our streets between tall houses, walking in

41

their shadow, and now and then there is a cross street down which a blaze of sunshine comes, and when we reach it, and the houses fall back, we see the blue beyond. But we go on, and we are in the shadow again. And so our earthly lives are passed, to a large extent, beneath the shade of the grimy buildings that we ourselves have put up, and which shut out heaven from us, and only now and then a slanting beam comes through some opening, and carries wistful thoughts and longings into the Empyrean beyond. And how feeble our faith, and how little of His power comes into our hearts, and how little of the joy of the Lord is realised in our daily experience we all know, and it is sometimes good for us to force ourselves to feel it is but an 'earnest' of the 'inheritance' that the best of us has.

'God has us.' Has He? Has He my will, which submits itself, and finds joy in submitting itself, to Him? How many competitors are there for my love which come in in front of Him, and we 'cannot get at Him for the press'! How many other motives are dominant in our lives, and how often we wrench ourselves away from our submission to Him, and try to set up a little dominion of our own, and say, 'Our lives are ours; who is lord over us?' Oh, brethren! we have God if we are Christians at all, and God has us. But alas! surely all honest experience tells us that there are awful gaps in the circle, and that our possession of Him, and His possession of us, are wofully incomplete.

Now, let me remind you that this incompleteness is mainly our own fault. Of course, I know that for the absolute completeness, either of my possession of God or of His of me, I must pass from out this world, and enter upon another stage and manner of being. But it is not being in the flesh, but it is being dominated by the flesh, that is the reason for the incompleteness of our mutual possession. And it is not being in the world, but it is being seduced and tyrannised over by the influx of worldly desires and thoughts, surging into our hearts, that drives God from out of our hearts, and draws us away from the sweet security of being possessed by, and living close to, Him. Death does a great deal for a man in advancing him in the scale of being, and in changing the centre of gravity, as it were, of this life. But there is no reason to believe that anything in death, or beyond it, will so alter the set and direction of his soul as that it will lead him into that possession of God, and being possessed by Him, which he has not here. There are many of us who, if we were to die this instant, would no more have God for ours, or belong to God, than we do now. It is our fault if the circle is broken into so many segments, if the moments of mutual love, communion, and indwelling are so rare and interrupted in our lives. The incompleteness which is due to our earthly condition is nothing as compared with the incompleteness which is due to our own sin.

But this incompleteness is one which may be progressively diminished, and we may be tending moment by moment, and year by year, nearer and nearer, and ever nearer, to the unreachable ideal of the entire possession of, and being possessed by, our God. There is a continual process of redemption of 'God's own possession' going on if a Christian man is true to himself and to that Divine Spirit which is the 'earnest' of the 'inheritance.' Mark that in my text, as it stands in our Bibles, and reads 'until the redemption,' there seems to be merely a pointing onwards to a future epoch, but that, in the more accurate rendering which you will find in the Revised Version, instead of 'until' we have 'unto,' and that teaches us that the Divine Spirit, which in one aspect is the 'earnest of the inheritance,' is also operating upon men's hearts and minds so as to bring about the gradual completion of the process of redemption.

So, dear brethren, seeing that by our own faults the possession is incomplete, and seeing that in the incompleteness there is given to each of us, if we rightly use it, a mighty power which is working ever towards the completion, it becomes us day by day to draw into our spirits more and more of that divine influence, and to let it work more fully upon the sins and faults which, far more than the body of flesh, or the connection with the world which it brings about, are the reasons for the incompleteness of the possession. We have, if we are wise, the task to discharge of daily enclosing, so to speak, more and more of the broad land which is all given over to us for our inheritance, but of which only so much as we fence in and cultivate, and make our own, is our own.

The incompleteness is progressively completed, and it is our work as much as God's work to complete it. For though in our text that redemption is conceived of as a divine act, it is not an act in which we are but passive. The air goes into the lungs, and that oxygenates the blood, but the lung has to inflate if the air is to penetrate all its vesicles. And so the Spirit which seals us unto the redemption of the possession has to be received, held, diffused throughout, and utilised by our own effort.

II. Now, secondly, notice the certainty of the completion of the incompleteness.

As I have already said, the clod of earth and the handful of grass, the servant's wages, the soldier's shilling, are all guarantees that the whole of the inheritance or of the pay will be forthcoming in due time. And so there emerges from this consideration of the Divine Spirit as the 'earnest,' the thought that the present experiences of a Christian soul are the surest proofs, and the irrefragable guarantees, of that perfect future. We ask for proofs of a future life. They may be very useful in certain states of mind, and to certain phases of opinion, but as it seems to me, far deeper than the region of logical understanding, and far more conclusive than anything that can be cast into the form of a syllogism, is the experience of a soul which knows that God is its, and that it is God's. 'I think, therefore, I am,' said the philosopher. 'I have God; therefore I shall always be,' says the Christian. Whilst that evidence is available only for himself, it is absolutely conclusive for himself. And the fact that it does spring in the hearts which are purest, because nearest God, is no small matter to be considered by men who may be groping for proofs of a life to come. If the selected moments of the purest devotion here on earth bring with them inevitably the confidence of the unending continuance of that communion, then those who do not believe in that future have to account for the fact as best they may. As for us who do know, though brokenly, and by reason of our own faults very imperfectly, what it is to have God, and be had by Him, we do not need to travel out to dim and doubtful analogies, nor do we even depend entirely upon the fact of a risen Christ ascended to the heavens, and living evermore, but we can say, 'I am God's; God is mine, and death has no power over such a mutual possession.'

The very incompleteness adds strength to the assurance, for the facts of the Christian life are such as to demand, both by its greatness and by its littleness, by its loftiness and by its lapses into lowliness, by the floodtide of devotion that sometimes sweeps rejoicingly over the mud-shoals and by the ebb that sometimes leaves them all black and festering, a future life wherein what was manifestly meant to be, and capable of being, dominant, supreme, but was hampered and hindered here, shall reach its full development, and where the plant that was dwarfed in this alien soil, transplanted into that higher house, shall blossom and bear immortal fruits. The new moon has a ragged edge, and each of the protrusions and concavities are the prophecy of the perfect orb which shall ere long fill the night with calm light from its silvery shield. The incompleteness prophesies completion.

And if the incompleteness is so blessed, what will the completeness be? A shilling to a million pounds, Knowledge which is partial and intermittent, like the twilight, as contrasted with the blaze of noonday, Joy like winter sunshine as compared with the warmth and heat of the midday sun at the zenith on the Equator. The 'earnest' of the 'inheritance' is wealth; the inheritance itself shall be unaccountable treasure.

III. And so, lastly, a word about the completion of the possession.

The 'earnest' is always of the same nature as, and a part of the 'inheritance.' Therefore, since the Holy Spirit is the earnest, the conclusion is plain, that the inheritance is nothing less than God Himself. Heaven is to possess God, and to be possessed by Him. That is the highest conception that we can form of that future life. And it is sorely to be lamented that subsidiary conceptions, which are all useful in their subordinate places, have, by popular Christianity, been far too much elevated into being the central blessedness of that future heaven. It is all right that we should cast the things which it is 'impossible for men to utter' into the shape of symbols which may a little relieve the necessary inarticulateness; but golden streets, and crystal pavements, and white robes, and golden palms, and all such representations, are but the dimmest shadows of that which they intend to express, and do often, as is the vice of all symbols, obscure. We can only conceive of a condition of which we have had no experience, by the two ways of symbolism and of negation. We can say, 'There shall be no night there; there shall be no curse there; they need no candle, neither light of the sun; they rest not day nor night; there shall be no more death, neither sorrow, nor crying, neither shall there be any more pain, for the former things are passed away.' But all these negations, like their sister symbols, are but surface work, and we have to go deeper than all of them.

But to possess God, and to be possessed by Him, and in either case fully, perfectly in degree, progressively in measure, eternal in duration, is the Heaven of heaven.

If that is the true conception of the inheritance, then it follows indubitably that such a Heaven is not for everybody. God would fain have us all for His there, as He would fain have each of us here and now, but it may not be. There are creatures which live beneath stones, and if you turn their coverings up, and let light fall on them, it kills them. And there are men who have refused to belong to God here, and refused to claim their portion in Him, and such cannot possess that true Heaven which is God Himself. Then, if its possession is not a mere matter of divine volition, giving a man what he is not capable of receiving, it plainly follows that the preparation must begin now and here by the incomplete possession of which my text is discoursing. And the way of such preparation is plain. The context says: 'In whom, after that ye believed, ye were sealed with that Holy Spirit of promise.' Faith in Jesus Christ, and trust in Him and His work as my forgiveness, my acceptance, my changed nature and heart-is the condition of being 'sealed' with that Spirit whose sealing of us is the condition of our love, our surrender, and mutual indwelling, which are our possession of God and being possessed by Him, and are the condition of our future complete possession of the 'inheritance.' We must begin with faith in Christ. Then comes the sealing, then comes the earnest, then comes the growing redemption, and in due time shall come the fulness of the possession. 'Believe on the Lord Jesus Christ' if thou wouldst have the earnest, whilst thou dost tabernacle in tents in the wilderness of Time, and if thou wouldst have the inheritance when thou crossest the flood into the goodly land.

GOD'S INHERITANCE IN THE SAINTS

Ephesians 1:18

The misery of Hope is that it so often owes its materials to the strength of our desires or to the activity of our imagination. But when mere wishes or fancies spin the thread, Hope cannot weave a lasting fabric. And so one of the old prophets, in speaking of the delusive hopes of man, says that they are like 'spiders' webs,' and 'shall not become garments.' Paul, then, having been asking for these Ephesian Christians that they might have hopes lofty and worthy, and such as God's summons to them would inspire, passes on to ask that they might have the material out of which they could weave such hope, namely, a sure and clear knowledge of the future blessings. The language in which he describes that future is remarkable-'the riches of the glory of His inheritance in the saints.' He calls it God's inheritance, not as meaning that God is the Inheritor, but the Giver. He speaks of it as 'in the saints,' meaning that, just as the land of Canaan was distributed amongst tribes and families, and each man got his own little plot, so that broad land is parted out amongst those who are 'partakers of the inheritance of the saints in light.'

And so my text suggests to me three points to which I seek to call your attention. First, the inheritance; second, the heirs; and third, the heirs' present knowledge of their future possession.

I. First, then, note the inheritance.

Now we must discharge from the word some of its ordinary associations. There is no reference to the thought of succession in it, as the mere English reader is accustomed to think-to whom inheritance means possession by the death of another. The idea is simply that of possession. The figure which underlies the word is, of course, that of the ancient partition of the land of Canaan amongst the tribes, but we must go a great deal deeper than that in order to understand its whole sweep and fulness of meaning.

48

What is the portion for a soul? God. God is Heaven, and Heaven is God. No interpretation of 'the inheritance,' however it may run into cheap and vulgar sensuous descriptions of a future glory, has come within sight of the meaning of the word, unless it has grasped this as the central thought: 'Whom have I in heaven but Thee? And there is none upon earth that I desire beside Thee.' Only God can be the portion of a human spirit. And none else can fill the narrowest and the smallest of man's needs.

So, then, if there were realised all the accumulated changes of progress in blessedness, and the withdrawal of all external causes of disquiet and weariness and weeping, still the heart would hunger and be empty of its true possession unless God Himself had flowed into it. It were but a poor advancement and the gain of a loss, if yearnings were made immortal, and the aching vacuity, which haunts every soul that is parted from God, were cursed with immortality. It would be so, if it be not true that the inheritance is nothing less than the fuller possession of God Himself.

And how do men possess God? How do we possess one another, here and now? By precisely the same way, only indefinitely expanded and exalted, do we possess Him here, and shall we possess Him hereafter. Heart to heart is joined by love which is mutual and interpenetrating possession; where 'mine' and 'thine' become blended, like the several portions of the one ray of white light, in the blessed word 'ours.' Contemplation makes us possessors of God. Assimilation to His character makes us own and have Him. They who love and gaze, and are being changed by still degrees into His likeness, possess Him. This is the central idea of man's future destiny and highest blessedness, a union with God closer and more intimate in degree, but yet essentially the same in kind, as is here possible amidst the shows and vanities and wearinesses of this mortal life. 'His servants shall serve Him, and see His face, and His name shall be on their foreheads.' Obedience, contemplation, transformation, these are the hands by which we here lay hold on God; and they in the heavens grasp Him just as we here on earth may do. The 'inheritance' is God Himself.

Surely that is in accordance with the whole teaching of Scripture, and is but the expansion of plain words which tell us that we 'are heirs of God.' If that be so, then all the other subsidiary blessings which have been, to the sore detriment of Christian anticipation and of Christian life in a hundred ways, elevated into disproportionate importance, fall into their right places, and are more when they are looked upon as secondary than when they are looked upon as primary.

Ah, brethren! neither the sensuous metaphors which, in accommodation to our weakness, Scripture has used to paint that future so that we may, in some measure, comprehend it, nor the translation of these, in so far as they refer to circumstances and externals, are enough for us. It is blessed to know that 'there shall be no night there'-blessed to grasp all those sweet negatives which contradict the miseries of the world, and to think of no sin, no curse, no tears, no sighing nor sorrow, neither any more pain, 'because the former things have passed away.' It is sweet and ennobling to think that, when we are discharged of the load of this cumbrous flesh, we shall be much more ourselves, and able to see where now is but darkness, and to feel where now is but vacancy. It is blessed to think of the recognising of lost and loved ones. But all these blessednesses, heaped together, as it seems to me, would become sickeningly the same if prolonged through eternity, unless we had God for our very own. Eternal is an awful word, even when the noun that goes with it is blessedness. And I know not how even the redeemed could be saved, as the long ages rolled on, from the oppression of monotony, and the feeling, 'I would not live always,' unless God was 'the strength of their hearts, and their portion for ever.' We must rise above everything that merely applies to changes in our own natures and in our relations to the external universe, and to other orders of creatures; and grasp, as the hidden sweetness that lies in the calyx of the gorgeous flower, the possession of God Himself as the rapture of our joy and the heaven of our heaven.

And if that be so, then these accumulated words with which the Apostle, in his fiery, impetuous way, tries to set forth the greatness of what he is speaking about, receive a loftier meaning than they otherwise would have.

'The riches of the glory of His inheritance'-now that word 'riches,' or 'wealth,' is a favourite of Paul's; and in this single letter occurs, if I count rightly, five times. In addition to our text, it is used twice in connection with God's grace, 'the riches of His grace' once in connection with Jesus, 'the unsearchable riches of Christ'; and once in a similar connection to, though with a different application from, our text, 'the riches of His glory.' Always, you see, it is applied to something that is special and properly divine. And here, therefore, it applies, not to the abundance of any creatural good, however exuberant and inexhaustible the store of it may be, but simply and solely to that unwearying energy, that self-feeding and ever-burning and never-decaying light, which is God. Of Him alone it can be said that work does not exhaust, nor Being tend to its own extinction, nor expenditure of resources to their diminution. The guarantee for eternal blessedness is the 'riches' of the eternal God, and so we may be sure that no time can exhaust, nor any expenditure empty, either His storehouse or our wealth.

And again, the 'glory' is not the lustrous light, however dazzling to our feeble eyes that may be, of any creature that reflects the light of God, but it is the far-flashing and never-dying radiance of His own manifestation of Himself to the hearts and souls of them that love Him. And so the 'inheritance is incorruptible and undefiled, and fadeth not away'; not merely by reason of the communicated will of God operating upon creatures whom He preserves untarnished by corruption, and ungnawed by decay, but because He Himself is the 'inheritance,' and on Him time hath no power. On His wealth all His creatures may hang for ever; and it shall be as it was in the sweet parable of the miracle of old, the fragments that remain will be more than when the meal began. 'The riches of the glory of His inheritance.'

II. Now notice, secondly, the heirs.

The words of my text receive, perhaps, their best commentary and explanation in those words which the writer of them heard, on the Damascus road, when the voice from heaven spoke to him about men 'obtaining an inheritance among them that are sanctified.' It almost sounds like an echo of that long past, but never-to-be-forgotten voice, when our Apostle writes as he does in our text.

Now what does he mean by 'saints'? Who are these amongst whom the broad acres of that infinite prairie are to be parted out? The word has attracted to itself contemptuous meanings and ascetical meanings, and meanings which really deny the true democracy of Christianity and the equality of all believers in the sight of God. But its scriptural use has none of these narrowing and confusing associations adhering to it, nor does it even directly and at first mean, as we generally take it to mean, pure men, holy in the sense of clean and righteous. But something goes before that phase of meaning, and it is this-a saint is a man separated and set apart for God, as His property. That is the true meaning of the word. It is its meaning as it is applied to the vessels of the Temple, the priests, the services, and the altar. It is its meaning, only with the necessary substitution of spirit for body, as it is applied in the New Testament as a designation co-extensive with that of believers.

How does a man belong to God?

We asked a minute or two ago how God belonged to men. The answer to the converse question is almost identical. A man belongs to God by the affection of his heart, by the submission of his will, by the reference of his actions to Him; and he who thus belongs to God, in the same act in which he gives himself to God, receives God as his possession. The thing must be reciprocal. 'All mine is Thine'; and God answers, 'And all Mine is thine.' He ever meets our 'O Lord, I yield myself to Thee,' with His 'And My child, I give Myself to thee.' It is so in regard of our earthly loves. It is so in regard of our relations to Him. And that being the case, purity, which is generally taken by careless readers as being the main idea of sanctity, will follow this self-surrender, which is the basis of all goodness, everywhere and always.

If that be true, and I do not think it can be effectively denied, then the next step is a very plain one, and that is that for the perfect possession of God, which is heaven, the same thing is needed in its perfection which is required for the partial possession of Him that makes the Christian life of earth. And just as here we get Him for ours in proportion as we give up ourselves to be His, so yonder the inheritance belongs, and can only belong to, 'the saints.' So, then, one can see that there is nothing arbitrary in this limitation of a possession, which in its very nature cannot go beyond the bounds which are thus marked out for it. If heaven were the vulgar thing that some of you think it, if that future life were desirable simply because you escaped from some external punishment and got all sorts of outward blessings and joys, felicities and advantages, hung round the neck, or pinned upon the breast, as they do to successful fighters, why then, of course, there might be partiality in the distribution of the decorations. But if that possession hinges upon our yielding ourselves to Him, then there is not an arbitrary link in the whole chain. Faith is set forth as the condition of heaven, because faith is the means of union with Christ, by and from whom alone we draw the motives for self-surrender and the power for sanctity. You cannot have heaven unless you have God. That is step number one. You cannot have God unless you have 'holiness, without which no man shall see the Lord.' That is step number two. You cannot have holiness without faith. That is step number three. 'An inheritance among them that are sanctified'; and then there is added, 'by faith which is in Me.'

It is clear, too, what a fatal delusion some of us are under who think that we shall, and fancy that we should like to, as we say, 'go to heaven when we die.' Why, heaven is here, round about you, a present heaven in the imitation of God, in the practice of righteousness, in the cultivation of dependence upon Him, in the yielding of yourselves up to Him. Heaven is here, and by your own choice you stop outside of it. There must be a correspondence between environment and nature for blessedness. 'The mind is its own place,' as the great Puritan poet taught us, 'and makes a heaven of hell, a hell of heaven.' Fishes die on the shore, and the man that drew them out dies in the water. Gills cannot breathe where lungs are useful, and lungs cannot, where gills come into play. If you have not here and now the holiness which knits you to God, and gives you possession of Him, you would not like 'heaven,' if it were possible to carry you to that place, in so far as it is a place. It is rather strange, if you hope to go to heaven when you die, that you should be very unwilling to spend a little time in it whilst you are alive, and that you should expect blessedness then from that presence of God which brings you no blessedness now.

III. Lastly, we have here the heirs' present knowledge of their future blessedness.

The Apostle asks that these men may know a thing that clearly seems unknowable. It is an impossible petition, we might be ready to say, because it is clear enough that there can be no true knowledge of the conditions and details of that future life. The dark mountains that lie between us and it hide their secret well, and few or no stray beams have reached us. An unborn babe, or a chrysalis in a hole in the ground or in a chink of a tree, might think as wisely about its future condition as we can do about that life beyond. There can be no knowledge until there is experience.

What, then, does Paul mean by framing such a petition as this? The answer is found in noticing that the knowledge which he is imploring here is a consequence of a previous knowledge. For, in a former verse, he prays that these men may have 'the spirit of wisdom in the knowledge of God'; and when they have got the knowledge of God he thinks that they will have got the knowledge of 'the riches of the glory of His inheritance in the saints.' Now, turn that into other words, and it is just this, that the knowledge of God, which comes by faith and love here, is in kind so identical with the fullest and loftiest riches of the knowledge of Him hereafter, that, if we have the one, we are not without the other. The one is in germ, the other, no doubt, full blown; the one is the twinkling of the rushlight, as it were, the other is the blaze of the sunshine. The two states of being are so correspondent that from the one we draw our clearest knowledge of the other. There are telescopes, in using which you do not look up when you want to see the stars, but down on to a reflecting mirror, and there you see them. Such a reflecting mirror, though it be sometimes muddied and dimmed and always very small, are the experiences of the Christian soul here.

So, dear friends, if we want to know as much as may be known of the blessedness of heaven, let us seek to possess as much as may be possessed of the knowledge and love of God on earth. Then we shall know the centre, at any rate; and that is light, though the circumference may be very dark. Much will remain obscure. That is of very small consequence to Hope, which does not need information half so much as it needs assurance. Like some flower in the cranny of the rock, it can spread a broad bright blossom on little soil, if only it be firmly rooted.

The path for us all is plain. Come to Jesus Christ as sinful men, and take what He has given, who has given Himself for us. Touched by His love, let us love Him back again, and yield ourselves to Him, and He will give Himself to us. They who can say, 'O Lord! I am Thine,' are sure to hear from heaven, 'I am thine.' And they who possess, in being possessed by, God Himself, do not need to die in order to go to heaven, but are at least doorkeepers in the house of the Lord now, and stand where they can see into the inner sanctuary which they will one day tread. A life of faith brings Heaven to us, and thereby gives us the surest and the clearest knowledge of what we shall be, and have, when we are brought to heaven.

THE MEASURE OF IMMEASURABLE POWER

Ephesians 1:19

'The riches of the glory of the inheritance' will sometimes quench rather than stimulate hope. He can have little depth of religion who has not often felt that the transcendent glory of that promised future sharpens the doubt-'and can I ever hope to reach it?' Our paths are strewn with battlefields where we were defeated; how should we expect the victor's wreath? And so Paul does not think that he has asked all which his friends in Ephesus need when he has asked that they may know the hope and the inheritance. There is something more wanted, something more even for our knowledge of these, and that is the knowledge of the power which alone can fulfil the hope and bring the inheritance. His language swells and peals and becomes exuberant and noble with his theme. He catches fire, as it were, as he thinks about this power that worketh in us. It is 'exceeding.' Exceeding what? He does not tell us, but other words in this letter, in the other great prayer which it contains, may help us to supply the missing words. He speaks of the 'love of Christ which passeth knowledge,' and of God being 'able to do exceeding abundantly above all that we can ask or think.' The power which is really at work in Christian men to-day is in its nature properly transcendent and immeasurable, and passes thought and desire and knowledge.

And yet it has a measure. 'According to the working of the strength of the might which He wrought in Christ.' Is that heaping together of synonyms or all but synonyms, mere tautology? Surely not. Commentators tell us that they can distinguish differences of meaning between the words, in that the first of them is the more active and outward, and the last of them is the more inward. And so they liken them to fruit and branch and root; but we need simply say that the gathering together of words so nearly co-extensive in their meaning is witness to the effort to condense the infinite within the bounds of human tongue, to speak the unspeakable; and that these reiterated expressions, like the blows of the billows that succeed one another on the beach, are hints of the force of the infinite ocean that lies behind.

And then the Apostle, when he has once come in sight of his risen Lord, as is his wont, is swept away by the ardour of his faith and the clearness of his vision, and breaks from his purpose in order to dilate on the glories of his King. We do not need to follow him into that. I limit myself now to the words which I have read as my text, with only such reference to the magnificent passage which succeeds as may be necessary for the exposition of this.

I. So, then, I ask you to look, first, at the measure and example of the immeasurable power that works in Christian men.

'According to the working of the strength of the might which He wrought in Christ'-the Resurrection, the Ascension, the session at the right hand of God, the rule over all creatures, and the exaltation above all things on earth or in the heavens-these are the facts which the Apostle brings before us as the pattern-works, the chefs-d'oeuvre of the power that is operating in all Christians. The present glories of the ascended Christ are glories possessed by a Man, and, that being so, they are available as evidences and measures of the power which works in believing souls. In them we see the possibilities of humanity, the ideal for man which God had when He created and breathed His blessing upon him. It is one of ourselves who has strength enough to bear the burden of the glory, one of ourselves who can stand within the blaze of encircling and indwelling Divinity and be unconsumed. The possibilities of human nature are manifest there. If we want to know what the Divine Power can make of us, let us turn to look with the eye of faith upon what it has made of Jesus Christ.

But such a thought, glorious as it is, still leaves room for doubt as to my personal attainment of such an ideal. Possibility is much, but we need solid certainty. And we find it in the truth that the bond between Christ and those who truly love and trust Him is such as that the possibility must become a reality and be consolidated into a certainty. The Vine and its branches, their Head and the members, the Christ and His Church, are knit together by such closeness of union as that wheresoever and whatsoever the one is, there and that must the others also be. Therefore, when doubts and fears, and consciousness of our own weakness, creep across us, and all our hopes are dimmed, as some star in the heavens is, when a light mist floats between us and it, let us turn away to Him our brother, bone of our bone and flesh of our flesh, and think that He, in His calm exaltation and regal authority and infinite blessedness, is not only the pattern of what humanity may be, but the pledge of what His Church must be. 'Where I am, there shall also My servant be.' 'The glory that Thou gavest Me I have given them.'

Nor is that all. Not only a possibility and a certainty for the future are for us the measure of the power that worketh in us, but as this same letter teaches us, we have, as Christians, a present scale by which we may estimate the greatness of the power. For in the next chapter, after that glorious burst as to the dignity of his Lord, which we have not the heart to call a digression, the Apostle, recurring to the theme of my text, goes on to say, 'And you hath He quickened,' and then, catching it up again a verse or two afterwards, he reiterates, clause by clause, what had been done on Jesus as having been done on us Christians. If that Divine Spirit raised Him from the dead, and set Him at His own right hand in the heavenly places, it is as true that the same power hath 'raised us up together, and made us sit together in heavenly places in Christ Jesus.' And so not only the far-off, though real and brilliant, and eye and heart-filling glories of the ascended Christ give us the measure of the power, but also the limited experience of the present Christian life, the fact of the resurrection from the true death, the death of sin, the fact of union with Jesus Christ so real and close as that they who truly experience it do live, as far as the roots of their lives and the scope and the aim of them are concerned, 'in the heavens,' and 'sit with Him in heavenly places'-these things afford us the measure of the power that worketh in us.

Then, because a Man is King of kings and Lord of lords; and because He who is our Life 'is exalted high above all principalities and powers';

and because from His throne He has quickened us from the death of sin, and has drawn us so near to Himself that if we are His we truly live beside Him, even whilst we stumble here in the darkness, we may know the exceeding greatness of His power, according to the working of the strength of the might which He wrought in Christ when He raised Him from the dead.

II. Secondly, notice the knowledge of the unknowable power.

We have already come across the same apparent paradox, covering a deep truth, in the former sections of this series of petitions. I need only remind you, in reference to this matter, that the knowledge which is here in question is not the intellectual perception of a fact as revealed in Scripture, but is that knowledge to which alone the New Testament gives the noble name, being knowledge verified by inward experience, and the result of one's own personal acquaintance with its object.

How do we know a power? By thrilling beneath its force. How are we to know the greatness of the power but because it comes surging and rejoicing into our aching emptiness, and lifts us buoyant above our temptations and weakness? Paul was not asking for these people theological conceptions. He was asking that their spirits might be so saturated with and immersed in that great ocean of force that pours from God as that they should never, henceforth, be able to doubt the greatness of that power which wrought in them. The knowledge that comes from experience is the knowledge that we all ought to seek. It is not merely to be desired that we should have right and just conceptions, but that we should have the vital knowledge which is, and which comes from, life eternal.

And that power, which thus we may all know by feeling it working upon ourselves, though it be immeasurable, has its measure; though it be, in its depth and fulness, unknowable and inexhaustible, may yet be really and truly known. You do not need a thunderstorm to experience the electric shock; a battery that you can carry in your pocket will do that for you. You do not need to have traversed all the length and breadth and depth and height of some newly-discovered country to be sure of its existence, and to have a real, though it may be a vague, conception of the magnitude of its shores. And so, really, though boundedly, we have the knowledge of God, and can rely upon it as valid, though partial; and similarly, by experience we have such a certified acquaintance with Him and His power as needs no enlargement to be trusted, and to become the source of blessings untold. We may see but a strip of the sky through the narrow chinks of our prison windows, and many a grating may further intercept the view, and much dust that might be cleared away may dim the glass but yet it is the sky that we see, and we can think of the great horizon circling round and round, and of the infinite depths above there, which neither eye nor thought can travel unwearied. Though all that we see be but an inch in breadth and a foot or two in height, yet we do see. We know the unknowable power that passeth knowledge.

And let me remind you of how large importance this knowledge of and constant reference to the measureless power manifested in Christ is for us. I believe there can be no vigorous, happy Christian life without it. It is our only refuge from pessimism and despair for the world. The old psalm said, 'Thou hast crowned Him with glory and honour, and hast given Him dominion over the works of Thy hands,' and hundreds of years afterwards the writer of the Epistle to the Hebrews commented on it thus, 'We see not yet all things put under Him.' Was the old vision a dream, was it never intended to be fulfilled? Apparently so, if we take the history of the past into account, and the centuries that have passed since have done nothing to make it more probable, apart from Jesus Christ, that man will rise to the height which the Psalmist dreamed of. When we look at the exploded Utopias that fill the past; when we think of the strange and apparently fatal necessity by which evil is developed from every stage of what men call progress, and how improvement is perverted, almost as soon as effected, into another fortress of weakness and misery; when we look on the world as it is to-day, I know not whence a man is to draw bright hopes, or what is to deliver him from pessimism as his last word about himself and his fellows, except the 'working of the strength of the might which He wrought in Christ.' 'We see not yet all things put under Him'-be it so, 'but we see Jesus,' and, looking to Him, hope is possible, reasonable, and imperative.

The same knowledge is our refuge from our own consciousness of weakness. We look up, as a climber may do in some Alpine ravine, upon the smooth gleaming walls of the cliff that rises above us. It is marble, it is fair, there are lovely lands on the summit, but nothing that has not wings can get there. We try, but slip backwards almost as much as we rise. What is to be done? Are we to sit down at the foot of the cliff, and say, 'We cannot climb, let us be content with the luscious herbage and sheltered ease below?' Yes! That is what we are tempted to say. But look! a mighty hand reaches over, an arm is stretched down, the hand grasps us, and lifts us, and sets us there.

'No man hath ascended up into heaven save He that came down from heaven,' and having returned thither stoops thence, and will lift us to Himself. I am a poor, weak creature. Yes! I am all full of sin and corruption. Yes! I am ashamed of myself every day. Yes! I am too heavy to climb, and have no wings to fly, and am bound here by chains manifold. Yes! But we know the exceeding greatness of the power, and we triumph in Him.

That knowledge should shame us into contrition, when we think of such force at our disposal, and such poor results. That knowledge should widen our conceptions, enlarge our desires, breathe a brave confidence into our hopes, should teach us to expect great things of God, and to be intolerant of present attainments whilst anything remains unattained. And it should stimulate our vigorous effort, for no man will long seek to be better, if he is convinced that the effort is hopeless.

Learn to realise the exceeding greatness of the power that will clothe your weakness. 'Lift up your eyes on high, and behold who hath created these things, for that He is strong in might, not one faileth.' That is wonderful, but here is a far nobler operation of the divine power. It is great to 'preserve the ancient heavens' fresh and strong by His might, but it is greater to come down to my weakness, to 'give power to the

61

faint,' and 'increase strength to them that have no might.' And that is what He will do with us.

III. Lastly, notice the conditions for the operations of the power.

'To usward who believe,' says Paul. He has been talking to these Ephesians, and saying 'ye,' but now, by that 'us,' he places himself beside them, identifies himself with them, and declares that all his gifts and strength come to him on precisely the same conditions on which theirs do to them; and that he, like them, is a waiter upon that grace which God bestows on them that trust Him.

'To usward who believe.' Once more we are back at the old truth which we can never make too emphatic and plain, that the one condition of the weakest among us being strong with the strength of the Lord is simple trust in Him, verified, of course, by continuance and by effort.

How did the water go into the Ship Canal at Eastham last week? First of all they cut a trench, and then they severed the little strip of land between the hole and the sea, and the sea did the rest. The wider and deeper the opening that we make in our natures by our simple trust in God, the fuller will be the rejoicing flood that pours into us. There is an old story about a Christian father, who, having been torturing himself with theological speculations about the nature of the Trinity, fell asleep and dreamed that he was emptying the ocean with a thimble! Well, you cannot empty it with a thimble, but you can go to it with one, and, if you have only a thimble in your hand, you will only bring away a thimbleful. The measure of your faith is the measure of God's power given to you.

There are two measures of the immeasurable power-the one is that infinite limit, of 'the power which He wrought in Christ,' and the other the practical limit. The working measure of our spiritual life is our faith. In plain English, we can have as much of God as we want. We do have as much as we want. And if, in touch with the power that can shatter a universe, we only get a little thrill that is scarcely perceptible to ourselves, and all unnoticed by others, whose fault is that? If, coming to the fountain that laughs at drought, and can fill a universe with its waters, we scarcely bear away a straitened drop or two, that barely refreshes our parched lips, and does nothing to stimulate the growth of the plants of holiness in our gardens, whose fault is that? The practical measure of the power is for us the measure of our belief and desire. And if we only go to Him, as I pray we all may, and continue there, and ask from Him strength, according to the riches that are treasured in Jesus Christ, we shall get the old answer, 'According to your faith be it unto you.'

EPHESIANS 2

EPHESIANS CHAPTER 2 CONTENTS

THE RESURRECTION OF DEAD SOULS

Ephesians 2:4-5

Scripture paints man as he is, in darker tints, and man as he may become, in brighter ones, than are elsewhere found. The range of this portrait painter's palette is from pitchiest black to most dazzling white, as of snow smitten by sunlight. Nowhere else are there such sad, stern words about the actualities of human nature; nowhere else such glowing and wonderful ones about its possibilities. This Physician knows that He can cure the worst cases, if they will take His medicine, and is under no temptation to minimise the severity of the symptoms or the fatality of the disease. We have got both sides in my text; man's actual condition, 'dead in trespasses'; man's possible condition, and the actual condition of thousands of men-made to live again in Jesus Christ, and with Him raised from the dead, and with Him gone up on high, and with Him sitting at God's right hand. That is what you and I may be if we will; if we will not, then we must be the other.

So there are three things here to look at for a few moments-the dead souls; the pitying love that looks down upon them; and the resurrection of the dead.

I. First, here is a picture, a dogmatic statement if you like, about the actual condition of human nature apart from Jesus Christ-'Dead in trespasses.'

The Apostle looks upon the world-many-coloured, full of activity, full of intellectual stir, full of human emotions, affections, joys, sorrows, fluctuations-as if it were one great cemetery, and on every gravestone there were written the same inscription. They all died of the same disease-'dead through sin,' as the original more properly means.

Now, I dare say many who are listening to me are saying in their hearts, 'Oh! Exaggeration! The old gloomy, narrow view of human nature cropping up again.' Well, I am not at all unwilling to acknowledge that truths like this have very often been preached both with a tone and in a manner that repels, and which is rightly chargeable with exaggeration and undue gloom and narrowness. But let me remind you that it is not the Evangelical preacher nor the Apostle only who have to bear the condemnation of exaggeration, if this representation of my text be not true to facts, but it is Jesus Christ too; for He says, 'Except ye eat the flesh and drink the blood of the Son of Man, ye have no life in you.' And I think that be He divine or not divine, His words about the religious condition of men go so surely to the mark that a man must be tolerably impregnable in his self-conceit who charges Him with narrowness and exaggeration. At all events, I am content to say after Him, and I pray that you and I, when we accept Him as our Teacher, may take not only His gracious, but His stern, words, assured that a deep graciousness lies in these, too, if we rightly understand them.

Let me remind you that the phrase of my text is by no means confined to Christian teachers, but that, in common speech, we hear from all high thinkers about the lower type of humanity being dead to the loftier thoughts in which they live and move and have their being. It has passed into a commonplace of language to speak of men being 'dead to honour,' 'dead to shame,' 'dead' to this, that, and the other good and noble and gracious thing. And the same metaphor, if you like, lies here in my text-that men who have given their wills and inmost natures over to the dominion of self-and that is the definition of sin-that such men are, ipso facto, by reason of that very surrender of themselves to their worst selves, dead on what I may call the top side of their nature, and that all that is there is atrophied and dwindling away.

Unconsciousness is one characteristic of death. And oh! as I look round I know that there are tens, and perhaps hundreds, of men and women who are all but utterly unconscious of a whole universe in which are the only realities, and to which it becomes them to have access. You live, in the physical sense, and move and have your being in God, and yet your inmost life would not be altered one hair's-breadth if there were no God at all. You pass the most resplendent instances and illustrations of His presence, His work, and you see nothing. You are blind on that side of your natures; or, as my text says, dead to the whole spiritual realm. Just as if there were a brick wall run against some man's windows so that he could see nothing out of them; so you, by your persistent adherence to the paltry present, the material, the visible, the selfish, have reared up a wall against the windows of your souls that look heavenwards; and of God, and all the lofty starry realities that cluster round Him, you are as unconscious as the corpse upon its bier is of the sunshine that plays upon its pallid features, or of the dew that falls on its stiffened limbs. Dead, because of sin-is that exaggeration? Is it exaggeration which charges all but absolute unconsciousness of spiritual realities upon worldly men like some of you?

And, then, take another illustration. Another of the signatures of death is inactivity. And oh! what faculties in some of my friends listening to me now are shrivelled and all but extinct! They are dormant, at any rate, to use another word, for the death of my text is not so absolute a death but that a resurrection is possible, and so dormant comes to express pretty nearly the same thing. Faculties of service, of enthusiasm, of life for God, of noble obedience to Him-what have you done with them? Left them there until they have stiffened like an unused lock, or rusted like the hinges of an unopened door; and you are as little active in all the noblest activities of spirit, which are activities in submission to and dependence upon Him, as if you were laid in your coffin with your idle hands crossed for evermore upon an unheaving breast.

There is another illustration that I may suggest for a moment. Decay is another characteristic and signature of death. And your best self, in some of you, is rotting to corruption by sin.

Ay! Dear brethren, when we think of these tragedies of suicide that are going on in thousands of men round about us to-day, it seems to me as if the metaphor and the reality were reversed; and instead of saying that my text is a violent metaphor, transferring the facts of material death and corruption to the spiritual realm, I am almost disposed to say it is the other way about, and the real death is the death of the spirit; and the outer dissolution and unconsciousness and inactivity of the material body is only a kind of parable to preach to men what are the awful invisible facts ever associated with the fact of transgression.

There are three lives possible for each of us; two of them involuntary, the third requiring our consent and effort, but all of them sustained by the same cause. The first of them is that which we call life, the activity and the consciousness of the bodily frame; and that continues as long as the power of God keeps the body in life. When He withdraws His hand there comes what the senses call death. Then there is the natural life of thinking, loving, willing, enjoying, sorrowing, and the like, and that continues as long as He who is the life and light of men breathes into them the breath of that life. And these two are lived or died largely without the man's own consent or choice.

But there is a third life, when all that lower is lifted to God, and thinking and willing and loving and enjoying and aspiring and trusting and obeying, and all these natural faculties find their home and their consecration and their immortality in Him. That life is only lived by our own will and it is the true life, and the others are, as I said, but parables, and envelopes, and vehicles, as it were, in which this life is carried, that is more precious than they. In the physical realm, separate the body from God, and it dies. In the natural conscious life, separate the soul, as we call it, from God, and it dies. And in the higher region, separate the spirit, which is the man grasping God, from God, and he dies; and that is the real death. Both the others are nothing in comparison with it.

It may co-exist with a large amount of intellectual and other forms of activity, as we see all round about us, and that makes it only the more ghastly and the sadder. You are full of energy in regard to all other subjects, but smitten into torpor about the highest; ready to live, to work, to enjoy, to think, to will, in all other directions, and utterly unconscious and unconcerned, or all but utterly unconscious and unconcerned, in regard to God.

Oh! a death which is co-existent with such feverish intensity of life as the most of you are expending all the week at your business and your daily pursuits is among the saddest of all the tragedies that angels are called upon to weep over, and that men are fools enough to enact. Brother! If the representation is a gloomy one, do not you think that it is better to ask the question-Is it a true one? than, Is it a cheerful one? I lay it upon your hearts that he that lives to God and with God is alive to the centre as well as out to the finger tips and circumference of his visible being. He that is dead to God is dead indeed whilst he lives.

II. Now, notice, in the second place, the pitying love that looks down on the cemetery.

'God, who is rich in mercy, for His great love wherewith He loved us.' Thus the great truth that is taught us here, first of all, is that that divine love of the Divine Father bends down over His dead children and cherishes them still. Oh! you can do much in separating yourselves from God through selfishness, selfwill, sensuality, or other forms of sin, but there is one thing you cannot do, you cannot prevent His loving you. If I might venture without seeming irreverent, I would point to that pathetic page in the Old Testament history where the king hears of the death, red-handed in treason, of his darling son, and careless of victory and forgetful of everything else, and oblivious that Absalom was a rebel, and only remembering that he was his boy, burst into that monotonous wail that has come down over all the centuries as the deepest expression of undying fatherly love. 'Oh! my son Absalom, my son, my son Absalom! Oh! Absalom, my son, my son!' The name and the relationship will well up out of the Father's heart, whatever the child's crime. We are all His Absaloms, and though we are dead in trespasses and in sins, God, who is rich in mercy, bends over us and loves us with His great love.

The Apostle might well expatiate in these two varying forms of speech, both of them intended to express the same thing-'rich in mercy' and 'great in love.' For surely a love which takes account of the sin that cannot repel it, and so shapes itself into mercy, sparing, and departing from the strict line of retribution and justice, is great. And surely a mercy

70

which refuses to be provoked by seventy times seven transgressions in an hour, not to say a day, is rich. That mercy is wider than all humanity, deeper than all sin, was before all rebellion, and will last for ever. And it is open for every soul of man to receive if he will.

But there is another point to be noticed in reference to this wonderful manifestation of the divine love looking down upon the myriads of men dead in sin, and that is that this love shapes the divine action. Mark the language of our text, in which the Apostle attributes a certain line of conduct in the divine dealings with us to the fact of His great love. Because 'He loved us' therefore He did so and so. Now about that I have only two remarks to make, and I will make them very briefly. The one is, here is a demonstration, for some of you people who do not believe in the Evangelical doctrine of an Atonement by the sacrifice of Jesus Christ, that the true scriptural representation of that doctrine is not that which caricaturists have represented it-viz. that the sacrifice of Jesus Christ changed in any manner the divine heart and disposition. It is not as unfriendly critics {who, perhaps, are not to be so much blamed for their unfriendliness as for their superficiality} would have us to believe, that the doctrine of Atonement says that God loves because Christ died. But the Apostle who preached that doctrine and looked upon it as the very heart and centre of his message to the world here puts as the true sequence-Christ died because God loves. Jesus Christ said the same thing, 'God so loved the world that He sent His Son, that whosoever believeth on Him should be saved.'

And that brings me to the second of the remarks which I wish briefly to make-viz. this, that the Divine Love, great, patient, wonderful, unrepelled by men's sin, as it is, has to adopt a process to reach its end. God by His love does not, because He cannot, raise these dead souls into a life of righteousness without Jesus Christ. And Jesus Christ comes to be the channel and the medium through which the love of God may attain its end. God's pitying love, because 'He is rich in mercy,' is not turned away by man's sin; and God's pitying love, because 'He is rich in mercy,' quickens men not by a bare will, but by the mission and work of His dear Son.

III. And so that is the last thing on which I speak a word-viz. the resurrection of the dead souls.

They died of sin. That was the disease that killed them. They cannot be quickened unless the disease be conquered. Dear brethren, I have to preach-not to argue, but to preach-and to press upon each soul the individual acceptance of the Death of Jesus Christ as being for each of us, if we will trust Him, the death of our death, and the death of our sin. By His great sacrifice and sufficient oblation He has borne the sins of the world and has taken away their guilt. And in Him the inmost reality of the spiritual death, and its outermost parable of corporeal dissolution, are equally and simultaneously overcome. If you will take Him for your Lord you will rise from the death of guilt, condemnation, selfishness, and sin into a new life of liberty, sonship, consecration, and righteousness, and will never see death.

And, on the other hand, the life of Jesus Christ is available for all of us. If we will put our trust in Him, His life will pass into our deadness; He Himself will vitalise our being, dormant capacities will be quickened and brought into blessed activity, a new direction will be given to the old faculties, desires, aspirations, emotions of our nature. The will will tower into new power because it obeys. The heart will throb with a better life because it has grasped a love that cannot change and will never die. And the thinking power will be brought into living, personal contact with the personal Truth, so that whatsoever darknesses and problems may still be left, at the centre there will be light and satisfaction and peace. You will live if you trust Christ and let Him be your Life.

And if thus, by simple faith in Him, knowing that the power of His atoning death has destroyed the burden of our guilt and condemnation, and knowing the quickening influences of His constraining love as drawing us to love new things and make us new creatures, we receive into our inmost spirits 'the law of the spirit of life' which was in Christ Jesus, and are thereby made 'free from the law of sin and death,' then it is only a question of time, when the vitalising force shall flow into all the cracks and crannies of our being and deliver us wholly from the bondage of corruption in the outer as well as in the inner life; for they who have learned that Christ is the life of their lives upon earth can never cease their appropriation of the fulness of His quickening power until He has 'changed the body of their humiliation into the likeness of the body of His glory, according to the working whereby He is able to subdue even all things unto Himself.'

Brethren! He Himself has said, and His words I beseech you to remember though you forget all mine, 'He that believeth in Me, though he were dead, yet shall he live, and he that liveth and believeth in Me shall never die.' 'Believest thou this?'

THE RICHES OF GRACE

Ephesians 2:7

One very striking characteristic of this epistle is its frequent reference to God's purposes, and what, for want of a better word, we must call His motives, in giving us Jesus Christ. The Apostle seems to rise even higher than his ordinary height, while he gazes up to the inaccessible light, and with calm certainty proclaims not only what God has done, but why He has done it. Through all the earlier portions of this letter, the things on earth are contemplated in the light of the things in heaven. The great work of redemption is illuminated by the thought of the will and meaning of God therein; for example, we read in Chapter i. that He 'hath blessed us with all spiritual blessings in Christ, according as He hath chosen us in Him,' and immediately after we read that He 'has predestinated us unto the adoption of children by Jesus Christ according to the good pleasure of His will.' Soon after, we hear that 'He hath revealed to us the mystery of His will, according to His good pleasure which He purposed in Himself'; and that our predestination to an inheritance in Christ is 'according to the purpose of Him who worketh all things after the counsel of His own will.'

Not only so, but the motive or reason for the divine action in the gift of Christ is brought out in a rich variety of expression as being 'the praise of the glory of His grace' {1-6}, or 'that He might gather together in one all things in Christ' {1-10}, or that 'we should be to the praise of His glory' {1-12}, or that 'unto the principalities and powers in heavenly places might be known by the Church the manifold wisdom of God.'

In like manner our text follows a sublime statement of what has been bestowed upon men in Jesus, with an equally sublime insight into the divine purpose of thereby showing 'the exceeding riches of His grace.' Such heights are not for our unaided traversing; it is neither reverent nor safe to speculate, and still less to dogmatise, concerning the meaning of the divine acts, but here, at all events, we have, as I believe, not a man

74

making unwarranted assertions about God's purposes, but God Himself by a man, letting us see so far into the depths of Deity as to know the very deepest meaning of His very greatest acts, and when God speaks, it is neither reverent nor safe to refuse to listen.

I. The purpose of God in Christ is the display of His grace.

Of course we cannot speak of motives in the divine mind as in ours; they imply a previous state of indecision and an act of choice, from which comes the slow emerging of a resolve like that of the moon from the sea. A given end being considered by us desirable, we then cast about for means to secure it, which again implies limitation of power. Still we can speak of God's motives, if only we understand, as this epistle puts it so profoundly, that His 'is an eternal purpose which He purposed in Himself,' which never began to be formed, and was not formed by reason of anything external.

With that caution Paul would have us think that God's chiefest purpose in all the wondrous facts which make up the Gospel is the setting forth of Himself, and that the chiefest part of Himself, which He desires that all men should come to know, is the glory of His grace. Of course very many and various reasons for these acts may be alleged, but this is the deepest of them all. It has often been misunderstood and made into a very hard and horrible doctrine, which really means little else than all-mighty selfishness, but it is really a most blessed one; it is the proclamation in tenderest, most heart-melting fashion of the truth that God is Love, and therefore delights in imparting that which is His creatures' life and blessedness; it bids us think that He, too, amidst the blessedness of His infinite Being, knows the joy of communicating which makes so large a part of the blessedness of our finite selves, and that He, too, is capable of being touched and gladdened by the joy of expression. As an artist in his noblest work paints or chisels simply for love of pouring out his soul, so, but in infinitely loftier fashion, the great Artist delights to manifest Himself, and in manifesting to communicate somewhat of Himself. Creation is divine self-revelation, and we might say, with all reverence, that God acts as birds sing, and fountains leap, and stars shine.

But our text leads us still farther into mysteries of glory, when it defines what it is in God that he most desires to set forth. It is the 'exceeding riches of Grace,' in which wonderful expression we note the Apostle's passionate accumulation of epithets which he yet feels to be altogether inadequate to his theme. It would carry us too far to attempt to bring out the whole wealth contained in these words which glide so easily over unthinking lips, but we may lovingly dwell for a few moments upon them. Grace, in Paul's language, means love lavished upon the undeserving and sinful, a love which is not drawn forth by the perception of any excellence in its objects, but wells up and out like a fountain, by reason of the impulse in its subject, and which in itself contains and bestows all good and blessing. There may be, as this very letter shows, other aspects of the divine nature which God is glad that man should know. His power and His wisdom have their noblest illustration in the work of Jesus, and are less conspicuously manifested in all His work; but His grace is shrined in Christ alone, and from Him flows forth into a thirsty world. That love, 'unmerited and free,' holds in solution power, wisdom and all the other physical or metaphysical perfections belonging to God with all their energies. It is the elixir in which they are all contained, the molten splendour into which have been dissolved gold and jewels and all precious things. When we look at Christ, we see the divinest thing in God, and that is His grace. The Christ who shows us and certifies to us the grace of God must surely be more than man. Men look at Him and see it; He shows us that grace because He was full of grace and truth.

But Paul is here not propounding theological dogmas, but pouring out a heart full of personal experience, and so adds yet other words to express what he himself has found in the Divine Grace, and speaks of its riches. He has learned fully to trust its fulness, and in his own daily life has had the witness of its inexhaustible abundance, which remains the same after all its gifts. It 'operates unspent.' That continually self-communicating love pours out in no narrower stream to its last recipient than to its first. All 'eat and are filled,' and after they are satisfied, twelve

76

baskets full of fragments are taken up. These riches are exceeding; they surpass all human conception, all parallel, all human needs; they are properly transcendent.

This, then, is what God would have us know of Himself. So His love is at once the motive of His great message to us in Jesus Christ, and is the whole contents of the message, like some fountain, the force of whose pellucid waters cleanses the earth, and rushes into the sunshine, being at once the reason for the flow and that which flows. God reveals because He loves, and His love is that which He reveals.

II. The great manifestation of grace is God's kindness to us in Christ.

All the revelation of God in Creation and Providence carries the same message, but it is often there hard to decipher, like some half-obliterated inscription in a strange tongue. In Jesus the writing is legible, continuous, and needs no elaborate commentary to make its meaning intelligible. But we may note that what the Apostle founds on here is not so much Christ in Himself, as that which men receive in Christ. As he puts it in another part of this epistle, it is 'through the Church' that 'principalities and powers in heavenly places' are made to 'know the manifold wisdom of God.' It is 'His kindness towards us' by which 'to the ages to come,' is made known the exceeding riches of grace, and that kindness can be best estimated by thinking what we were, namely, dead in trespasses and sins; what we are, namely, quickened together in Christ; raised up with Him, and with Him made to sit in heavenly places, as the immediately preceding clauses express it. All this marvellous transformation of conditions and of self is realised 'in Christ Jesus.' These three words recur over and over again in this profound epistle, and may be taken as its very keynote. It would carry us beyond all limits to deal with the various uses and profound meanings of this phrase in this letter, but we may at least point out how intimately and inseparably it is intertwined with the other aspect of our relations to Christ in which He is mainly regarded as dying for us, and may press upon you that these two are not, as they have sometimes been taken to be, antagonistic but complementary. We shall never understand the depths of the one

Apostolic conception unless we bring it into closest connection with the other. Christ is for us only if we are in Christ; we are in Christ only because He died for us.

God's kindness is all 'in Christ Jesus'; in Him is the great channel through which His love comes to men, the river of God which is full of water. And that kindness is realised by us when we are 'in Christ.' Separated from Him we do not possess it; joined to Him as we may be by true faith in Him, it is ours, and with it all the blessings which it brings into our else empty and thirsting hearts. Now all this sets in strong light the dignity and work of Christian men; the profundity and clearness of their religious character is the great sign to the world of the love of God. The message of Christ to man lacks one chief evidence of its worth if they who profess to have received it do not, in their lives, show its value. The characters of Christian people are in every age the clearest and most effectual witnesses of the power of the Gospel. God's honour is in their hands. The starry heavens are best seen by reflecting telescopes, which, in their field, mirror the brightness above.

III. The manifestation of God through men 'in Christ' is for all ages.

In our text the ages to come open up into a vista of undefined duration, and, just as in another place in this epistle, Paul regards the Church as witnessing to the principalities and powers in heavenly places, so here he regards it as the perennial evidence to all generations of the ever-flowing riches of God's grace. Whatever may have been the Apostle's earlier expectations of the speedy coming of the day of the Lord, here he obviously expects the world to last through a long stretch of undefined time, and for all its changing epochs to have an unchanging light. That standing witness, borne by men in Christ, of the grace which has been so kind to them, is not to be antiquated nor superseded, but is as valid to-day as when these words gushed from the heart of Paul. Eyes which cannot look upon the sun can see it as a golden glory, tinging the clouds which lie cradled around it. And as long as the world lasts, so long will Christian men be God's witnesses to it.

There are then two questions of infinite importance to us-do we show in character and conduct the grace which we have received by reverently submitting ourselves to its transforming energy? We need to be very close to Him for ourselves if we would worthily witness to others of what we have found Him to be. We have but too sadly marred our witness, and have been like dim reflectors round a lamp which have received but little light from it, and have communicated even less than we have received. Do we see the grace that shines so brightly in Jesus Christ? God longs that we should so see; He calls us by all endearments and by loving threats to look to that Incarnation of Himself. And when we lift our eyes to behold, what is it that meets our gaze? Intolerable light? The blaze of the white throne? Power that crushes our puny might? No! the 'exceeding riches of grace.' The voice cries, 'Behold your God!' and what we see is, 'In the midst of the throne a lamb as it had been slain.'

SALVATION: GRACE: FAITH

Ephesians 2:8

Here are three of the key-words of the New Testament-'grace,' 'saved,' 'faith.' Once these terms were strange and new; now they are old and threadbare. Once they were like lava, glowing and cast up from the central depths; but it is a long while since the eruption, and the blocks have got cold, and the corners have been rubbed off them. I am afraid that some people, when they read such a text, will shrug the shoulder of weariness, and think that they are in for a dreary sermon.

But the more familiar a word is, the more likely are common ideas about it to be hazy. We substitute acquaintance with the sound for penetration into the sense. A frond of sea-weed, as long as it is in the ocean, unfolds its delicate films and glows with its subdued colours. Take it out, and it is hard and brown and ugly, and you have to plunge it into the water again before you see its beauty. So with these well-worn Christian terms; you have to put them back, by meditation and thought, especially as to their bearing on yourself, in order to understand their significance and to feel their power. And, although it is very hard, I want to try and do that for a few moments with this grand thought that lies in my text.

I. Here we have the Christian view of man's deepest need, and God's greatest gift.

'Ye have been saved.' Now, as I have said, 'saved,' and 'salvation,' and 'Saviour,' are all threadbare words. Let us try to grasp the whole throbbing meaning that is in them. Well, to begin with, and in its original and lowest application, this whole set of expressions is applied to physical danger from which it delivers, and physical disease which it heals. So, in the Gospels, for instance, you find 'Thy faith hath made thee whole'-literally, 'saved thee' And you hear one of the Apostles crying, in an excess of terror and collapse of faith, 'Save! Master! we perish!' The two notions that are conveyed in our familiar expression

80

'safe and sound,' both lie in the word-deliverance from danger, and healing of disease.

Then, when you lift it up into the loftier region, into which Christianity buoyed it up, the same double meaning attaches to it. The Christian salvation is, on its negative side, a deliverance from something impending-peril-and a healing of something infecting us-the sickness of sin.

It is a deliverance; what from? Take, in the briefest possible language, three sayings of Scripture to answer that question-what am I to be saved from? 'His name shall be called Jesus, for He shall save His people from their sins.' He 'delivers'-or saves-'us from the wrath to come.' He 'saves a soul from death.' Sin, wrath death, death spiritual as well as physical, these are the dangers which lie in wait; and the enemies which have laid their grip upon us. And from these, as the shepherd drags the kid from the claws of the lion or the bear's hug, the salvation of the Gospel wrenches and rescues men.

The same general conceptions emerge, if we notice, on the other side-what are the things which the New Testament sets forth as the opposites of its salvation? Take, again, a brief reference to Scripture words: 'The Son of Man came not to condemn the world, but that the world through Him might be saved.' So the antithesis is between judgment or condemnation on the one hand, and salvation on the other. That suggests thoughts substantially identical with the preceding but still more solemn, as bringing in the prospect a tribunal and a judge. The Gospel then reveals the Mighty Power that lifts itself between us and judgment, the Mighty Power that intervenes to prevent absolute destruction, the Power which saves from sin, from wrath, from death.

Along with them we may take the other thought, that salvation, as the New Testament understands it, is not only the rescue and deliverance of a man from evils conceived to lie round about him, and to threaten his being from without, but that it is his healing from evils which have so wrought themselves into his very being, and infected his whole nature, as that the emblem for them is a sickness unto death for the healing from which this mighty Physician comes. These are the negative sides of this great Christian thought.

But the New Testament salvation is more than a shelter, more than an escape. It not only trammels up evil possibilities, and prevents them from falling upon men's heads, but it introduces all good. It not only strips off the poisoned robe, but it invests with a royal garb. It is not only negatively the withdrawal from the power, and the setting above the reach, of all evil, in the widest sense of that word, physical and moral, but it is the endowment with every good, in the widest sense of that word, physical and moral, which man is capable of receiving, or God has wealth to bestow. And this positive significance of the Christian salvation, which includes not only pardon, and favour, and purity, and blessedness here in germ, and sure and certain hope of an overwhelming glory hereafter-this is all suggested to us by the fact that in Scripture, more than once, to 'have everlasting life,' and to 'enter into the Kingdom of God,' are employed as equivalent and alternative expressions for being saved with the salvation of God.

And that leads me to another point-my text, as those of you who have used the Revised Version will observe, is there slightly modified in translation, and reads 'Ye have been saved,'-a past act, done once, and with abiding present consequences, which are realised progressively in the Christian life, and reach forward into infinitude. So the Scripture sometimes speaks of salvation as past, 'He saved us by His mercy': sometimes of it as present and progressive, 'The Lord added to the Church daily those that were {in process of} being saved': sometimes of it as future, 'now is our salvation nearer than when we believed.' In that future all that is involved in the word will be evolved from it in blessed experience onwards through eternity.

I have said that we should try to make an effort to fathom the depth of meaning in this and other familiar commonplace terms of Scripture. But no effort prior to experience will ever fathom it. There was in the papers some time ago an account of some extraordinary deep-sea soundings that have been made away down in the South Pacific, 29,400 feet and no bottom, and the wire broke. The highest peak of the Himalayas might be put into that abyss, and there would be hundreds of feet between it and the surface. He 'casts all our sins,' mountainous as they are, behind His back 'into the depths of the sea'; and no plummet that man can drop will ever reach its profound abyss. 'Thy judgments are a great deep,' and deeper than the judgments is the depth of Thy salvation.

And now, brethren, before I go further, notice the-I was going to say theory, but that is a cold word-the facts of man's condition and need that underlie this great Christian term of salvation-viz. we are all in deadly peril; we are all sick of a fatal disease. 'Ah!' you say, 'that is Paul.' Yes! it is Paul. But it is not Paul only; it is Paul's Master, and, I hope, your Master; for He not only spoke loving, gentle words to and about men, and not only was grace poured into His lips, but there is another side to His utterances. No one ever spoke sadder, sterner words about the real condition of men than Jesus Christ did. Lost sheep, lost coins, prodigal sons, builders of houses on the sand that are destined to be blown down and flooded away, men in danger of an undying worm and unquenchable fire-these are parts of Christ's representations of the condition of humanity, and these are the conceptions that underlie this great thought of salvation as being man's deepest need.

It goes far deeper down than any of the superficial constructions of what humanity requires, which are found among non-Christian, social and economical, and intellectual and political reformers. It includes all that is true in the estimate of any of these people, and it supplies all that they aim at. But it goes far beyond them. And as they stand pottering round the patient, and administering-what shall I say? 'pills for the earthquake,' as we once heard-it comes and brushes them aside and says, 'Physicians of no value! here is the thing that is wanted-salvation that comes from God.'

Brother! it is what you need. Do not be led away by the notion that wealth, or culture, or anything less than Christ's gift to men will meet your necessities. If once we catch a glimpse of what we really are, there will be no words wanted to enforce the priceless value of the salvation that the Gospel offers. It is sure to be an uninteresting word and thing to a man who does not feel himself to be a sinner. It is sure to be of perennial worth to a man who does. Life-belts lie unnoticed on the cabin-shelf above the berth as long as the sun is bright, and the sea calm, and everything goes well; but when the ship gets on the rocks the passengers fight to get them. If you know yourself, you will know that salvation is what you need.

II. Here we have the Christian unfolding of the source of salvation.

'By grace ye have been saved.' There is another threadbare word. It is employed in the New Testament with a very considerable width of signification, which we do not need to attend to here. But, in regard of the present context, let me just point out that the main idea conveyed by the word is that of favour, or lovingkindness, or goodwill, especially when directed to inferiors, and most eminently when given to those who do not deserve it, but deserve its opposite. 'Grace' is love that stoops and that requites, not according to desert, but bestows upon those who deserve nothing of the kind; so when the Apostle declares that the source of salvation is 'grace.' he declares two things. One is that the fountain of all our deliverance from sin, and of our healing of our sicknesses, lies in the deep heart of God, from which it wells up undrawn, unmotived, uncaused by anything except His own infinite lovingkindness. People have often presented the New Testament teaching about salvation as if it implied that God's love was brought to man because Jesus Christ died, and turned the divine affections. That is not New Testament teaching. Christ's death is not the cause of God's love, but God's love is the cause of Christ's death. 'God so loved the world that He gave His only begotten Son.'

When we hear in the Old Testament, 'I am that I am,' we may apply it to this great subject. For that declaration of the very inmost essence of the divine nature is not merely the declaration, in half metaphysical terms, of a self-substituting, self-determining Being, high above limitation and time and change, but it is a declaration that when He loves He loves freely and unmodified save by the constraint of His own Being. Just as the light, because it is light and must radiate, falls upon dunghills and diamonds, upon black rocks and white snow, upon ice-peaks and fertile fields, so the great fountain of the Divine Grace pours out upon men by reason only of its own continual tendency to communicate its own fulness and blessedness.

There follows from that the other thought, on which the Apostle mainly dwells in our context, that the salvation which we need, and may have, is not won by desert, but is given as a gift. Mark the last words of my text- 'that not of yourselves it is the gift of God.' They have often been misunderstood, as if they referred to the faith which is mentioned just before. But that is a plain misconception of the Apostle's meaning, and is contradicted by the whole context. It is not faith that is the gift of God, but it is salvation by grace. That is plain if you will read on to the next verse. 'By grace are ye saved through faith, and that not of yourselves; it is the gift of God; not of works lest any man should boast.' What is it that is 'not of works'? Faith? certainly not. Nobody would ever have thought it worth while to say, 'faith is not of works,' because nobody would have said that it was. The two clauses necessarily refer to the same thing, and if the latter of them must refer to salvation by grace, so must the former. Thus, the Apostle's meaning is that we get salvation, not because we work for it but because God gives it as a free gift, for which we have nothing to render, and which we can never deserve.

Now, I am sure that there are some of you who are saying to yourselves, 'This is that old, threadbare, commonplace preaching again!' Well! shame on us preachers if we have made a living Gospel into a dead theology. And shame no less on you hearers if by you the words that should be good news that would make the tongue of the dumb sing, and the lame man leap as a hart, have been petrified and fossilised into a mere dogma.

I know far better than you do how absolutely inadequate all my words are, but I want to bring it to you and to lay it not on your heads only but on your hearts, as the good news that we all need, that we have not to buy, that we have not to work to get salvation, but that having got it we have to work thereafter. 'What shall we do that we might work the works of God?' A whole series of diverse, long, protracted, painful toils? Christ swept away the question by striking out the 's' at the end of the word, and answered, 'This is the work' {not 'works'} 'of God,' the one thing which will open out into all heroism and practical obedience, 'that ye believe on Him to whom He hath sent.'

III. That leads me to the last point-viz. the Christian requirement of the condition of salvation.

Note the precision of the Apostle's prepositions: 'Ye have been saved by grace'; there is the source-'Ye have been saved by grace, through faith'-there is the medium, the instrument, or, if I may so say, the channel; or, to put it into other words, the condition by which the salvation which has its source in the deep heart of God pours its waters into my empty heart. 'Through faith,' another threadbare word, which, withal, has been dreadfully darkened by many comments, and has unfortunately been so represented as that people fancy it is some kind of special attitude of mind and heart, which is only brought to bear in reference to Christ's Gospel. It is a thousand pities, one sometimes thinks, that the word was not translated 'trust' instead of 'faith,' and then we should have understood that it was not a theological virtue at all, but just the common thing that we all know so well, which is the cement of human society and the blessedness of human affection, and which only needs to be lifted, as a plant that had been running along the ground, and had its tendrils bruised and its fruit marred might be lifted, and twined round the pillar of God's throne, in order to grow up and bear fruit that shall be found after many days unto praise, and honour, and glory.

Trust; that is the condition. The salvation rises from the heart of God. You cannot touch the stream at its source, but you can tap it away down in its flow. What do you want machinery and pumps for? Put a yard of wooden pipe into the river, and your house will have all the water it needs.

So, dear brethren, here is the condition-it is a condition only, for there is no virtue in the act of trust, but only in that with which we are brought into living union when we do trust. When salvation comes, into my heart by faith it is not my faith but God's grace that puts salvation there.

Faith is only the condition, ay! but it is the indispensable condition. How many ways are there of getting possession of a gift? One only, I should suppose, and that is, to put out a hand and take it. If salvation is by grace it must be 'through faith.' If you will not accept you cannot have. That is the plain meaning of what theologians call justification by faith; that pardon is given on condition of taking it. If you do not take it you cannot have it. And so this is the upshot of the whole-trust, and you have.

Oh, dear friends! open your eyes to see your dangers. Let your conscience tell you of your sickness. Do not try to deliver, or to heal yourselves. Self-reliance and self-help are very good things, but they leave their limitations, and they have no place here. 'Every man his own Redeemer' will not work. You can no more extricate yourself from the toils of sin than a man can release himself from the folds of a python. You can no more climb to heaven by your own effort than you can build a railway to the moon. You must sue in forma pauperis, and be content to accept as a boon an unmerited place in your Father's heart, an undeserved seat at His bountiful table, an unearned share in His wealth, from the hands of your Elder Brother, in whom is all His grace, and who gives salvation to every sinner if he will trust Him. 'By grace have ye been saved through faith.'

GOD'S WORKMANSHIP AND OUR WORKS

Ephesians 2:10

The metal is molten as it runs out of the blast furnace, but it soon cools and hardens. Paul's teaching about salvation by grace and by faith came in a hot stream from his heart, but to this generation his words are apt to sound coldly, and hardly theological. But they only need to be reflected upon in connection with our own experience, to become vivid and vital again. The belief that a man may work towards salvation is a universal heresy. And the Apostle, in the context, summons all his force to destroy that error, and to substitute the great truth that we have to begin with an act of God's, and only after that can think about our acts. To work up towards salvation is, in the strict sense of the words, preposterous; it is inverting the order of things. It is beginning at the wrong end. It is saying X Y Z before you have learnt to say A B C. We are to work downwards from salvation because we have it, not that we may get it. And whatever 'good works' may mean, they are the consequences, not the causes, of 'salvation,' whatever that may mean. But they are consequences, and they are the very purpose of it. So says Paul in the archaic language of my text-which only wants a little steadfast looking at to be turned into up-to-date gospel-'We are His workmanship, created unto good works'; and the fact that we are is one great reason for the assertion which he brings it in to buttress, that we are saved by grace, not by works. Now, I wish, in the simplest possible way, to deal with these great words, and take them as they lie before us.

I. We have, first, then, this as the root of everything, the divine creation.

Now, you will find that in this profound letter of the Apostle there are two ideas cropping up over and over again, both of them representing the facts of the Christian life and of the transition from the unchristian to the Christian; and the one is Resurrection and the other is Creation. They have this in common, that they suggest the idea that the great gift which Christianity brings to men-no, do not let me use the abstract word

'Christianity'-the great gift which Christ brings to men-is a new life. The low popular notion that salvation means mainly and primarily immunity from the ultimate, most lasting future consequences of transgression, a change of place or of condition, infects us all, and is far too dominant in our popular notions of Christianity and of salvation. And it is because people have such an unworthy, narrow, selfish idea of what 'salvation' is that they fall into the bog of misconception as to how it is to be attained. The ordinary man's way of looking at the whole matter is summed up in a sentence which I heard not long since about a recently deceased friend of the speaker's, and the like of which you have no doubt often heard and perhaps said, 'He is sure to be saved because he has lived so straight.' And at the foundation of that confident epitaph lay a tragical, profound misapprehension of what salvation was.

For it is something done in you; it is not something that you get, but it is something that you become. The teaching of this letter, and of the whole New Testament, is that the profoundest and most precious of all the gifts which come to us in Jesus Christ, and which in their totality are summed up in the one word that has so little power over us, because we understand it so little, and know it so well-'salvation'-is a change in a man's nature so deep, radical, vital, as that it may fairly be paralleled with a resurrection from the dead.

Now, I venture to believe that it is something more than a strong rhetorical figure when that change is described as being the creation of a new man within us. The resurrection symbol for the same fact may be treated as but a symbol. You cannot treat the teaching of a new life in Christ as being a mere figure. It is something a great deal more than that, and when once a man's eye is opened to look for it in the New Testament it is wonderful how it flashes out from every page and underlies the whole teaching. The Gospel of John, for example, is but one long symphony which has for its dominant theme 'I am come that they might have life.' And that great teaching-which has been so vulgarised, narrowed, and mishandled by sacerdotal pretensions and sacramentarian superstitions-that great teaching of Regeneration, or the new birth, rests upon this as its very basis, that what takes place when a man turns to Jesus Christ, and is saved by Him, is that there is communicated to him not in symbol but in spiritual fact {and spiritual facts are far more true than external ones which are called real} a spark of Christ's own life, something of 'that spirit of life which was in Christ Jesus,' and by which, and by which alone, being transfused into us, we become 'free from the law of sin and death.' I beseech you, brethren, see that, in your perspective of Christian truth, the thought of a new life imparted to us has as prominent and as dominant a place as it obviously has in the teaching of the New Testament. It is not so dominant in the current notions of Christianity that prevail amongst average people, but it is so in all men who let themselves be guided by the plain teaching of Christ Himself and of all His servants. Salvation? Yes! And the very essence of the salvation is the breathing into me of a divine life, so that I become partaker of 'the divine nature.'

Now, there is another step to be taken, and that is that this new life is realised in Christ Jesus. Now, this letter of the Apostle is distinguished even amongst his letters by the extraordinary frequency and emphasis with which he uses that expression 'in Christ Jesus.' If you will take up the epistle, and run your eye over it at your leisure, I think you will be surprised to find how, in all connections, and linked with every sort of blessing and good as its condition, there recurs that phrase. It is 'in Christ' that we obtain the inheritance; it is 'in Christ' that we receive 'redemption, even the forgiveness of sins'; it is in Him that we are 'builded together for a habitation of God'; it is in Him that all fulness of divine gifts, and all blessedness of spiritual capacities, is communicated to us; and unless, in our perspective of the Christian life, that expression has the same prominence as it has in this letter, we have yet to learn the sweetest sweetness, and have yet to receive the most mighty power, of the Gospel that we profess. 'In Christ'-a union which leaves the individuality of the Saviour and of the saint unimpaired, because without such individuality sweet love were slain, and there were no communion possible, but which is so close, so real, so vital, as that only the separating wall of personality and individual consciousness comes in between-that is the New Testament teaching of the relation of the Christian to Christ. Is it your experience, dear brother? Do not be frightened by talking about mysticism. If a Christianity has no mysticism it has no life. There is a wholesome mysticism and there is a morbid one, and the wholesome one is the very nerve of the Gospel as it is presented by Jesus Himself: 'I am the Vine, ye are the branches. Abide in Me, and I in you.' If our nineteenth century busy Christianity could only get hold of that truth as firmly as it grasps the representative and sacrificial character of Christ's work, I believe it would come like a breath of spring over 'the winter of our discontent,' and would change profoundly and blessedly the whole contexture of modern Christianity.

And now there is another step to take, and that is that this union with Christ, which results in the communication of a new life, or, as my text puts it, a new creation, depends upon our faith. We are not passive in the matter. There is the condition on which the entrance of the life into our spirits is made possible. You must open the door, you must fling wide the casement, and the blessed warm morning air of the sun of righteousness, with healing in its beams, will rush in, scatter the darkness and raise the temperature. 'Faith' by which we simply mean the act of the mind in accepting and of the will and heart in casting one's self upon Christ as the Saviour-that act is the condition of this new life. And so each Christian is 'God's workmanship, created in Christ Jesus.'

And now, says Paul-and here some of us will hesitate to follow him-that new creation has to go before what you call 'good works.' Now, do not let us exaggerate. There has seldom been a more disastrous and untrue thing said than what one of the Fathers dared to say, that the virtues of godless men were 'splendid vices.' That is not so, and that is not the New Testament teaching. Good is good, whoever does it. But, then, no man will say that actions, however they may meet the human conception of excellence, however bright, pure, lofty in motive and in aim they may be, reach their highest possible radiance and are as good as they ought to be, if they are done without any reference to God and His love. Dear brethren, we surely do not need to have the alphabet of morality repeated to us, that the worth of an action depends upon its motive, that no motive is correspondent to our capacities and our relation to God and our consequent responsibilities, except the motive of loving obedience to

Him. Unless that be present, the brightest of human acts must be convicted of having dark shadows in it, and all the darker because of the brightness that may stream from it. And so I venture to assert that since the noblest systems of morality, apart from religion, will all coincide in saying that to be is more than to do, and that the worth of an action depends upon its motive, we are brought straight up to the 'narrow, bigoted' teaching of the New Testament, that unless a man is swayed by the love of God in what he does, you cannot, in the most searching analysis, say that his deed is as good as it ought to be, and as it might be. To be good is the first thing, to do good is the second. Make the tree good and its fruit good. And since, as we have made ourselves we are evil, there must come a re-creation before we can do the good deeds which our relation to God requires at our hands.

II. I ask you to look at the purpose of this new creation brought out in our text.

'Created in Christ Jesus unto good works.' That is what life is given to you for. That is why you are saved, says Paul. Instead of working upwards from works to salvation, take your stand at the received salvation, and understand what it is for, and work downwards from it.

Now, do not let us take that phrase, 'good works,' which I have already said came hot from the Apostle's heart, and is now cold as a bar of iron, in the limited sense which it has come to bear in modern religious phraseology. It means something a great deal more than that. It covers the whole ground of what the Apostle, in another of his letters, speaks of when he says, 'Whatsoever things are lovely and of good report, if there be any virtue'-to use for a moment the world's word, which has such power to conjure in Greek ethics-'or if there be any praise'-to use for a moment the world's low motive, which has such power to sway men-'think of these things,' and these things do. That is the width of the conception of 'good works'; everything that is 'lovely and of good report.' That is what you receive the new life for.

Contrast that with other notions of the purpose of revelation and redemption. Contrast it with what I have already referred to, and so need not enlarge upon now, the miserably inadequate and low notions of the essentials of salvation which one hears perpetually, and which many of us cherish. It is no mere immunity from a future hell. It is no mere entrance into a vague heaven. It is not escaping the penalty of the inexorable law, 'Whatsoever a man soweth that shall he also reap,' that is meant by 'salvation,' any more than it is putting away the rod, which the child would be all the better for having administered to him, that is meant by 'forgiveness.' But just as forgiveness, in its essence, means not suspension nor abolition of penalty, but the uninterrupted flow of the Father's love, so salvation in its essence means, not the deliverance from any external evil or the alteration of anything in the external position, but the revolution and the re-creation of the man's nature. And the purpose of it is that the saved man may live in conformity with the will of God, and that on his character there may be embroidered all the fair things which God desires to see on His child's vesture.

Contrast it with the notion that an orthodox belief is the purpose of revelation. I remember hearing once of a man that 'he was a very shady character, but sound on the Atonement.' What is the use of being 'sound on the Atonement' if the Atonement does not make you live the Christ life? And what is the good of all your orthodoxy unless the orthodoxy of creed issues in orthopraxy of conduct? There are far too many of us who half-consciously do still hold by the notion that if a man believes rightly then that makes him a Christian. My text shatters to pieces any such conception. You are saved that you may be good, and do good continually; and unless you are so doing you may be steeped to the eyebrows in the correctest of creeds, and it will only drown you.

Contrast this conception of the purpose of Christianity with the far too common notion that we are saved, mainly in order that we may indulge in devout emotions, and in the outgoing of affection and confidence to Jesus Christ. Emotional Christianity is necessary, but Christianity, which is mainly or exclusively emotional, lives next door to hypocrisy, and there is a door of communication between them. For there is nothing more certain and more often illustrated in experience than that there is a strange underground connection between a Christianity which is mainly fervid and a very shady life. One sees it over and over again. And the cure of that is to apprehend the great truth of my text, that we are saved, not in order that we may know aright, nor in order that we may feel aright, but in order that we may be good and do 'good works.' In the order of things, right thought touches the springs of right feeling, and right feeling sets going the wheels of right action. Do not let the steam all go roaring out of the waste-pipe in however sacred and blessed emotions. See that it is guided so as to drive the spindles and the shuttles and make the web.

III. And now, lastly, and only a word-here we have the field provided for the exercise of the 'good works.'

'Created unto good works which God has before prepared'-before the re-creation-'that we should walk in them.' That is to say, the true way to look at the life is to regard it as the exercising-ground which God has prepared for the development of the life that, through Christ, is implanted in us. He cuts the channels that the stream may flow. That is the way to look at tasks, at difficulties. Difficulty is the parent of power, and God arranges our circumstances in order that, by wrestling with obstacles, we may gain the 'thews that throw the world,' and in order that in sorrows and in joys, in the rough places and the smooth, we may find occasions for the exercise of the goodness which is lodged potentially in us, when He creates us in Christ Jesus. So be sure that the path and the power will always correspond. God does not lead us on roads that are too steep for our weakness, and too long for our strength. What He bids us do He fits us for; what He fits us for He thereby bids us do.

And so, dear brother, take heed that you are fulfilling the purpose for which you receive this new life. And let us all remember the order in which being and doing come. We must be good first, and then, and only then, shall we do good. We must have Christ for us first, our sacrifice and our means of receiving that new life, and then, Christ in us, the soul of our souls, the Life of our lives, the source of all our goodness.

'If any power we have, it is to ill,
And all the power is Thine to do and eke to will.'

THE CHIEF CORNERSTONE

Ephesians 2:20

The Roman Empire had in Paul's time gathered into a great unity the Asiatics of Ephesus, the Greeks of Corinth, the Jews of Palestine, and men of many another race, but grand and imposing as that great unity was, it was to Paul a poor thing compared with the oneness of the Kingdom of Jesus Christ. Asiatics of Ephesus, Greeks of Corinth, Jews of Palestine and members of many another race could say, 'Our citizenship is in heaven.' The Roman Eagle swept over wide regions in her flight, but the Dove of Peace, sent forth from Christ's hand, travelled further than she. As Paul says in the context, the Ephesians had been strangers, 'aliens from the commonwealth of Israel,' wandering like the remnants of some 'broken clans,' but now they are gathered in. That narrow community of the Jewish nation has expanded its bounds and become the mother-country of believing souls, the true 'island of saints.' It was not Rome which really made all peoples one, but it was the weakest and most despised of her subject races. 'Of Zion it shall be said,' 'Lo! this and that man was born in her.'

To emphasise the thought of the great unity of the Church, the Apostle uses here his often-repeated metaphor of a temple, of which the Ephesian Christians are the stones, apostles and prophets the builders, and Christ Himself the chief corner-stone. Of course the representation of the foundation, as being laid by apostles and prophets, refers to them as proclaiming the Gospel. The real laying of the foundation is the work of the divine power and love which gave us Christ, and it is the Divine Voice which proclaims, 'Behold I lay in Zion a foundation!' But that divine work has to be made known among men, and it is by the making of it known that the building rises course by course. There is no contradiction between the two statements, 'I have laid the foundation' and Paul's 'As a wise master-builder I have laid the foundation.'

A question may here rise as to the meaning of 'prophets.' Unquestionably the expression in other places of the Epistle does mean New Testament prophets, but seeing that here Jesus is designated as the foundation stone which, standing beneath two walls, has a face into each, and binds them strongly together, it is more natural to see in the prophets the representatives of the great teachers of the old dispensation as the apostles were of the new. The remarkable order in which these two classes are named, the apostles being first, and the prophets who were first in time being last in order of mention, confirms this explanation, for the two co-operating classes are named in the order in which they lie in the foundation. Digging down you come to the more recent first, to the earlier second, and deep and massive, beneath all, to the corner-stone on whom all rests, in whom all are united together. Following the Apostle's order we may note the process of building; beneath that, the foundation on which the building rests; and beneath it, the corner-stone which underlies and unites the whole.

I. The process of building.

In the previous clauses the Apostle has represented the condition of the Ephesian Christians before their Christianity as being that of strangers and foreigners, lacking the rights of citizenship anywhere, a mob rather than in any sense a society. They had been like a confused heap of stones flung fortuitously together; they had become fellow-citizens with the saints. The stones had been piled up into an orderly building. He is not ignoring the facts of national, political, or civic relationships which existed independent of the new unity realised in a common faith. These relationships could not be ignored by one who had had Paul's experience of their formidable character as antagonists of him and of his message, but they seemed to him, in contrast with the still deeper and far more perfect union, which was being brought about in Christ, of men of all nationalities and belonging to mutually hostile races, to be little better than the fortuitous union of a pile of stones huddled together on the roadside. Measured against the architecture of the Church, as Paul saw it in his lofty idealism, the aggregations of men in the world do not deserve the name of buildings. His point of view is the exact opposite of that which is common around us, and which, alas! finds but too much support in the present aspects of the so-called churches of this day.

It is to be observed that in our text these stones are, in accordance with the propriety of the metaphor, regarded as being built, that is, as in some sense the subjects of a force brought to bear upon them, which results in their being laid together in orderly fashion and according to a plan, but it is not to be forgotten that, according to the teaching, not of this epistle alone, but of all Paul's letters, the living stones are active in the work of building, as well as beings subject to an influence. In another place of the New Testament we read the exhortation to 'build up yourselves on your most holy faith,' and the means of discharging that duty are set forth in the words which follow it; as being 'Praying in the Holy Spirit, keeping yourselves in the love of God, and looking for the mercy of our Lord Jesus Christ.'

Throughout the Pauline letters we have frequent references to edifying, a phrase which has been so vulgarised by much handling that its great meaning has been all but lost, but which still, rightly understood, presents the Christian life as one continuous effort after developing Christian character. Taking into view the whole of the apostolic references to this continuous process of building, we cannot but recognise that it all begins with the act of faith which brings men into immediate contact and vital union with Jesus Christ, and which is, if anything that a man does is, the act of his very inmost self passing out of its own isolation and resting itself on Jesus. It is by the vital and individual act of faith that any soul escapes from the dreary isolation of being a stranger and a foreigner, wandering, homeless and solitary, and finds through Jesus fellowship, an elder Brother, a Father, and a home populous with many brethren. But whilst faith is the condition of beginning the Christian life, which is the only real life, that life has to be continued and developed towards perfection by continuous effort. 'Tis a life-long toil till the lump be leavened.'

One of the passages already referred to varies the metaphor of building, in so far as it seems to represent 'your most holy faith' as the foundation, and may be an instance of the doubtful New Testament usage of 'faith,' as meaning the believed Gospel, rather than the personal act of believing. But however that may be, context of the words clearly suggests the practical duties by which the Christian life is preserved and strengthened. They who build up themselves do so, mainly, by keeping themselves in the love of God with watchful oversight and continual preparedness for struggle against all foes who would drag them from that safe fortress, and subsidiarily, by like continuity in prayer, and in fixing their meek hope on the mercy of our Lord Jesus Christ unto eternal life. If Christian character is ever to be made more Christian, it must be by a firmer grasp and a more vivid realisation of Christ and His truth. The more we feel ourselves to be lapped in the love of God, the more shall we be builded up on our most holy faith. There is no mystery about the means of Christian progress. That which, at the beginning, made a man a Christian shapes his whole future course; the measure of our faith is the measure of our advance.

But the Apostle, in the immediately following words, goes on to pass beyond the bounds of his metaphor, and with complete indifference to the charge of mixing figures, speaks of the building as growing. That thought leads us into a higher region than that of effort. The process by which a great forest tree thickens its boles, expands the sweep of its branches and lifts them nearer the heavens, is very different from that by which a building rises slowly and toilsomely and with manifest incompleteness all the time, until the flag flies on the roof-tree. And if we had not this nobler thought of a possible advance by the increasing circulation within us of a mysterious life, there would be little gospel in a word which only enjoined effort as the condition of moral progress, and there would be little to choose between Paul and Plato. He goes on immediately to bring out more fully what he means by the growth of the building, when he says that if Christians are in Christ, they are 'built up for an habitation of God in the Spirit.' Union with Christ, and a consequent life in the Spirit, are sure to result in the growth of the individual soul and of the collective community. That divine Spirit dwells in and works through every believing soul, and while it is possible to grieve and to quench It, to resist and even to neutralise Its workings, these are the true sources of all our growth in grace and knowledge. The process of building may be and will be slow. Sometimes lurking enemies will pull down in a night what we have laboured at for many days. Often our hands will be slack and our hearts will droop. We shall often be tempted to think that our progress is so slow that it is doubtful if we have ever been on the foundation at all or have been building at all. But 'the Spirit helpeth our infirmities,' and the task is not ours alone but His in us. We have to recognise that effort is inseparable from building, but we have also to remember that growth depends on the free circulation of life, and that if we are, and abide in, Jesus, we cannot but be built 'for an habitation of God in the Spirit.' We may be sure that whatever may be the gaps and shortcomings in the structures that we rear here, none will be able to say of us at the last, 'This man began to build and was not able to finish.'

II. The foundation on which the building rests.

In the Greek, as in our version, there is no definite article before 'prophets,' and its absence indicates that both sets of persons here mentioned come under the common vinculum of the one definite article preceding the first named. So that apostles and prophets belong to one class. It may be a question whether the foundation is theirs in the sense that they constitute it, an explanation in favour of which can be quoted the vision in the Apocalypse of the new Jerusalem, in the twelve foundations of which were written the names of the twelve apostles of the Lamb, or whether, as is more probable, the foundation is conceived of as laid by them. In like manner the Apostle speaks to the Corinthians of having 'as a wise master-builder laid the foundation,' and to the Romans of making it his aim to preach especially where Christ was not already named, that he might 'not build upon another man's foundation.' Following these indications, it seems best to understand the preaching of the Gospel as being the laying of the foundation.

Further, the question may be raised whether the prophets here mentioned belong to the Old Testament or to the New. The latter alternative has been preferred on the ground that the apostles are named first, but, as we have already noticed, the order here begins at the top and goes downwards, what was last in order of time being first in order of mention. We need only recall Peter's bold words that 'all the prophets, as many as have spoken, have told of the days' of Christ, or Paul's sermon in the synagogue of Antioch in which he passionately insisted on the Jewish crime of condemning Christ as being the fulfilment of the voices of the prophets, and of the Resurrection of Jesus as being God's fulfilment of the promise made unto the fathers to understand how here, as it were, beneath the foundation laid by the present preaching of the apostles, Paul rejoices to discern the ancient stones firmly laid by long dead hands.

The Apostle's strongest conviction was that he himself had become more and not less of a Jew by becoming a Christian, and that the Gospel which he preached was nothing more than the perfecting of that Gospel before the Gospel, which had come from the lips of the prophets. We know a great deal more than he did as to the ways in which the progressive divine revelation was presented to Israel through the ages, and some of us are tempted to think that we know more than we do, but the true bearing of modern criticism, as applied to the Old Testament, is to confirm, even whilst it may to some extent modify, the conviction common to all the New Testament writers, and formulated by the last of the New Testament prophets, that 'the testimony of Jesus is the spirit of prophecy.' Whatever new light may shine on the questions of the origin and composition of the books of the Old Testament, it will never obscure the radiance of the majestic figure of the Messiah which shines from the prophetic page. The inner relation between the foundation of the apostles and that of the prophets is best set forth in the solemn colloquy on the Mount of Transfiguration between Moses and Elias and Jesus. They 'were with Him' as witnessing to Him to whom law and ritual and prophecy had pointed, and they 'spake of His decease which He should accomplish at Jerusalem' as being the vital centre of all His work which the lambs slain according to ritual had foreshadowed, and the prophetic figure of the Servant of the Lord 'wounded for our transgressions and bruised for our iniquities' had more distinctly foretold.

III. The corner-stone which underlies and unites the whole.

Of course the corner-stone here is the foundation-stone and not 'the head-stone of the corner.' Jesus Christ is both. He is the first and the last; the Alpha and Omega. In accordance with the whole context, in which the prevailing idea is that which always fired Paul's imagination, viz. that of reconciling Jew and Gentile in one new man, it is best to suppose a reference here to the union of Jew and Gentile. The stone laid beneath the two walls which diverge at right angles from each other binds both together and gives strength and cohesion to the whole. In the previous context the same idea is set forth that Christ 'preached peace to them that were afar off {Gentiles} and to them that were nigh {Jews}.' By His death He broke down another wall, the middle wall of partition between them, and did so by abolishing 'the law of commandments contained in ordinances.' The old distinction between Jew and Gentile, which was accentuated by the Jew's rigid observance of ordinances and which often led to bitter hatred on both sides, was swept away in that strange new thing, a community of believers drawn together in Jesus Christ. The former antagonistic 'twain' had become one in a third order of man, the Christian man. The Jew Christian and the Gentile Christian became brethren because they had received one new life, and they who had common feelings of faith and love to the same Saviour, a common character drawn from Him, and a common destiny open to them by their common relation to Jesus, could never cherish the old emotions of racial hate.

When we, in this day, try to picture to ourselves that strange new thing, the love which bound the early Christians together and buried as beneath a rushing flood the formidable walls of separation between them, we may well penitently ask ourselves how it comes that Jesus seems to have so much less power to triumph over the divisive forces that part us from those who should be our hearts' brothers. In our modern life there are no such gulfs of separation from one another as were filled up unconsciously in the experience of the first believers, but the narrower chinks seem to remain in their ugliness between those who profess a common faith in one Lord, and who are all ready to assert that they are built on the foundation of the Apostles and prophets, and that Jesus Christ is from them the chief corner-stone.

If in reality He is so to us, and He is so if we have been builded upon Him through our faith, the metaphor of corner-stone and building will fail to express the reality of our relation to Him, for our corner-stone has in it an infinite vitality which rises up through all the courses of the living stones, and moulds each 'into an immortal feature of loveliness and perfection.' So it shall be for each individual, though here the appropriation of the perfect gift is imperfect. So it shall be in reference to the history of the world. Christ is its centre and foundation-stone, and as His coming makes the date from which the nations reckon, and all before it was in the deepest sense preparatory to His incarnation, all which is after it is in the deepest sense the appropriating of Him and the developing of His work. The multitudes which went before and that followed cried, saying, 'Blessed is He that cometh in the name of the Lord.'

EPHESIANS 3

EPHESIANS CHAPTER 3 CONTENTS

THE WHOLE FAMILY

Ephesians 3:15

Grammatically, we are driven to recognise that the Revised Version is more correct than the Authorised, when it reads 'every family,' instead of 'the whole family.' There is in the expression no reference to the thought, however true it is in itself, that the redeemed in heaven and the believers on earth make up but one family. The thought rather is, that, as has been said, 'the father makes the family,' and if any community of intelligent beings, human, or angelic, bears the great name of family, the great reason for that lies 'in God's paternal relationship.'

But my present purpose in selecting this text is not so much to speak of it as to lay hold of the probably incorrect rendering in the Authorised Version, as suggesting, though here inaccurately, the thought that believers struggling here and saints and angels glorious above 'but one communion make,' and in the light of that thought, to consider the meaning of the Lord's Supper. I am, of course, fully conscious that in thus using the words, I am diverting them from their original purpose; but possibly in this case, open confession, my open confession, may merit your forgiveness and at all events, it, in some degree, brings me my own.

I. Consider the Lord's Supper as a sign that the Church on earth is a family.

The Passover was essentially a family feast, and the Lord's Supper, which was grafted on it, was plainly meant to be the same. The domestic character of the rite shines clearly out in the precious simplicity of the arrangements in the upper room. When Christ and the twelve sat down there, it was a family meal at which they sat. He was the head of the household; they were members of His family. The early examples of the rite, when the disciples 'gathered together to break bread,' obviously preserved the same familiar character, and stand in extraordinary

106

contrast to the splendours of high mass in a Roman Catholic Cathedral. The Church, as a whole, is a household, and the very form of the rite proclaims that 'we, being many, are one bread.' The conception of a family brings clearly into view the deepest ground of Christian unity. It is the possession of a common life, just as men are born into an earthly family, not of their own will, nor of their own working, and come without any action of their own into bonds of blood relationship with brothers and sisters. When we become sons of God and are born again, we become brethren of all His children. That which gives us life in Him makes us kindred with all through whose veins flows that same life. It is the common partaking in the one bread which makes us one. The same blood flows in the veins of all the children.

Hence, the only ground on which the Church rests is this common possession of the life of Christ, and that ground makes, and ought to be felt to make, Christian union a far deeper, more blessed, and more imperative bond than can be found in any shallow similarities of aim-or identities of opinion or feeling. The deepest fact of Christian consciousness is the foundation fact of Christian brotherhood; each is nearer to every Christian than to any besides. A very solemn view of Christian duty arises from these thoughts, familiar as they are:

'No distance breaks the tie of blood,
Brothers are brothers ever more.'

and every tongue is loud in condemnation of any man who is ashamed or afraid to recognise his brother and stand by him, whatever may be the difference in their worldly positions. 'Every one who loveth Him that begat, loveth Him also that is begotten of Him.'

II. The Lord's Supper as a prophecy of the family at home above.

The prophetic character was stamped on the first institution of the Lord's Supper by Christ's own words 'until it be fulfilled in the kingdom of God,' and by His declaration that He appointed unto them a kingdom, that they might eat and drink at His table in His kingdom. We may also recall the mysterious feast spread on the shore of the lake, where, with obvious allusion both to his earlier miracles and to the sad hour in the upper room, he came 'and taketh the bread and gave it to them.' Blending these two together we get most blessed, though dim, thoughts of that future; they speak to us of an eternal home, an eternal feast, and an eternal society. We have to reverse not a few of the characteristics of the upper room in order to reach those of the table in the kingdom. The Lord's Supper was followed for Him by Gethsemane and Calvary, and for them by going out to betray and to deny and to forsake Him. From that better table there is no more going out. The servant comes in from the field, spent with toil and stained with many a splash, but the Master Himself comes forth and serves His servant.

In the eternal feast, which is spread above, the bread as well as the wine is new, even whilst it is old, for there will be disclosed new depths of blessing and power in the old Christ, and new draughts of joy and strength in the old wine which will make the feasters say, in rapture and astonishment, to the Master of the feast, 'Thou hast kept the good wine until now.' There and then all broken ties will be re-knit, all losses supplied, and no shadow of change, nor fear of exhaustion, pass across the calm hearts.

III. The Lord's Supper is a token of the present union of the two.

If it thus prophesies the perfectness of heaven, it also shows us how the two communities of earth and heaven are united. They, as we, live by derivation of the one life; they, as we, are fed and blessed by the one Lord. The occupations and thoughts of Christian life on earth and of the perfect life of Saints above are one. They look to Christ as we do, when we live as Christians, though the sun which is the light of both regions shows there a broader disc, and pours forth more fervid rays, and is never obscured by clouds, nor ever sets in night. Whether conscious of us or not, they are doing there, in perfect fashion, what we imperfectly attempt, and partially accomplish.

108

'The Saints on earth and all the Dead
But one communion make.'

Heaven and earth are equally mansions in the Father's house.

To the faith which realises this great truth, death dwindles to a small matter. The Lord's table has an upper and a lower level. Sitting at the lower, we may feel that those who have gone from our sides, and have left empty places which never can be filled, are gathered round Him in the upper half, and though a screen hangs between the two, yet the feast is one and the family is one. Singly our dear ones go, and singly we all shall go. The table spread in the presence of enemies will be left vacant to its last place, and the one spread above will be filled to its last place, and so shall we ever be with the Lord, and the unity which was always real be perfectly and permanently manifested at the last.

STRENGTHENED WITH MIGHT

Ephesians 3:16

In no part of Paul's letters does he rise to a higher level than in his prayers, and none of his prayers are fuller of fervour than this wonderful series of petitions. They open out one into the other like some majestic suite of apartments in a great palace-temple, each leading into a loftier and more spacious hall, each drawing nearer the presence-chamber, until at last we stand there.

Roughly speaking, the prayer is divided into four petitions, of which each is the cause of the following and the result of the preceding-'That He would grant you, according to the riches of His glory, to be strengthened with might by His Spirit in the inner man'-that is the first. 'In order that Christ may dwell in your hearts by faith,' 'ye being rooted and grounded in love'-such is the second, the result of the first, and the preparation for the third. 'That ye may be able to comprehend with all saints ... and to know the love of Christ which passeth knowledge,' such is the third, and all lead up at last to that wonderful desire beyond which nothing is possible-'that ye might be filled with all the fulness of God.'

I venture to contemplate dealing with these four petitions in successive sermons, in order, God helping me, that I may bring before you a fairer vision of the possibilities of your Christian life than you ordinarily entertain. For Paul's prayer is God's purpose, and what He means with all who profess His name is that these exuberant desires may be fulfilled in them. So let us now listen to that petition which is the foundation of all, and consider that great thought of the divine strength-giving power which may be bestowed upon every Christian soul.

I. First, then, I remark that God means, and wishes, that all Christians should be strong by the possession of the Spirit of might.

It is a miserably inadequate conception of Christianity, and of the gifts which it bestows, and the blessings which it intends for men, when it is limited, as it practically is, by a large number-I might almost say the majority-of professing Christians to a simple means of altering their relation to the past, and to the broken law of God and of righteousness. Thanks be to His name! His great gift to the world begins in each individual case with the assurance that all the past is cancelled. He gives that blessed sense of forgiveness, which can never be too highly estimated unless it is forced out of its true place as the introduction, and made to be the climax and the end, of His gifts. I do not know what Christianity means, unless it means that you and I are forgiven for a purpose; that the purpose, if I may so say, is something in advance of the means towards the purpose, the purpose being that we should be filled with all the strength and righteousness and supernatural life granted to us by the Spirit of God.

It is well that we should enter into the vestibule. There is no other path to the throne but through the vestibule. But do not let us forget that the good news of forgiveness, though we need it day by day, and need it perpetually repeated, is but the introduction to and porch of the Temple, and that beyond it there towers, if I cannot say a loftier, yet I may say a further gift, even the gift of a divine life like His, from whom it comes, and of which it is in reality an effluence and a spark. The true characteristic blessing of the Gospel is the gift of a new power to a sinful weak world; a power which makes the feeble strong, and the strongest as an angel of God.

Oh, brethren! we who know how, 'if any power we have, it is to ill'; we who understand the weakness, the unaptness of our spirits to any good, and our strength for every vagrant evil that comes upon them to tempt them, should surely recognise as a Gospel in very deed that which proclaims to us that the 'everlasting God, the Lord, the Creator of the ends of the earth,' who Himself 'fainteth not, neither is weary.' hath yet a loftier display of His strength-giving power than that which is visible in the heavens above, where, 'because He is strong in might not one faileth.' That heaven, the region of calm completeness, of law unbroken and therefore of power undiminished, affords a lesser and dimmer manifestation of His strength than the work that is done in the hell of a human heart that has wandered and is brought back, that is stricken with the weakness of the fever of sin, and is healed into the strength of obedience and the omnipotence of dependence. It is much to say 'for that He is strong in might, not one of these faileth;' it is more to say 'He giveth power to them that have failed; and to them that have no might He increaseth strength.' The Gospel is the gift of pardon for holiness, and its inmost and most characteristic bestowment is the bestowment of a new power for obedience and service.

And that power, as I need not remind you, is given to us through the gift of the Divine Spirit. The very name of that Spirit is the 'Spirit of Might.' Christ spoke to us about being 'endued with power from on high.' The last of His promises that dropped from His lips upon earth was the promise that His followers should receive the power of the Spirit coming upon them. Wheresoever in the early histories we read of a man who was full of the Holy Ghost, we read that he was 'full of power.' According to the teaching of this Apostle, God hath given us the 'Spirit of power,' which is also the Spirit 'of love and of a sound mind.' So the strength that we must have, if we have strength at all, is the strength of a Divine Spirit, not our own, that dwells in us, and works through us.

And there is nothing in that which need startle or surprise any man who believes in a living God at all, and in the possibility, therefore, of a connection between the Great Spirit and all the human spirits which are His children. I would maintain, in opposition to many modern conceptions, the actual supernatural character of the gift that is bestowed upon every Christian soul. My reading of the New Testament is that as distinctly above the order of material nature as is any miracle, is the gift that flows into a believing heart. There is a direct passage between God and my spirit. It lies open to His touch; all the paths of its deep things can be trodden by Him. You and I act upon one another from without, He acts upon us within. We wish one another blessings; He gives the blessings. We try to train, to educate, to incline, and dispose, by the presentation of motives and the urging of reasons; He can plant in a heart by His own divine husbandry the seed that shall blossom into immortal life. And so the Christian Church is a great, continuous, supernatural community in the midst of the material world; and every believing soul, because it possesses something of the life of Jesus Christ, has been the seat of a miracle as real and true as when He said 'Lazarus, come forth!' Precisely this teaching does our Lord Himself present for our acceptance when He sets side by side, as mutually illustrative, as belonging to the same order of supernatural phenomena, 'the hour is coming when the dead shall hear the voice of the Son of God and they that hear shall live,' which is the supernatural resurrection of souls dead in sin,-and 'the hour is coming in the which all that are in the graves shall hear His voice, and shall come forth,' which is the future resurrection of the body, in obedience to His will.

So, Christian men and women, do you set clearly before you this: that God's purpose with you is but begun when He has forgiven you, that He forgives you for a design, that it is a means to an end, and that you have not reached the conception of the large things which He intends for you unless you have risen to this great thought-He means and wishes that you should be strong with the strength of His own Divine Spirit.

II. Now notice, next, that this Divine Power has its seat in, and is intended to influence the whole of, the inner life.

As my text puts it, we may be 'strengthened with might by His Spirit in the inner man.' By the 'inner man' I suppose, is not meant the new creation through faith in Jesus Christ which this Apostle calls 'the new man,' but simply what Peter calls the 'hidden man of the heart' the 'soul,' or unseen self as distinguished from the visible material body which it animates and informs. It is this inner self, then, in which the Spirit of God is to dwell, and into which it is to breathe strength. The leaven is hid deep in three measures of meal until the whole be leavened. And the point to mark is that the whole inward region which makes up the true man is the field upon which this Divine Spirit is to work. It is not a bit of your inward life that is to be hallowed. It is not any one aspect of it that is to be strengthened, but it is the whole intellect, affections, desires, tastes, powers of attention, conscience, imagination, memory, will. The whole inner man in all its corners is to be filled, and to come under the influence of this power, 'until there be no part dark, as when the bright shining of a candle giveth thee light.'

There is no part of my being that is not patent to the tread of this Divine Guest. There are no rooms of the house of my spirit into which He may not go. Let Him come with the master key in His hand into all the dim chambers of your feeble nature; and as the one life is light in the eye, and colour in the cheek, and deftness in the fingers, and strength in the arm, and pulsation in the heart, so He will come with the manifold results of the one gift to you. He will strengthen your understandings, and make you able for loftier tasks of intellect and of reason than you can face in your unaided power; He will dwell in your affections and make them vigorous to lay hold upon the holy things that are above their natural inclination, and will make it certain that their reach shall not be beyond their grasp, as, alas! it so often is in the sadness and disappointments of human love. He will come into that feeble, vacillating, wayward will of yours, that is only obstinate in its adherence to the low and the evil, as some foul creature, that one may try to wrench away, digs its claws into corruption and holds on by that. He will lift your will and make it fix upon the good and abominate the evil, and through the whole being He will pour a great tide of strength which shall cover all the weakness. He will be like some subtle elixir which, taken into the lips, steals through a pallid and wasted frame, and brings back a glow to the cheek and a lustre to the eye, and swiftness to the brain, and power to the whole nature. Or as some plant, drooping and flagging beneath the hot rays of the sun, when it has the scent of water given to it, will, in all its parts, stiffen and erect itself, so, when the Spirit is poured out on men, their whole nature is invigorated and helped.

That indwelling Spirit will be a power for suffering. The parallel passage to this in the twin epistle to the Colossians is-'strengthened with all might unto all patience and long-suffering with gentleness.' Ah, brethren! unless this Divine Spirit were a power for patience and endurance it were no power suited to us poor men. So dark at times is every life; so full at times of discouragements, of dreariness, of sadness, of loneliness, of bitter memories, and of fading hopes does the human heart become, that if we are to be strong we must have a strength that will manifest itself most chiefly in this, that it teaches us how to bear, how to weep, how to submit.

And it will be a power for conflict. We have all of us, in the discharge of duty and in the meeting of temptation, to face such tremendous antagonisms that unless we have grace given to us which will enable us to resist, we shall be overcome and swept away. God's power given by the Divine Spirit does not absolve us from the fight, but it fits us for the fight. It is not given in order that, holiness may be won without a struggle, as some people seem to think, but it is given to us in order that in the struggle for holiness we may never lose 'one jot of heart or hope,' but may be 'able to withstand in the evil day, and having done all to stand.'

It is a power for service. 'Tarry ye in Jerusalem till ye be endued with power from on high.' There is no such force for the spreading of Christ's Kingdom, and the witness-bearing work of His Church, as the possession of this Divine Spirit. Plunged into that fiery baptism, the selfishness and the sloth, which stand in the way of so many of us, are all consumed and annihilated, and we are set free for service because the bonds that bound us are burnt up in the merciful furnace of His fiery power.

'Ye shall be strengthened with might by His Spirit in the inner man'-a power that will fill and flood all your nature if you will let it, and will make you strong to suffer, strong to combat, strong to serve, and to witness for your Lord.

III. And now, lastly, let me point you still further to the measure of this power. It is limitless with the boundlessness of God Himself. 'That he would grant you' is the daring petition of the Apostle, 'according to the riches of His glory to be strengthened.'

There is the measure. There is no limit except the uncounted wealth of His own self-manifestation, the flashing light of revealed divinity. Whatsoever there is of splendour in that, whatsoever there is of power there, in these and in nothing on this side of them, lies the limit of the possibilities of a Christian life. Of course there is a working limit at each moment, and that is our capacity to receive; but that capacity varies, may vary indefinitely, may become greater and greater beyond our count or measurement. Our hearts may be more and more capable of God; and in the measure in which they are capable of Him they shall be filled by Him. A limit which is always shifting is no limit at all. A kingdom, the boundaries of which are not the same from one year to another, by reason of its own inherent expansive power, may be said to have no fixed limit. And so we appropriate and enclose, as it were, within our own little fence, a tiny portion of the great prairie that rolls boundlessly to the horizon. But to-morrow we may enclose more, if we will, and more and more; and so ever onwards, for all that is God's is ours, and He has given us His whole self to use and to possess through our faith in His Son. A thimble can only take up a thimbleful of the ocean, but what if the thimble be endowed with a power of expansion which has no term known to men? May it not, then, be that some time or other it shall be able to hold so much of the infinite depth as now seems a dream too audacious to be realised?

So it is with us and God. He lets us come into the vaults, as it were, where in piles and masses the ingots of uncoined and uncounted gold are stored and stacked; and He says, 'Take as much as you like to carry.' There is no limit except the riches of His glory.

And now, dear friends, remember that this great gift, offered to each of us, is offered on conditions. To you professing Christians especially I speak. You will never get it unless you want it, and some of you do not want it. There are plenty of people who call themselves Christian men that would not for the life of them know what to do with this great gift if they had it. You will get it if you desire it. 'Ye have not because ye ask not.'

Oh! when one contrasts the largeness of God's promises and the miserable contradiction to them which the average Christian life of this generation presents, what can we say? 'Hath His mercy clean gone for ever? Doth His promise fail for evermore?' Ye weak Christian people, born weakling and weak ever since, as so many of you are, open your mouths wide. Rise to the height of the expectations and the desires which it is our sin not to cherish; and be sure of this, as we ask so shall we receive. 'Ye are not straitened in God.' Alas! alas! 'ye are straitened in yourselves.'

And mind, there must be self-suppression if there is to be the triumph of a divine power in you. You cannot fight with both classes of weapons. The human must die if the divine is to live. The life of nature, dependence on self, must be weakened and subdued if the life of God is to overcome and to fill you. You must be able to say 'Not I!' or you will never be able to say 'Christ liveth in me.' The patriarch who overcame halted on his thigh; and all the life of nature was lamed and made impotent that the life of grace might prevail. So crush self by the power and for the sake of the Christ, if you would that the Spirit should bear rule over you.

See to it, too, that you use what you have of that Divine Spirit. 'To him that hath shall be given.' What is the use of more water being sent down the mill lade, if the water that does come in it all runs away at the bottom, and none of it goes over the wheel? Use the power you have, and power will come to the faithful steward of what he possesses. He that is faithful in a little shall get much to be faithful over. Ask and use, and the ancient thanksgiving may still come from your lips. 'In the day when I cried, Thou answeredst me, and strengthenedst me with strength in my soul.'

THE INDWELLING CHRIST

Ephesians 3:17

We have here the second step of the great staircase by which Paul's fervent desires for his Ephesian friends climbed towards that wonderful summit of his prayers-which is ever approached, never reached,-'that ye might be filled with all the fulness of God.'

Two remarks of an expository character will prepare the way for the lessons of these verses. The first is as to the relation of this clause to the preceding. It might appear at first sight to be simply parallel with the former, expressing substantially the same ideas under a somewhat different aspect. The operation of the strength-giving Spirit in the inner man might very naturally be supposed to be equivalent to the dwelling of Christ in our hearts by faith. So many commentators do, in fact, take it; but I think that the two ideas may be distinguished, and that we are to see in the words of our text, as I have said, the second step in this prayer, which is in some sense a result of the 'strengthening with might by the Spirit in the inner man.' I need not enter in detail into the reasons for taking this view of the connection of the clause, which is obviously in accordance with the climbing-up structure of the whole verse. It is enough to point it out as the basis of my further remarks.

And now the second observation with which I will trouble you, before I come to deal with the thoughts of the verse, is as to the connection of the last words of it. You may observe that in reading the words of my text I omitted the 'that' which stands in the centre of the verse. I did so because the words, 'Ye being rooted and grounded in love,' in the original, do stand before the 'that,' and are distinctly separated by it from the subsequent clause. They ought not, therefore, to be shifted forward into it, as our translators and the Revised Version have, I think, unfortunately done, unless there were some absolute necessity either from meaning or from construction. I do not think that this is the case; but on the contrary, if they are carried forward into the next clause,

118

which describes the result of Christ's dwelling in our hearts by faith, they break the logical flow of the sentence by mixing together result and occasion. And so I attach them to the first part of this verse, and take them to express at once the consequence of Christ's dwelling in the heart by faith, and the preparation or occasion for our being able to comprehend and know the love of Christ which passeth knowledge. Now that is all with which I need trouble you in the way of explanation of the meaning of the words. Let us come now to deal with their substance.

I. Consider the Indwelling of Christ, as desired by the Apostle for all Christians.

To begin with, let me say in the plainest, simplest, strongest way that I can, that that dwelling of Christ in the believing heart is to be regarded as being a plain literal fact.

To a man who does not believe in the divinity of Jesus Christ, of course that is nonsense, but to those of us who do see in Him the manifested incarnate God, there ought to be no difficulty in accepting this as the simple literal force of the words before us, that in every soul where faith, howsoever feeble, has been exercised, there Jesus Christ does verily abide.

It is not to be weakened down into any notion of participation in His likeness, sympathy with His character, submission to His influence, following His example, listening to His instruction, or the like. A dead Plato may so influence his followers, but that is not how a living Christ influences His disciples. What is meant is no mere influence derived but separable from Him, however blessed and gracious that influence might be, but it is the presence of His own self, exercising influences which are inseparable from His presence, and only to be realised when He dwells in us.

I think that Christian people as a rule do far too little turn their attention to this aspect of the Gospel teaching, and concentrate their thoughts far too much upon that which is unspeakably precious in itself, but does not exhaust all that Christ is to us, viz. the work that He wrought for us upon Calvary; or to take a step further, the work that He is now carrying on for us as our Intercessor and Advocate in the heavens. You who listen to me Sunday after Sunday will not suspect me of seeking to minimise either of these two aspects of our Lord's mission and operation, but I do believe that very largely the glad thought of an indwelling Christ, who actually abides and works in our hearts, and is not only for us in the heavens, or with us by some kind of impalpable and metaphorical presence, but in simple, that is to say, in spiritual reality is in our spirits, has faded away from the consciousness of the Christian Church.

And so we are called 'mystics' when we preach Christ in the heart. Ah, brother! unless your Christianity be in the good deep sense of the word 'mystical,' it is mechanical, which is worse. I preach, and rejoice that I have to preach, a 'Christ that died, yea! rather that is risen again; who is even at the right hand of God, who also maketh intercession for us.' Nor do I stop there, but I preach a Christ that is in us, dwelling in our hearts if we be His at all.

Well, then, further observe that the special emphasis of the prayer here is that this 'indwelling' may be an unbroken and permanent one. Any of you who can consult the original for yourselves will see that the Apostle here uses a compound word which conveys the idea of intensity and continuity. What he desires, then, is not merely that these Ephesian Christians may have occasional visits of the indwelling Lord, or that at some lofty moments of spiritual enthusiasm they may be conscious that He is with them, but that always, in an unbroken line of deep, calm receptiveness, they may possess, and know that they possess, an indwelling Saviour.

And this, I think, is one of the reasons why we may and must distinguish between the apparently very similar petition in the previous verse, about which we spoke in the last sermon, and the petition which is now occupying us; for, as I shall have to show you, it is only as 'strengthened with might by His Spirit in the inner man' that we are capable of the continuous abiding of that Lord within us.

Oh! what a contrast to that idea of a perpetual unbroken inhabitation of Jesus in our spirits and to our consciousness is presented by our ordinary life! 'Why shouldst Thou be as a wayfaring man that turneth aside to tarry for a night?' may well be the utterance of the average Christian. We might, with unbroken blessedness, possess Him in our hearts, and instead, we have only 'visits short and far between' Alas, alas, how often do we drive away that indwelling Christ, because our hearts are 'foul with sin,' so that He

'Can but listen at the gate
And hear the household jar within.'

Christian men and women! here is the ideal of our lives, capable of being approximated to {if not absolutely in its entirety reached} with far more perfection than it ever has yet been by us. There might be a line of light never interrupted running all through our religious experience. Instead of that there is a light point here, and a great gap of darkness there, like the straggling lamps by the wayside in the half-lighted squalid suburbs of some great city. Is that your Christian life, broken by many interruptions, and having often sounding through it the solemn words of the retreating divinity which the old profound legend tells us were heard the night before the Temple on Zion was burnt:-'Let us depart?' 'I will arise and return unto My place till they acknowledge their offences.' God means and wishes that Christ may continuously dwell in our hearts. Does He to your own consciousness dwell in yours?

And then the last thought connected with this first part of my subject is that the heart, strengthened by the Spirit, is fitted to be the Temple of the indwelling Christ. How shall we prepare the chamber for such a guest? How shall some poor occupant of some wretched hut by the wayside fit it up for the abode of a prince? The answer lies in these words that precede my text. You cannot strengthen the rafters and lift the roof and adorn the halls and furnish the floor in a manner befitting the coming of the King; but you can turn to that Divine Spirit who will expand and embellish and invigorate your whole spirit, and make it capable of receiving the indwelling Christ.

That these two things which are here considered as cause and effect may, in another aspects be considered as but varying phases of the same truth, is only part of the depth and felicity of the teaching that is here; for if you come to look more deeply into it, the Spirit that strengtheneth with might is the Spirit of Christ; and He dwells in men's hearts by His own Spirit. So that the apparent confusion, arising from what in other places are regarded as identical being here conceived as cause and effect, is no confusion at all, but is explained and vindicated by the deep truth that nothing but the indwelling of the Christ can fit for the indwelling of the Christ. The lesser gift of His presence prepares for the greater measure of it; the transitory inhabitation for the more permanent. Where He comes in smaller measure He opens the door and makes the heart capable of His own more entire indwelling. 'Unto him that hath shall be given.' It is Christ in the heart that makes the heart fit for Christ to dwell in the heart. You cannot do it by your own power; turn to Him and let Him make you temples meet for Himself.

II. So now, in the second place, notice the open door through which the Christ comes in to dwell-'that He may dwell in your hearts by faith.'

More accurately we may render 'through faith' and might even venture to suppose that the thought of faith as an open door through which Christ passes into the heart, floated half distinctly before the Apostle's mind. Be that as it may, at all events faith is here represented as the means or condition through which this dwelling takes effect. You have but to believe in Him and He comes, drawn from heaven, floating down on a sunbeam, as it were, and enters into the heart and abides there.

Trust, which is faith, is self-distrust. 'I dwell in the high and holy place, with him also that is of a contrite and humble spirit.' Rivers do not run on the mountain tops, but down in the valleys. So the heart that is lifted up and self-complacent has no dew of His blessing resting upon it, but has the curse of Gilboa adhering to its barrenness; but the low lands, the humble and the lowly hearts, are they in which the waters that go softly scoop their course and diffuse their blessings. Faith is self-distrust. Self-distrust brings the Christ.

Faith is desire. Never, never in the history of the world has it been or can it be that a longing towards Him shall be a longing thrown back unsatisfied upon itself. You have but to trust, and you possess. We open the door for the entrance of Christ by the simple act of faith, and blessed be His name! He can squeeze Himself through a very little chink, and He does not require that the gates should be flung wide open in order that, with some of His blessings, He may come in.

Mystical Christianity of the false sort has much to say about the indwelling of God in the soul, but it spoils all its teaching by insisting upon it that the condition on which God dwells in the soul is the soul's purifying itself to receive Him. But you cannot cleanse your hearts so as to bring Christ into them, you must let Him come and cleanse them by the process of His coming, and fit them thereby for His own indwelling. And, assuredly, He will so come, purging us from our evil and abiding in our hearts.

But do not forget that the faith which brings Christ into the spirit must be a faith which works by love, if it is to keep Christ in the spirit. You cannot bring that Lord into your hearts by anything that you do. The man who cleanses his own soul by his own strength, and so expects to draw God into it, has made the mistake which Christ pointed out when He told us that when the unclean spirit is gone out of a man he leaves his house empty, though it be swept and garnished. Moral reformation may turn out the devils, it will never bring in God, and in the emptiness of the swept and garnished heart there is an invitation to the seven to come back again and fill it.

And whilst that is true, remember, on the other hand, that a Christian man can drive away his Master by evil works. The sweet song-birds and the honey-making bees are said always to desert a neighbourhood before a pestilence breaks out in it. And if I may so say, similarly quick to feel the first breath of the pestilence is the presence of the Christ which cannot dwell with evil. You bring Christ into your heart by faith, without any work at all; you keep Him there by a faith which produces holiness.

III. And the last point is the gifts of this indwelling Christ,-'ye being,' or as the words might more accurately be translated, 'Ye having been rooted and grounded in love.'

Where He comes He comes not empty-handed. He brings His own love, and that, consciously received, produces a corresponding and answering love in our hearts to Him. So there is no need to ask the question here whether 'love' means Christ's love to me, or my love to Christ. From the nature of the case both are included-the recognition of His love and the response by mine are the result of His entering into the heart. This love, the recognition of His and the response by mine, is represented in a lovely double metaphor in these words as being at once the soil in which our lives are rooted and grow, and the foundation on which our lives are built and are steadfast.

There is no need to enlarge upon these two things, but let me just touch them for a moment. Where Christ abides in a man's heart, love will be the very soil in which his life will be rooted and grow. That love will be the motive of all service, it will underlie, as its productive cause, all fruitfulness. All goodness and all beauty will be its fruit. The whole life will be as a tree planted in this rich soil. And so the life will grow not by effort only, but as by an inherent power drawing its nourishment from the soil. This is blessedness. It is heaven upon earth that love should be the soil in which our obedience is rooted, and from which we draw all the nutriment that turns to flowers and fruit.

Where Christ dwells in the heart, love will be the foundation upon which our lives are builded steadfast and sure. The blessed consciousness of His love, and the joyful answer of my heart to it, may become the basis upon which my whole being shall repose, the underlying thought that gives security, serenity, steadfastness to my else fluctuating life. I may so plant myself upon Him, as that in Him I shall be strong, and then my life will not only grow like a tree and have its leaf green and broad, and its fruit the natural outcome of its vitality, but it will rise like some stately building, course by course, pillar by pillar, until at last the shining topstone is set there. He that buildeth on that foundation shall never be confounded.

For, remember that, deepest of all, the words of my text may mean that the Incarnate Personal Love becomes the very soil in which my life is set and blossoms, on which my life is founded.

'Thou, my Life, O let me be
Rooted, grafted, built in Thee.'

Christ is Love, and Love is Christ. He that is rooted and grounded in love has the roots of his being, and the foundation of his life fixed and fastened in that Lord.

So, dear brethren, go to Christ like those two on the road to Emmaus; and as Fra Angelico has painted them on his convent wall, put out your hands and lay them on His, and say, 'Abide with us. Abide with us!' And the answer will come:-'This is my rest for ever; here'-mystery of love!-'will I dwell, for I have desired it,' even the narrow room of your poor heart.

THE PARADOX OF LOVE'S MEASURE

Ephesians 3:18

Of what? There can, I think, be no doubt as to the answer. The next clause is evidently the continuation of the idea begun in that of our text, and it runs: 'And to know the love of Christ which passeth knowledge.' It is the immeasurable measure, then; the boundless bounds and dimensions of the love of Christ which fire the Apostle's thoughts here. Of course, he had no separate idea in his mind attaching to each of these measures of magnitude, but he gathered them together simply to express the one thought of the greatness of Christ's love. Depth and height are the same dimension measured from opposite ends. The one begins at the top and goes down, the other begins at the bottom and goes up, but the distance is the same in either case. So we have the three dimensions of a solid here-breadth, length, and depth.

I suppose that I may venture to use these expressions with a somewhat different purpose from that for which the Apostle employs them; and to see in each of them a separate and blessed aspect of the love of God in Jesus Christ our Lord.

I. What, then, is the breadth of that love?

It is as broad as humanity. As all the stars lie in the firmament, so all creatures rest in the heaven of His love. Mankind has many common characteristics. We all suffer, we all sin, we all hunger, we all aspire, hope, and die; and, blessed be God! we all occupy precisely the same relation to the divine love which lies in Jesus Christ. There are no step-children in God's great family, and none of them receives a more grudging or a less ample share of His love and goodness than every other. Far-stretching as the race, and curtaining it over as some great tent may enclose on a festal day a whole tribe, the breadth of Christ's love is the breadth of humanity.

And it is universal because it is divine. No human mind can be stretched so as to comprehend the whole of the members of mankind, and no human heart can be so emptied of self as to be capable of this absolute universality and impartiality of affection. But the intellectual difficulties which stand in the way of the width of our affections, and the moral difficulties which stand still more frowningly and forbiddingly in the way, have no power over that love of Christ's which is close and tender, and clinging with all the tenderness and closeness and clingingness of a human affection and lofty and universal and passionless and perpetual, with all the height and breadth and calmness and eternity of a divine heart.

And this broad love, broad as humanity, is not shallow because it is broad. Our love is too often like the estuary of some great stream which runs deep and mighty as long as it is held within narrow banks, but as soon as it widens becomes slow and powerless and shallow. The intensity of human affection varies inversely as its extension. A universal philanthropy is a passionless sentiment. But Christ's love is deep though it is wide, and suffers no diminution because it is shared amongst a multitude. It is like the great feast that He Himself spread for five thousand men, women, and children, all seated on the grass, 'and they did all eat and were filled.'

The whole love is the property of each recipient of it. He does not love as we do, who give a part of our heart to this one and a part to that one, and share the treasure of our affections amongst a multitude. All this gift belongs to every one, just as all the sunshine comes to every eye, and as every beholder sees the moon's path across the dark waters, stretching from the place where He stands to the centre of light.

This broad love, universal as humanity, and deep as it is broad, is universal because it is individual. You and I have to generalise, as we say, when we try to extend our affections beyond the limits of household and family and personal friends, and the generalising is a sign of weakness and limitation. Nobody can love an abstraction, but God's love and Christ's love do not proceed in that fashion. He individualises, loving each and therefore loving all. It is because every man has a space in His heart singly and separately and conspicuously, that all men have a place there. So our task is to individualise this broad, universal love, and to say, in the simplicity of a glad faith, 'He loved me and gave Himself for me.' The breadth is world-wide, and the whole breadth is condensed into, if I may so say, a shaft of light which may find its way through the narrowest chink of a single soul. There are two ways of arguing about the love of Christ, both of them valid, and both of them needing to be employed by us. We have a right to say, 'He loves all, therefore He loves me.' And we have a right to say, 'He loves me, therefore He loves all.' For surely the love that has stooped to me can never pass by any human soul.

What is the breadth of the love of Christ? It is broad as mankind, it is narrow as myself.

II. Then, in the next place, what is the length of the love of Christ?

If we are to think of Him only as a man, however exalted and however perfect, you and I have nothing in the world to do with His love. When He was here on earth it may have been sent down through the ages in some vague way, as the shadowy ghost of love may rise in the heart of a great statesman or philanthropist for generations yet unborn, which He dimly sees will be affected by His sacrifice and service. But we do not call that love. Such a poor, pale, shadowy thing has no right to the warm throbbing name; has no right to demand from us any answering thrill of affection. Unless you think of Jesus Christ as something more and other than the purest and the loftiest benevolence that ever dwelt in human form, I know of no intelligible sense in which the length of His love can be stretched to touch you.

If we content ourselves with that altogether inadequate and lame conception of Him and of His nature, of course there is no present bond between any man upon earth and Him, and it is absurd to talk about His present love as extending in any way to me. But we have to believe, rising to the full height of the Christian conception of the nature and person of Christ, that when He was here on earth the divine that dwelt in Him so informed and inspired the human as that the love of His man's heart was able to grasp the whole, and to separate the individuals who should make up the race till the end of time; so as that you and I, looking back over all the centuries, and asking ourselves what is the length of the love of Christ, can say, 'It stretches over all the years, and it reached then, as it reaches now, to touch me, upon whom the ends of the earth have come.' Its length is conterminous with the duration of humanity here or yonder.

That thought of eternal being, when we refer it to God, towers above us and repels us; and when we turn it to ourselves and think of our own life as unending, there come a strangeness and an awe that is almost shrinking, over the thoughtful spirit. But when we transmute it into the thought of a love whose length is unending, then over all the shoreless, misty, melancholy sea of eternity, there gleams a light, and every wavelet flashes up into glory. It is a dreadful thing to think, 'For ever, Thou art God.' It is a solemn thing to think, 'For ever I am to be'; but it is life to say: 'O Christ! Thy love endureth from everlasting to everlasting; and because it lives, I shall live also'-'Oh! give thanks unto the Lord, for He is good, for His mercy endureth for ever.'

There is another measure of the length of the love of Christ. 'Master! How often shall my brother sin against me, and I forgive him?-I say not unto thee until seven times, but until seventy times seven.' So said the Christ, multiplying perfection into itself twice-two sevens and a ten-in order to express the idea of boundlessness. And the law that He laid down for His servant is the law that binds Himself. What is the length of the love of Christ? Here is one measure of it-howsoever long drawn out my sin may be, this is longer; and the white line of His love runs out into infinity, far beyond the point where the black line of my sin stops. Anything short of eternal patience would have been long ago exhausted by your sins and mine, and our brethren's. But the pitying Christ, the eternal Lover of all wandering souls, looks down from heaven upon every one of us; goes with us in all our wanderings, bears with us in all our sins, in all our transgressions still is gracious. His pleadings sound on, like some stop in an organ continuously persistent through all the other notes. And round His throne are written the divine words which have been spoken about our human love modelled after His: 'Charity suffereth long and is kind; is not easily provoked, is not soon angry, beareth all things.' The length of the love of Christ is the length of eternity, and outmeasures all human sin.

III. Then again, what is the depth of that love?

Depth and height, as I said at the beginning of these remarks, are but two ways of expressing the same dimension. For the one we begin at the top and measure down, for the other we begin at the bottom and measure up. The top is the Throne; and the downward measure, how is it to be stated? In what terms of distance are we to express it? How far is it from the Throne of the Universe to the manger of Bethlehem, and the Cross of Calvary, and the sepulchre in the garden? That is the depth of the love of Christ. Howsoever far may be the distance from that loftiness of co-equal divinity in the bosom of the Father, and radiant with glory, to the lowliness of the form of a servant, and the sorrows, limitations, rejections, pains and death-that is the measure of the depth of Christ's love. We can estimate the depth of the love of Christ by saying, 'He came from above, He tabernacled with us,' as if some planet were to burst from its track and plunge downwards in amongst the mist and the narrowness of our earthly atmosphere.

A well-known modern scientist has hazarded the speculation that the origin of life on this planet has been the falling upon it of the fragments of a meteor, or an aerolite from some other system, with a speck of organic life upon it, from which all has developed. Whatever may be the case in regard to physical life, that is absolutely true in the case of spiritual life. It all originates because this heaven-descended Christ has come down the long staircase of Incarnation, and has brought with Him into the clouds and oppressions of our terrestrial atmosphere a germ of life which He has planted in the heart of the race, there to spread for ever. That is the measure of the depth of the love of Christ.

And there is another way to measure it. My sins are deep, my helpless miseries are deep, but they are shallow as compared with the love that goes down beneath all sin, that is deeper than all sorrow, that is deeper than all necessity, that shrinks from no degradation, that turns away from no squalor, that abhors no wickedness so as to avert its face from it. The purest passion of human benevolence cannot but sometimes be aware of disgust mingling with its pity and its efforts, but Christ's love comes down to the most sunken. However far in the abyss of degradation any human soul has descended, beneath it are the everlasting arms, and beneath it is Christ's love. When a coalpit gets blocked up by some explosion, no brave rescuing party will venture to descend into the lowest depths of the poisonous darkness until some ventilation has been restored. But this loving Christ goes down, down, down into the thickest, most pestilential atmosphere, reeking with sin and corruption, and stretches out a rescuing hand to the most abject and undermost of all the victims. How deep is the love of Christ! The deep mines of sin and of alienation are all undermined and countermined by His love. Sin is an abyss, a mystery, how deep only they know who have fought against it; but

'O love! thou bottomless abyss,
My sins are swallowed up in thee.'

'I will cast all their sins into the depths of the sea.' The depths of Christ's love go down beneath all human necessity, sorrow, suffering, and sin.

IV. And lastly, what is the height of the love of Christ?

We found that the way to measure the depth was to begin at the Throne, and go down to the Cross, and to the foul abysses of evil. The way to measure the height is to begin at the Cross and the foul abysses of evil, and to go up to the Throne. That is to say, the topmost thing in the Universe, the shining apex and pinnacle, glittering away up there in the radiant unsetting light, is the love of God in Jesus Christ. Other conceptions of that divine nature spring high above us and tower beyond our thoughts, but the summit of them all, the very topmost as it is the very bottommost, outside of everything, and therefore high above everything, is the love of God which has been revealed to us all, and brought close to us sinful men in the manhood and passion of our dear Christ.

And that love which thus towers above us, and gleams like the shining cross on the top of some lofty cathedral spire, does not flash up there inaccessible, nor lie before us like some pathless precipice, up which nothing that has not wings can ever hope to rise, but the height of the love of Christ is an hospitable height, which can be scaled by us. Nay, rather, that heaven of love which is 'higher than our thoughts,' bends down, as by a kind of optical delusion the physical heaven seems to do towards each of us, only with this blessed difference, that in the natural world the place where heaven touches earth is always the furthest point of distance from us: and in the spiritual world the place where heaven stoops to me is always right over my head, and the nearest possible point to me. He has come to lift us to Himself, and this is the height of His love, that it bears us, if we will, up and up to sit upon that throne where He Himself is enthroned.

So, brethren, Christ's love is round about us all, as some sunny tropical sea may embosom in its violet waves a multitude of luxuriant and happy islets. So all of us, islanded on our little individual lives, lie in that great ocean of love, all the dimensions of which are immeasurable, and which stretches above, beneath, around, shoreless, tideless, bottomless, endless.

But, remember, this ocean of love you can shut out of your lives. It is possible to plunge a jar into mid-Atlantic, further than soundings have ever descended, and to bring it up on deck as dry inside as if it had been lying on an oven. It is possible for men and women-and I have them listening to me at this moment-to live and move and have their being in that sea of love, and never to have let one drop of its richest gifts into their hearts or their lives. Open your hearts for Him to come in, by humble faith in His great sacrifice for you. For if Christ dwell in your heart by faith, then and only then will experience be your guide; and you will be able to comprehend the boundless greatness, the endless duration, and absolute perfection, and to know the love of Christ which passeth knowledge.

THE CLIMAX OF ALL PRAYER

Ephesians 3:19

The Apostle's many-linked prayer, which we have been considering in successive sermons, has reached its height. It soars to the very Throne of God. There can be nothing above or beyond this wonderful petition. Rather, it might seem as if it were too much to ask, and as if, in the ecstasy of prayer, Paul had forgotten the limits that separate the creature from the Creator, as well as the experience of sinful and imperfect men, and had sought to 'wind himself too high for mortal life beneath the sky.' And yet Paul's prayers are God's promises; and we are justified in taking these rapturous petitions as being distinct declarations of God's desire and purpose for each of us; as being the end which He had in view in the unspeakable gift of His Son; and as being the certain outcome of His gracious working on all believing hearts.

It seems at first a paradoxical impossibility; looked at more deeply and carefully it becomes a possibility for each of us, and therefore a duty; a certainty for all the redeemed in fullest measure hereafter; and, alas! a rebuke to our low lives and feeble expectations. Let us look, then, at the petition, with the desire of sounding, as we may, its depths and realising its preciousness.

I. First of all, think with me of the significance of this prayer.

'The fulness of God' is another expression for the whole sum and aggregate of all the energies, powers, and attributes of the divine nature, the total Godhead in its plenitude and abundance.

'God is love,' we say. What does that mean, but that God desires to impart His whole self to the creatures whom He loves? What is love in its lofty and purest forms, even as we see them here on earth; what is love except the infinite longing to bestow one's self? And when we proclaim that which is the summit and climax of the revelation of our Father in the person of His Son, and say with the last utterances of Scripture that 'God is love,' we do in other words proclaim that the very nature and deepest desire and purpose of the divine heart is to pour itself on the emptiness and need of His lowly creatures in floods that keep back nothing. Lofty, wonderful, incomprehensible to the mere understanding as this thought may be, clearly it is the inmost meaning of all that Scripture tells us about God as being the 'portion of His people,' and about us, as being by Christ and in Christ 'heirs of God,' and possessors of Himself.

We have, then, as the promise that gleams from these great words, this wonderful prospect, that the divine love, truth, holiness, joy, in all their rich plenitude of all-sufficient abundance, may be showered upon us. The whole Godhead is our possession; for the fulness of God is no far-off remote treasure that lies beyond human grasp and outside of human experience. Do not we believe that, to use the words of this Apostle in another letter, 'it pleased the Father that in Him should all the fulness dwell'? Do we not believe that, to use the words of the same epistle, 'In Christ dwelleth all the fulness of the Godhead bodily'? Is not that abundance of the resources of the whole Deity insphered and incarnated in Jesus Christ our Lord, that it may be near us, and that we may put out our hand and touch it? This may be a paradox for the understanding, full of metaphysical puzzles and cobwebs, but for the heart that knows Christ, most true and precious. God is gathered into Jesus Christ, and all the fulness of God, whatever that may mean, is embodied in the Man Christ Jesus, that from Him it may be communicated to every soul that will.

For, to quote other words of another of the New Testament teachers, 'Of His fulness have all we received, and grace for grace,' and to quote words in another part of the same epistle, we may 'all come to a perfect man, to the measure of the stature of the fulness of Christ.' High above us, then, and inaccessible though that awful thought, 'the fulness of God,' may seem, as the zenith of the unscaleable heavens seems to us poor creatures creeping here upon the flat earth, it comes near, near,

near, ever nearer, and at last tabernacles among us, when we think that in Him all the fulness dwells, and it comes nearer yet and enters into our hearts when we think that 'of His fulness have we all received.'

Then, still further, observe another of the words in this petition:-'That ye may be filled.' That is to say, Paul's prayer and God's purpose and desire concerning us is, that our whole being may be so saturated and charged with an indwelling divinity as that there shall be no room in our present stature and capacity for more, and no sense of want or aching emptiness.

Ah, brethren! when we think of how eagerly we have drunk at the stinking puddles of earth, and how after every draught there has yet been left a thirst that was pain, it is something for us to hear Him say:-'The water that I shall give him shall be in him a well of water springing up into everlasting life,'-and 'he that drinketh of this water shall never thirst.' Our empty hearts, with their experiences of the insufficiency and the vanity of all earthly satisfaction, stand there like the water-pots at the rustic marriage, and the Master says, 'Fill them to the brim.' And then, by His touch, the water of our poor savourless, earthly enjoyments is transmuted and elevated into the new wine of His Kingdom. We may be filled, satisfied with the fulness of God.

There is another point as to the significance of this prayer, on which I must briefly touch. As our Revised Version will tell you, the literal rendering of my text is, 'filled unto' {not exactly with} 'all the fulness of God'; which suggests the idea not of a completed work but of a process, and of a growing process, as if more and more of that great fulness might pass into a man. Suppose a number of vessels, according to the old illustration about degrees of glory in heaven; they are each full, but the quantity that one contains is much less than that which the other may hold. Add to the illustration that the vessels can grow, and that filling makes them grow; as a shrunken bladder when you pass gas into it will expand and round itself out, and all the creases will be smoothed away. Such is the Apostle's idea here, that a process of filling goes on which may satisfy the then desires, because it fills us up to the then capacities of our spirits; but in the very process of so filling and satisfying makes those spirits capable of containing larger measures of His fulness, which therefore flow into it. Such, as I take it, in rude and faint outline, is the significance of this great prayer.

II. Now turn, in the next place, to consider briefly the possibility of the accomplishments of this petition.

As I said, it sounds as if it were too much to desire. Certainly no wish can go beyond this wish. The question is, can a sane and humble wish go as far as this; and can a man pray such a prayer with any real belief that he will get it answered here and now? I say yes!

There are two difficulties that at once start up.

People will say, does such a prayer as this upon man's lips not forget the limits that bound the creature's capacity? Can the finite contain the Infinite?

Well, that is a verbal puzzle, and I answer, yes! The finite can contain the Infinite, if you are talking about two hearts that love, one of them God's and one of them mine. We have got to keep very clear and distinct before our minds the broad, firm line of demarcation between the creature and the Creator, or else we get into a pantheistic region where both creature and Creator expire. But there is a Christian as well as an atheistic pantheism, and as long as we retain clearly in our minds the consciousness of the personal distinction between God and His child, so as that the child can turn round and say, 'I love Thee' and God can look down and say, 'I bless thee'; then all identification and mutual indwelling and impartation from Him of Himself are possible, and are held forth as the aim and end of Christian life.

Of course in a mere abstract and philosophical sense the Infinite cannot be contained by the finite; and attributes which express infinity, like omnipresence and omniscience and omnipotence and so on, indicate things in God that we can know but little about, and that cannot be communicated. But those are not the divinest things in God. 'God is love.' Do you believe that that saying unveils the deepest things in Him? God is light, 'and in Him is no darkness at all.' Do you believe that His light and His love are nearer the centre than these attributes of power and infinitude? If we believe that, then we can come back to my text and say, 'The love, which is Thee, can come into me; the light, which is Thee, can pour itself into my darkness; the holiness, which is Thee, can enter into my impurity. The heaven of heavens cannot contain Thee. Thou dwellest in the humble and in the contrite heart.'

So, dear brethren, the old legends about mighty forms that contracted their stature and bowed their divine heads to enter into some poor man's hut, and sit there, are simple Christian realities. And instead of puzzling ourselves with metaphysical difficulties which are mere shadows, and the work of the understanding or the spawn of words, let us listen to the Christ when He says, 'We will come unto him and make our abode with him' and believe that it was no impossibility which fired the Apostle's hope when he prayed, and in praying prophesied, that we might be filled with all the fulness of God.

Then there is another difficulty that rises before our minds; and Christian men say, 'How is it possible, in this region of imperfection, compassed with infirmity and sin as we are, that such hopes should be realised for us here?' Well, I would rather answer that question by retorting and saying: 'How is it possible that such a prayer should have come from inspired lips unless the thing that Paul was asking might be?' Did he waste his breath when he thus prayed? Are we not as Christian men bound, instead of measuring our expectations by our attainments, to try to stretch our attainments to what are our legitimate expectations, and to hear in these words the answer to the faithless and unbelieving doubt whether such a thing is possible, and the assurance that it is possible.

An impossibility can never be a duty, and yet we are commanded: 'Be ye perfect, as your Father in heaven is perfect.' An impossibility can never be a duty, and yet we are commanded to let Christ abide in our hearts.

Oh! if we believed less in the power of our sin it would have less power upon us. If we believed more in the power of an indwelling Christ He would have more power within us. If we said to ourselves, 'It is possible,' we should make it possible. The impossibility arises only from our own weakness, from our own sinful weakness; and though it may be true, and is true, that none of us will live without sin as long as we abide here, it is also true that each moment of interruption of our communion with Christ and therefore each moment of interruption of that being 'filled with the fulness of God,' might have been avoided. We know about every such time that we could have helped it if we had liked, and it is no use bringing any general principles about sin cleaving to men in order to break the force of that conviction. But if that conviction be a real one, and if whenever a Christian man loses the consciousness of God in his heart, making him blessed, he is obliged to say: 'It was my own fault and Thou wouldst have stayed if I had chosen,' then there follows from this, that it is possible, notwithstanding all the imperfection and sin of earth, that we may be 'filled with all the fulness of God.'

So, dear brethren, take you this prayer as the standard of your expectations; and oh! take it as we must all take it, as the sharpest of rebukes to our actual attainments in holiness and in likeness to our Master. Set by the side of these wondrous and solemn words-'filled with the fulness of God,' the facts of the lives of the average professing Christians of this generation, and of this congregation; their emptiness, their ignorance of the divine indwelling, their want of anything in their experience that corresponds in the least degree to such words as these. Judge whether a man is not more likely to be bowed down in wholesome sense of his own sinfulness and unworthiness, if he has before him such an ideal as this of my text, than if it, too, has faded out of his life. I believe, for my part, that one great cause of the worldliness and the sinfulness and mechanical formalities that are eating the life out of the Christianity of this generation is the fact of the Church having largely lost any real belief in the possibility that Christian men may possess the fulness of God as their present experience. And so, when they do not find it in themselves they say: 'Oh! it is all right; it is the necessary result of our imperfect fleshly condition.' No! It is all wrong; and His purpose is that we should possess Him in the fulness of His gladdening and hallowing power, at every moment in our happy lives.

III. One word to close with, as to the means by which this prayer may be fulfilled.

Remember, it comes as the last link in a chain. I shall have wasted my breath for a month, as far as you are concerned, if you do not feel that the preceding links are needful before this can be attained.

But I only touch upon the nearest of them and remind you that it must be Christ dwelling in our hearts, that fills them with the fulness of God. Where He comes God comes. And where does He come? He comes where faith opens the door for Him. If you will trust Jesus Christ, if you will distrust yourselves, if you will turn your thoughts and your hearts to Him, if you will let Him come into your souls, and not shut Him out because your souls are so full that there is no room for Him there, then when He comes He will not come empty-handed, but will bring the full Godhead with Him.

There must be the emptying of self, if there is to be the filling with God. And the emptying of self is realised in that faith which forsakes self-confidence, self-righteousness, self-dependence, self-control, self-pleasing, and yields itself wholly to the dear Lord.

There is another condition that is required, and that is the previous link in this braided chain. The conscious experience of the love which is in Christ will bring to us 'the fulness of God.' Love is power; love is God; and when we live in the sense and experience of God's love to us then we have the power and we have the God. It is as in some of these petrifying streams, the water is charged with particles which it deposits upon everything that is laid in its course. So, if we plunge our hearts into that fountain of the love of Christ, as it flows it will clothe us with all the divine energies which are held in solution in the divinest thing in God-His own love. Plunged into the love we are filled with the fulness.

Then keep near your Master. It all comes to that. Meditate upon Him; do not let days pass, as they do pass, without a thought being turned to Him. Do not go about your daily work without a remembrance of Him. Keep yourselves in Christ. Seek to experience His love, that love which passeth knowledge, and is only known by them who possess it. And then, as the old painters with deep truth used to paint the Apostle of Love with a face like his Master, living near Christ and looking upon Him you will receive of His fulness, and 'we all, with open face, beholding the glory, shall be changed into the glory.'

MEASURELESS POWER AND ENDLESS GLORY

Ephesians 3:20

One purpose and blessing of faithful prayer is to enlarge the desires which it expresses, and to make us think more loftily of the grace to which we appeal. So the Apostle, in the wonderful series of supplications which precedes the text, has found his thought of what he may hope for his brethren at Ephesus grow greater with every clause. His prayer rises like some songbird, in ever-widening sweeps, each higher in the blue, and nearer the throne; and at each a sweeter, fuller note.

'Strengthened with might by His Spirit'; 'that Christ may dwell in your hearts by faith'; 'that ye may be able to know the love of Christ'; 'that ye might be filled with all the fulness of God.' Here he touches the very throne. Beyond that nothing can be conceived. But though that sublime petition may be the end of thought, it is not the end of faith. Though God can give us nothing more than it is, He can give us more than we think it to be, and more than we ask, when we ask this. Therefore the grand doxology of our text crowns and surpasses even this great prayer. The higher true prayer climbs, the wider is its view; and the wider is its view, the more conscious is it that the horizon of its vision is far within the borders of the goodly land. And as we gaze into what we can discern of the fulness of God, prayer will melt into thanksgiving and the doxology for the swift answer will follow close upon the last words of supplication. So is it here; so it may be always.

The form of our text then marks the confidence of Paul's prayer. The exuberant fervour of his faith, as well as his natural impetuosity and ardour, comes out in the heaped-up words expressive of immensity and duration. He is like some archer watching, with parted lips, the flight of his arrow to the mark. He is gazing on God confident that he has not asked in vain. Let us look with him, that we, too, may be heartened to expect great things of God. Notice then-

142

I. The measure of the power to which we trust.

This epistle is remarkable for its frequent references to the divine rule, or standard, or measure, in accordance with which the great facts of redemption take place. The 'things on the earth'-the historical processes by which salvation is brought to men and works in men-are ever traced up to the 'things in heaven'; the divine counsels from which they have come forth. That phrase, 'according to,' is perpetually occurring in this connection in the epistle. It is applied mainly in two directions. It serves sometimes to bring into view the ground, or reason, of the redemptive facts, as, for instance, in the expression that these take place 'according to His good pleasure which He hath purposed in Himself' It serves sometimes to bring into view the measure by which the working of these redemptive facts is determined; as in our text, and in many other places.

Now there are three main forms under which this standard, or measure, of the Redeeming Power is set forth in this epistle, and it will help us to grasp the greatness of the Apostle's thought if we consider these.

Take, then, first, that clause in the earlier portion of the preceding prayer, 'that He would grant you according to the riches of His glory.' The measure, then, of the gift that we may hope to receive is the measure of God's own fulness. The 'riches of His glory' can be nothing less than the whole uncounted abundance of that majestic and far-shining Nature, as it pours itself forth in the dazzling perfectness of its own Self-manifestation. And nothing less than this great treasure is to be the limit and standard of His gift to us. We are the sons of the King, and the allowance which He makes us even before we come to our inheritance is proportionate to our Father's wealth. The same stupendous thought is given us in that prayer, heavy with the blessed weight of unspeakable gifts, 'that ye might be filled with all the fulness of God.' This, then, is the measure of the grace that we may possess. This limitless limit alone bounds the possibilities for every man, the certainties for every Christian.

The effect must be proportioned to the cause. And what effect will be adequate as the outcome of such a cause as 'the riches of His glory'? Nothing short of absolute perfectness, the full transmutation of our dark, cold being into the reflected image of His own burning brightness, the ceaseless replenishing of our own spirits with all graces and gladnesses akin to His, the eternal growth of the soul upward and Godward. Perfection is the sign manual of God in all His works, just as imperfection and the falling below our thought and wish is our 'token in every epistle' and deed of ours. Take the finest needle, and put it below a microscope, and it will be all ragged and irregular, the fine, tapering lines will be broken by many a bulge and bend, and the point blunt and clumsy. Put the blade of grass to the same test, and see how regular its outline, how delicate and true the spear-head of its point. God's work is perfect, man's is clumsy and incomplete. God does not leave off till He has finished. When He rests, it is because, looking on His work, He sees it all 'very good.' His Sabbath is the Sabbath of an achieved purpose, of a fulfilled counsel. The palaces which we build are ever like that one in the story, where one window remains dark and unjewelled, while the rest blaze in beauty. But when God builds, none can say, 'He was not able to finish.' In His great palace He makes her 'windows of agates' and all her 'borders of pleasant stones.'

So we have a right to enlarge our desires and stretch our confidence of what we may possess and become to this, His boundless bound-'The riches of glory.'

But another form in which the standard, or measure, is stated in this letter is: 'The working of His mighty power, which He wrought in Christ, when He raised Him from the dead' {i.19, 20}; or, as it is put with a modification, 'grace according to the measure of the gift of Christ' {iv.7}. That is to say, we have not only the whole riches of the divine glory as the measure to which we may lift our hopes, but lest that celestial brightness should seem too high above us, and too far from us, we have Christ in His human-divine manifestation, and especially in the great fact of the Resurrection, set before us, that by Him we may learn what God wills we should become. The former phase of the standard may sound abstract, cloudy, hard to connect with any definite anticipations; and so this form of it is concrete, historical, and gives human features to the fair ideal. His Resurrection is the high-water mark of the divine power, and to the same level it will rise again in regard to every Christian. The Lord, in the glory of His risen life, and in the riches of the gifts which He received when He ascended up on high, is the pattern for us, and the power which fulfils its own pattern. In Him we see what man may become, and what His followers must become. The limits of that power will not be reached until every Christian soul is perfectly assimilated to that likeness, and bears all its beauty in its face, nor till every Christian soul is raised to participation in Christ's dignity and sits on His throne. Then, and not till then, shall the purpose of God be fulfilled and the gift which is measured by the riches of the Father's glory, and the fulness of the Son's grace, be possessed or conceived in its measureless measure.

But there is a third form in which this same standard is represented. That is the form which is found in our text, and in other places of the epistle: 'According to the power that worketh in us.'

What power is that but the power of the Spirit of God dwelling in us? And thus we have the measure, or standard, set forth in terms respectively applying to the Father, the Son, and the Holy Ghost. For the first, the riches of His glory; for the second, His Resurrection and Ascension; for the third, His energy working in Christian souls. The first carries us up into the mysteries of God, where the air is almost too subtle for our gross lungs; the second draws nearer to earth and points us to an historical fact that happened in this everyday world; the third comes still nearer to us, and bids us look within, and see whether what we are conscious of there, if we interpret it by the light of these other measures, will not yield results as great as theirs, and open before us the same fair prospect of perfect holiness and conformity to the divine nature.

There is already a Power at work within us, if we be Christians, of whose workings we may be aware, and from them forecast the measure of the gifts which it can bestow upon us. We may estimate what will be by what we know has been, and by what we feel is. That is to say, in other words, the effects already produced, and the experiences we have already had, carry in them the pledge of completeness.

I suppose that if the mediaeval dream had ever come true, and an alchemist had ever turned a grain of lead into gold, he could have turned all the lead in the world in time, and with crucibles and furnaces enough. The first step is all the difficulty, and if you and I have been changed from enemies into sons, and had one spark of love to God kindled in our hearts, that is a mightier change than any that remains to be effected in order to make us perfect. One grain has been changed, the whole mass will be so in due time.

The present operations of that power carry in them the pledge of their own completion. The strange mingling of good and evil in our present nature, our aspirations so crossed and contradicted, our resolution so broken and falsified, the gleams of light, and the eclipses that follow-all these in their opposition to each other, are plainly transitory, and the workings of that Power within us, though they be often overborne, are as plainly the stronger in their nature, and meant to conquer and to endure. Like some half-hewn block, such as travellers find in long abandoned quarries, whence Egyptian temples, that were destined never to be completed, were built, our spirits are but partly 'polished after the similitude of a palace,' while much remains in the rough. The builders of these temples have mouldered away and their unfinished handiwork will lie as it was when the last chisel touched it centuries ago, till the crack of doom; but stones for God's temple will be wrought to completeness and set in their places. The whole threefold divine cause of our salvation supplies the measure, and lays the foundation for our hopes, in the glory of the Father, the grace of the Son, the power of the Holy Ghost. Let us lift up our cry: 'Perfect that which concerneth me, forsake not the works of thine own hands,' and we shall have for answer the ancient word, fresh as when it sounded long ago from among the stars to the sleeper at the ladder's foot, 'I will not leave thee, until I have done that which I have spoken to thee of.'

II. Notice the relation of the divine working to our thoughts and desires.

The Apostle in his fervid way strains language to express how far the possibility of the divine working extends. He is able, not only to do all things, but 'beyond all things'-a vehement way of putting the boundless reach of that gracious power. And what he means by this 'beyond all things' is more fully expressed in the next words, in which he labours by accumulating synonyms to convey his sense of the transcendent energy which waits to bless: 'exceeding abundantly above what we ask.' And as, alas! our desires are but shrunken and narrow beside our thoughts, he sweeps a wider orbit when he adds 'above what we think.' He has been asking wonderful things, and yet even his farthest-reaching petitions fall far on this side of the greatness of God's power. One might think that even it could go no further than filling us 'with all the fulness of God.' Nor can it; but it may far transcend our conceptions of what that is, and astonish us by its surpassing our thoughts, no less than it shames us by exceeding our prayers.

Of course, all this is true, and is meant to apply, only about the inward gifts of God's grace. I need not remind you that, in the outer world of Providence and earthly gifts, prayers and wishes often surpass the answers; that there a deeper wisdom often contradicts our thoughts and a truer kindness refuses our petitions, and that so the rapturous words of our text are only true in a very modified and partial sense about God's working for us in the world. It is His work in us concerning which they are absolutely true.

Of course we know that in all regions of His working He is able to surpass our poor human conceptions, and that, properly speaking, the most familiar, and, as we insolently call them, 'smallest' of His works holds in it a mystery-were it none other than the mystery of Being-against which Thought has been breaking its teeth ever since men began to think at all.

But as regards the working of God on our spiritual lives, this passing beyond the bounds of thought and desire is but the necessary result of the fact already dealt with, that the only measure of the power is God

Himself, in that Threefold Being. That being so, no plummet of our making can reach to the bottom of the abyss; no strong-winged thought can fly to the outermost bound of the encircling heaven. Widely as we stretch our reverent conceptions, there is ever something beyond. After we have resolved many a dim nebula in the starry sky, and found it all ablaze with suns and worlds, there will still hang, faint and far before us, hazy magnificences which we have not apprehended. Confidently and boldly as we may offer our prayers, and largely as we may expect, the answer is ever more than the petition. For indeed, in every act of His quickening grace, in every God-given increase of our knowledge of God, in every bestowment of His fulness, there is always more bestowed than we receive, more than we know even while we possess it. Like some gift given in the dark, its true preciousness is not discerned when it is first received. The gleam of the gold does not strike our eye all at once. There is ever an unknown margin felt by us to be over after our capacity of receiving is exhausted. 'And they took up of the fragments that remained, twelve baskets full.'

So, then, let us remember that while our thoughts and prayers can never reach to the full perception, or reception either, of the gift, the exuberant amplitude with which it reaches far beyond both is meant to draw both after it. And let us not forget either that, while the grace which we receive has no limit or measure but the fulness of God, the working limit, which determines what we receive of the grace, is these very thoughts and wishes which it surpasses. We may have as much of God as we can hold, as much as we wish. All Niagara may roar past a man's door, but only as much as he diverts through his own sluice will drive his mill, or quench his thirst. God's grace is like the figures in the Eastern tales, that will creep into a narrow room no bigger than a nutshell, or will tower heaven high. Our spirits are like the magic tent whose walls expanded or contracted at the owner's wish-we may enlarge them to enclose far more of the grace than we have ever possessed. We are not straitened in God, but in ourselves. He is 'able to do exceeding abundantly above what we ask or think.' Therefore let us stretch desires and thoughts to their utmost, remembering that, while they can never reach the measure of His grace in itself, they make the practical measure of our possession of it. 'According to thy faith' is the real measure of the gift received, even though 'according to the riches of His glory' be the measure of the gift bestowed. Note, again,

III. The glory that springs from the divine work.

'The glory of God' is the lustre of His own perfect character, the bright sum total of all the blended brilliances that compose His name. When that light is welcomed and adored by men, they are said to 'give glory to God,' and this doxology is at once a prophecy that the working of God's power on His redeemed children will issue in setting forth the radiance of His Name yet more, and a prayer that it may. So we have here the great thought expressed in many places of Scripture, that the highest exhibition of the divine character for the reverence and love-of the whole universe, shall we say?-lies in His work on Christian souls, and the effect produced thereby on them. God takes His stand, so to speak, on this great fact in His dealings, and will have His creatures estimate Him by it. He reckons it His highest praise that He has redeemed men, and by His dwelling in them fills them with His own fulness. And this chiefest praise and brightest glory accrues to Him 'in the Church in Christ Jesus.' The weakening of the latter word into by Christ Jesus,' as in the English version, is to be regretted, as substituting another thought, Scriptural no doubt and precious, for the precise shade of meaning in the Apostle's mind here. As has been well said, 'the first words denote the outward province; the second, the inward and spiritual sphere in which God was to be praised.' His glory is to shine in the Church, the theatre of His power, the standing demonstration of the might of redeeming love. By this He will be judged, and this He will point to if any ask what is His divinest work, which bears the clearest imprint of His divinest self. His glory is to be set forth by men on condition that they are 'in Christ,' living and moving in Him, in that mysterious but most real union without which no fruit grows on the dead branches, nor any music of praise breaks from the dead lips.

So, then, think of that wonder that God sets His glory in His dealings with us. Amid all the majesty of His works and all the blaze of His

creation, this is what He presents as the highest specimen of His power-
the Church of Jesus Christ, the company of poor men, wearied and
conscious of many evils, who follow afar off the footsteps of their Lord.
How dusty and toil-worn the little group of Christians that landed at
Puteoli must have looked as they toiled along the Appian Way and
entered Rome! How contemptuously emperor and philosopher and
priest and patrician would have curled their lips, if they had been told
that in that little knot of Jewish prisoners lay a power before which theirs
would cower and finally fade! Even so is it still. Among all the splendours
of this great universe, and the mere obtrusive tawdrinesses of earth,
men look upon us Christians as poor enough; and yet it is to His
redeemed children that God has entrusted His praise, and in their hands
that He has lodged the sacred deposit of His own glory.

Think loftily of that office and honour, lowly of yourselves who have it
laid upon you as a crown. His honour is in our hands. We are the
'secretaries of His praise.' This is the highest function that any creature
can discharge. The Rabbis have a beautiful bit of teaching buried among
their rubbish about angels. They say that there are two kinds of angels-
the angels of service and the angels of praise, of which two orders the
latter is the higher, and that no angel in it praises God twice, but having
once lifted up his voice in the psalm of heaven, then perishes and
ceases to be. He has perfected his being, he has reached the height of
his greatness, he has done what he was made for, let him fade away.
The garb of legend is mean enough, but the thought it embodies is that
ever true and solemn one, without which life is nought-'Man's chief end
is to glorify God.'

And we can only fulfil that high purpose in the measure of our union with
Christ. 'In Him' abiding, we manifest God's glory, for in Him abiding we
receive God's grace. So long as we are joined to Him, we partake of His
life, and our lives become music and praise. The electric current flows
from Him through all souls that are 'in Him' and they glow with fair
colours which they owe to their contact with Jesus. Interrupt the
communication, and all is darkness. So, brethren, let us seek to abide in
Him, severed from whom we are nothing. Then shall we fulfil the

purpose of His love, who 'hath shined in our hearts' that we might give to others 'the light of the knowledge of the glory of God in the face of Jesus Christ' Notice, lastly,

IV. The eternity of the work and of the praise.

As in the former clauses the idea of the transcendent greatness of the power of God was expressed by accumulated synonyms, so here the kindred thought of its eternity, and consequently of the ceaseless duration of the resulting glory, is sought to be set forth by a similar aggregation. The language creaks and labours, as it were, under the weight of the great conception. Literally rendered, the words are-'to all generations of the age of the ages'-a remarkable fusing together of two expressions for unbounded duration, which are scarcely congruous. We can understand 'to all generations' as expressive of duration as long as birth and death shall last. We can understand 'the age of the ages' as pointing to that endless epoch whose moments are 'ages'; but the blending of the two is but an unconscious acknowledgment that the speech of earth, saturated, as it is, with the colouring of time, breaks down in the attempt to express the thought of eternity. Undoubtedly that solemn conception is the one intended by this strange phrase.

The work is to go on for ever and ever, and with it the praise. As the ages which are the beats of the pendulum of eternity come and go, more and more of God's power will flow out to us, and more and more of God's glory will be manifested in us. It must be so; for God's gift is infinite, and man's capacity of reception is indefinitely capable of increase. Therefore eternity will be needful in order that redeemed souls may absorb all of God which He can give or they can take. The process has no limits, for there is no bound to be set to the possible approaches of the human spirit to the divine, and none to the exuberant abundance of the beauty and glory which God will give to His child. Therefore we shall live for ever: and for ever show forth His praise and blaze out like the sun with the irradiation of His glory. We cannot die till we have exhausted God. Till we comprehend all His nature in our thoughts, and reflect all His beauty in our character; till we have attained all the bliss that we can think, and received all the good that we can ask; till Hope has nothing before her to reach towards, and God is left behind: we 'shall not die, but live, and declare the works of the Lord.'

Let His grace work on you, and yield yourselves to Him, that His fulness may fill your emptiness. So on earth we shall be delivered from hopes which mock and wishes that are never fulfilled. So in heaven, after 'ages of ages' of growing glory, we shall have to say, as each new wave of the shoreless, sunlit sea bears us onward, 'It doth not yet appear what we shall be.'

EPHESIANS 4

EPHESIANS CHAPTER 4 CONTENTS

THE CALLING AND THE KINGDOM

Ephesians 4:1; Revelation 3:4

The estimate formed of a centurion by the elders of the Jews was, 'He is worthy for whom Thou shouldst do this' and in contrast therewith the estimate formed by himself was, 'I am not worthy that Thou shouldst come under my roof.' From these two statements we deduce the thought that merit has no place in the Christian's salvation, but all is to be traced to undeserved, gracious love. But that principle, true and all-important as it is, like every other great truth, may be exaggerated, and may be so isolated as to become untrue and a source of much evil. And so I desire to turn to the other side of the shield, and to emphasise the place that worthiness has in the Christian life, and its personal results both here and hereafter. To say that character has nothing to do with blessedness is untrue, both to conscience and to the Christian revelation; and however we trace all things to grace, we must also remember that we get what we have fitted ourselves for.

Now, my two texts bring out two aspects which have to be taken in conjunction. The one of them speaks about the present life, and lays it as an imperative obligation on all Christian people to be worthy of their Christianity, and the other carries us into the future and shows us that there it is they who are 'worthy' who attain to the Kingdom. So I think I shall best bring out what I desire to emphasise if I just take these two points-the Christian calling and the life that is worthy of it, and the Christian heaven and the life that is worthy of it.

I. The Christian calling and the life that is worthy of it.

'I beseech you that ye walk worthy of the vocation wherewith ye are called.' Now, that thought recurs in other places in the Apostle's writings, somewhat modified in expression. For instance, in one passage he speaks of 'walking worthily of the God who has called us to His kingdom and glory,' and in another of the Christian man's duty to 'walk worthily of the Lord unto all pleasing.' There is a certain vocation to which a Christian man is bound to make his life correspond, and his conduct should be in some measure worthy of the ideal that is set before it. Now, we shall best understand what is involved in such worthiness if we make clear to ourselves what the Apostle means by this 'calling' to which he appeals as containing in itself a standard to which our lives are to be conformed.

Suppose we try to put away the technical word 'calling' and instead of 'calling' say 'summons,' which is nearer the idea, because it conveys the notions more fully of the urgency of the voice, and of the authority of the voice, which speaks to us. And what is that summons? How do we hear it? One of the other Apostles speaks of God as calling us 'by His own glory and virtue,' that is to say, wherever God reveals Himself in any fashion, and by any medium, to a man, the man fails to understand the deepest meaning of the revelation unless his purged ear hears in it the great voice saying, 'Come up hither.' For all God's self-manifestation, in the creatures around us, in the deep voice of our own souls, in the mysteries of our own personal lives, and in the slow evolution of His purpose through the history of the world, all these revelations of God bear in them the summons to us that hear and see them to draw near to Him, and to mould ourselves into His likeness. And thus, just as the sun by the effluence of its beams gathers all the ministering planets, as it were, round its feet, and draws them to itself, so God, raying Himself out into the waste, fills the waste with magnetic influences which are meant to draw men to nobleness, goodness, God-pleasingness, and God-likeness.

But in another place in this Apostle's writings we read of 'the high calling of God in Christ Jesus.' Yes, there, as focussed into one strong voice, all the summonses are concentrated and gathered. For in Jesus Christ we see the possibilities of humanity realised, and we have the pattern of what we ought to be, and are called thereby to be. And in Christ we get the great motives which make this summons, as it comes mended from His lips, no longer the mere harsh voice of an authoritative legislator, but the gentle invitation, 'Come unto Me, ... and ye shall find rest unto your souls.' The summons is honeyed, sweetened, and made infinitely mightier when we hear it from His gracious lips. It is the blessed peculiarity of the Christian ideal, that the manifestation of the ideal carries with it the power to realise it. And just as the increasing strength of the spring sunshine summons the buds from out of their folds, and the snowdrops hear the call and force themselves through the frozen soil, so when Christ summons He inclines the ears that hear, and enables the men that own them to obey the summons, and to be what they are commanded. And thus we have 'the high calling of God in Christ Jesus.'

Now, if that is the call, if the life of Christ is that to which we are summoned, and the death of Christ is that by which we are inclined to obey the summons, and the Spirit of Christ is that by which we are enabled to do so, what sort of a life will be worthy of these? Well, the context supplies part of the answer. 'I beseech you that ye walk worthy of the vocation ... with all meekness and lowliness, with long-suffering, forbearing one another in love.' That is one side of the vocation, and the life that is worthy of it will be a life emancipated from the meanness of selfishness, and delivered from the tumidities of pride and arrogance, and changed into the sweetness of gentleness and the royalties of love.

And then, on the other side, in one of the other texts where the same general set of ideas is involved, we get a yet more wondrous exhibition of the life which the Apostle considered to be worthy. I simply signalise its points of detail without venturing to dwell upon them. 'Unto all pleasing'; the first characteristic of life that is 'worthy of our calling' and to which, therefore, every one of us Christian people is imperatively bound, is that it shall, in all its parts, please God, and that is a large demand. Then follow details: 'Fruitful in every good work'-a many-sided fruitfulness, an encyclopaediacal beneficent activity, covering all the ground of possible excellence; and that is not all; 'increasing in the knowledge of God,'-a life of progressive acquaintance with Him; and that is not all:-'strengthened with all might unto all patience and long-suffering'; nor is that all, for the crown of the whole is 'giving thanks unto the Father.' So, then, 'ye see your calling, brethren.' A life that is 'worthy of the vocation wherewith ye are called' is a life that conforms to the divine will, that is 'fruitful in all good,' that is progressive in its acquaintance with God, that is strengthened for all patience and long-suffering, and that in everything is thankful to Him. That is what we are summoned to be, and unless we are in some measure obeying the summons, and bringing out such a life in our conduct, then, notwithstanding all that we have to say about unmerited mercy, and free grace, and undeserved love, and salvation being not by works but by faith, we have no right to claim the mercy to which we say we trust.

Now, this necessity of a worthy life is perfectly harmonious with the great truth that, after all, every man owes all to the undeserved mercy of God. The more nearly we come to realise the purpose of our calling, the more 'worthy' of it we are, the deeper will be our consciousness of our unworthiness. The more we approximate to the ideal, and come closer up to it, and so see its features the better, the more we shall feel how unlike we are to it. The law for Christian progress is that the sense of unworthiness increases in the precise degree in which the worthiness increases. The same man that said, 'Of whom {sinners} I am chief,' said to the same reader, 'I have kept the faith, henceforth there is laid up for me a crown of righteousness.' And so the two things are not contradictory but complementary. On the one side 'worthy' has nothing to do with the outflow of Christ's love to us; on the other side we are to 'walk worthy of the vocation wherewith we are called.'

II. And now, let us turn to the other thought, the Christian heaven and the life that is worthy of it.

Some of you, I have no doubt, would think that that was a tremendous heresy if there were not Scriptural words to buttress it. Let us see what it means. My text out of the Revelation says, 'They shall walk with Me in white, for they are worthy.' And the same voice that spake these, to some of us, astounding, words, said, when He was here on earth, 'They which shall be counted worthy to attain to the life of the resurrection from the dead,' etc. The text brings out very clearly the continuity and congruity between the life on earth and the life in heaven. Who is it of whom it is said that 'they are worthy' to 'walk in white'? It is the 'few

158

names even in Sardis which have not defiled their garments.' You see the connection; clean robes here and shining robes hereafter; the two go together, and you cannot separate them. And no belief that salvation, in its incipient germ here, and salvation in its fulness hereafter, are the results 'not of works of righteousness which we have done, but of His mercy,' is to be allowed to interfere with that other truth that they who are worthy attain to the Kingdom.

I must not be diverted from my main purpose, tempting as the theme would be, to say more than just a sentence about what is included in that great promise, 'They shall walk with Me in white' And if I do touch upon it at all, it is only in order to bring out more clearly that the very nature of the heavenly reward demands this worthiness which the text lays down as the condition of possessing it. 'They shall walk'-activity on an external world. That opens a great door, but perhaps we had better be contented just with looking in. 'They shall walk'-progress; 'with me'-union with Jesus Christ; 'in white'-resplendent purity of character. Now take these four things-activity on an outward universe, progress, union with Christ, resplendent purity of character, and you have almost all that we know of the future; the rest is partly doubtful and is mostly symbolical or negative, and in any case subordinate. Never mind about 'physical theories of another life'; never mind about all the questions-to some of us how torturing they sometimes are!-concerning that future life. The more we keep ourselves within the broad limits of these promises that are intertwined and folded up together in that one saying, 'They shall walk with Me in white,' the better, I think, for the sanity and the spirituality of our conception of a future life.

That being understood, the next thing clearly follows, that only those who in the sense of the word as it is used here, are 'worthy,' can enter upon the possession of such a heaven. From the nature of the gift it is clear that there must be a moral and religious congruity between the gift and the recipient, or, to put it into plainer words, you cannot get heaven unless your nature is capable of receiving these great gifts which constitute heaven. People talk about the future state as being 'a state of retribution.' Well! that is not altogether a satisfactory form of expression, for retribution may convey the idea, such as is presented in earthly rewards and punishments, of there being no natural correspondence between the crime and its punishment, or the virtue and its reward. A bit of bronze shaped into the form of a cross may be the retribution 'For Valour,' and a prison cell may be the retribution by legal appointment for a certain crime. But that is not the way that God deals out rewards and punishments in the life which is to come. It is not a case of retribution, meaning thereby the arbitrary bestowment of a certain fixed gift in response to certain virtues, but it is a case of outcome, and the old metaphor of sowing and reaping is the true one. We sow here and we reap yonder. We pass into that future, 'bringing our sheaves with us,' and we have to grind the corn and make bread of it, and we have to eat the work of our own hands. They drink as they have brewed. 'Their works do follow them,' or they go before them and 'receive them into everlasting habitations.' Outcome, the necessary result, and not a mere arbitrary retribution, is the relation which heaven bears to earth.

That is plain, too, from our own nature. We carry ourselves with us wherever we go. The persistence of character, the continuity of personal being, the continuity of memory, the unobliterable-if I may coin a word-results upon ourselves of our actions, all these things make it certain that what looks to us a cleft, deep and broad, between the present life and the next, is to those that have passed it, and see it from the other side, but a little crack in the soil scarcely observable, and that we carry on into another world the selves that we have made here. Whatever death does-and it does a great deal that we do not know of-it does not alter, it only brings out, and, as I suppose, intensifies, the main drift and set of a character. And so they who 'have not defiled their garments shall walk with Me in white, for they are worthy.'

Ah, brethren! how solemn that makes life; the fleeting moment carries Eternity in its bosom. It passes, and the works pass, but nothing human ever dies, and we bear with us the net results of all the yesterdays into that eternal to-day. You write upon a thin film of paper and there is a black leaf below it. Yes, and below the black leaf there is another sheet, and all that you write on the top one goes through the dark interposed page, and is recorded on the third, and one day that will be taken out of the book, and you will have to read it and say, 'What I have written I have written.'

So, dear friends, whilst we begin with that unmerited love, and that same unmerited love is the sole ground on which the gates of the kingdom of heaven are by the Death and Resurrection and Ascension of Jesus Christ opened to believers, their place there depends not only on faith but on the work which is the fruit of faith. There is such a thing as being 'saved yet so as by fire,' and there is such a thing as 'having an entrance ministered abundantly unto us'; we have to make the choice. There is such a thing as the sore punishment of which they are thought worthy who have rejected the Son of God, and counted the blood of the Covenant an unholy thing; and there is such a thing as a man saying, 'I am not worthy that Thou shouldest come unto me,' and Christ answering, 'He shall walk with Me in white, for he is worthy' and we have to make that choice also.

THE THREEFOLD UNITY

Ephesians 4:5

The thought of the unity of the Church is very prominent in this epistle. It is difficult for us, amidst our present divisions, to realise how strange and wonderful it then was that a bond should have been found which drew together men of all nations, ranks, and characters. Pharisee and philosopher, high-born women and slaves, Roman patricians and gladiators, Asiatic Greeks and Syrian Jews forgot their feuds and sat together as one in Christ. It is no wonder that Paul in this letter dwells so long and earnestly on that strange fact. He is exhorting here to a unity of spirit corresponding to it, and he names a seven-fold oneness-one body and one spirit, one hope, one Lord, one faith, one baptism, one God and Father of all. The outward institution of the Church, as a manifest visible fact, comes first in the catalogue. One Father is last, and between these there lie the mention of the one Spirit and the one Lord. The 'body' is the Church. 'Spirit, Lord, God,' are the triune divine personality. Hope and faith are human acts by which men are joined to God; Baptism is the visible symbol of their incorporation into the one body. These three clauses of our text may be considered as substantially including all the members of the series. We deal with them quite simply now, and consider them in the order in which they stand here.

I. The one Lord.

The deep foundation of Christian unity is laid in the divine Christ. Here, as generally in the New Testament, the name 'Lord' designates Christ in His authority as ruler of men and in His divinity as Incarnation of God. It would not be going too far to suggest that we have in the name, standing as it does, for the most part, in majestic simplicity, a reference to the Old Testament name of Jehovah, which in the Greek translation familiar to Paul is generally rendered by this same word. Nor can we ignore the fact that in this great catalogue of the Christian unities the Lord stands in the centre of the three personalities named, and is regarded as being at once the source of the Spirit and the manifestation of the Father. The place which this name occupies in relation to the Faith which is next named suggests that the living personal Christ is the true uniting principle amongst men. The one body realises its oneness in its common relation to the one Lord. It is one, not because of identity in doctrine, not because of any of the bonds which hold men together in human associations, precious and sacred as many of these are, but 'we being many are one bread, for we are all partakers of that one bread.' The magnet draws all the particles to itself and holds them in a mysterious unity.

II. One faith.

The former clause set forth in one great name all the objective elements of the Church's oneness; this clause sets forth, with equally all-comprehending simplicity, the subjective element which makes a Christian. The one Lord, in the fulness of His nature and the perfectness of His work, is the all-inclusive object of faith. He, in His own living person, and not any dogmas about Him, is regarded as the strong support round which the tendrils of faith cling and twine and grow. True, He is made known to us as possessing certain attributes and as doing certain things which, when stated in words, become doctrines, and a Christ without these will never be the object of faith. The antithesis which is so often drawn between Christ's person and Christian doctrines is by no means sound, though the warning not to substitute the latter for the former is only too necessary at all times.

The subjective act which lays hold of Christ is faith, which in our text has its usual meaning of saving trust, and is entirely misconceived if it is taken, as it sometimes is, to mean the whole body of beliefs which make up the Christian creed. That which unites us to Jesus Christ is an infinitely deeper thing than the acceptance of any creed. A man may believe thirty-nine or thirty-nine hundred articles without having any real or vital connection with the one Lord. The faith which saves is the outgoing of the whole self towards Christ. In it the understanding, the emotions, and the will are all in action. The New Testament faith is absolutely identical with the Old Testament trust, and the prophet who exhorted Israel, 'Trust ye in the Lord for ever, for in the Lord Jehovah is everlasting strength,' was preaching the very same message as the Apostle who cried, 'Believe on the Lord Jesus Christ and thou shalt be saved.'

That 'saving faith' is the same in all Christians, however different they may be in condition and character and general outlook and opinion upon many points of Christian knowledge. The things on which they differ are on the surface, and sometimes by reason of their divergencies Christians stand like frowning cliffs that look threateningly at one another across a narrow gorge, but deep below ground they are continuous and the rock is unbroken. In many and melancholy ways 'the unity of faith and knowledge' is contradicted in the existing organisations of the Church, and we are tempted to postpone its coming to the day of the new Jerusalem which is compact together; but the clarion note of this great text may encourage us to hope, and to labour in our measure for the fulfilment of the hope, that all, who by one faith have been joined to the one Lord, may yet know themselves to be one in Him, and present to the world the fair picture of one body animated by one spirit.

III. One baptism.

Obviously in Paul's mind baptism here means, not the baptism with the Spirit, but the rite, one and the same for all, by which believers in Christ enter into the fellowship of the Church. It was then a perpetual rite administered as a matter of course to all who professed to have been joined to the one Lord by their one faith. The sequence in the three clauses of our text is perfectly clear. Baptism is the expression and consequence of the faith which precedes it. Surely there is here a most distinct implication that it is a declaration of personal faith. Without enlarging on the subject, I venture to think that the order of the Apostle's thought negatives other conceptions of Christian baptism, such as, that it is a communication of Grace, or an expression of the feelings and desires of parents, or a declaration of some truth about redeemed humanity. Paul's order is Christ's when He said, 'He that believeth and is baptized shall be saved.'

It is very remarkable and instructive that whilst thus our text shows that baptism was a matter of course and universally practised, the references to it in the epistles are so few. The inference is not that it was neglected, but that, as being a rite, it could not be as important as were Christian truths and Christian character. May we, in a word, suggest the contrast between the frequency and tone of the Apostolic references to baptism and those which we find in many quarters to-day?

It is remarkable that here the Lord's Supper is not mentioned, and all the more so, that in Paul's letter to the Corinthians, the passage which we have already quoted does put emphasis upon it as a token of Christian unity. The explanation of the omission may be found in the fact that, in these early days, the Lord's Supper was not a separate rite, but was combined with ordinary meals, or perhaps more probably in the consideration that baptism was what the Lord's Supper was not-an initial rite which incorporated the possessors of one faith into the one body.

THE MEASURE OF GRACE

Ephesians 4:7

The Apostle here makes a swift transition from the thought of the unity of the Church to the variety of gifts to the individual. 'Each' is contrasted with 'all.' The Father who stands in so blessed and gracious a relationship to the united whole also sustains an equally gracious and blessed relationship to each individual in that whole. It is because each receives His individual gift that God works in all. The Christian community is the perfection of individualism and of collectivism, and this rich variety of the gifts of grace is here urged as a reason additional to the unity of the one body, for the exhortation to the endeavour to maintain the unity of the spirit in the bond of peace.

I. Each Christian soul receives grace through Christ.

The more accurate rendering of the Revised Version reads 'the grace,' and the definite article points to it as a definite and familiar fact in the Ephesian believers to which the Apostle could point with the certainty that their own consciousness would confirm his statement. The wording of the Greek further implies that the grace was given at a definite point in the past, which is most naturally taken to have been the moment in which each believer laid hold on Jesus by faith. It is further to be noted that the content of the gift is the grace itself and not the graces which are its product and manifestation in the Christian life. And this distinction, which is in accordance with Paul's habitual teaching, leads us to the conclusion, that the essential character of the grace given through the act of our individual faith is that of a new vital force, flowing into and transforming the individual life. From that unspeakable gift which Paul supposed to be verifiable by the individual experience of every Christian, there would follow the graces of Christian character in which would be included the deepening and purifying of all the natural capacities of the individual self, and the casting out from thence of all that was contrary to the transforming power of the new life.

Such an utterance as this, so quietly and confidently taking for granted that the experience of every believer verifies it in his own case, may well drive us all to look more earnestly into our own hearts, to see whether in them are any traces of a similar experience. If it be true, that to every one of us is given the grace, how comes it that so many of us dare not profess to have any vivid remembrance of possessing it, of having possessed it, or of any clear consciousness of possessing it now? There may be gifts bestowed upon unconscious receivers, but surely this is not one of these. If we do not know that we have it, it must at least remain very questionable whether we do have it at all, and very certain that we have it in scant and shrivelled fashion.

The universality of the gift was a startling thing in a world which, as far as cultivated heathenism was concerned, might rightly be called aristocratic, and by the side of a religion of privilege into which Judaism had degenerated. The supercilious sarcasm in the lips of Pharisees, 'This people which knoweth not the law are cursed,' but too truly expresses the gulf between the Rabbis and the 'folk of the earth' as the masses were commonly and contemptuously designated by the former. Into the midst of a society in which such distinctions prevailed, the proclamation that the greatest gift was bestowed upon all must have come with revolutionary force, and been hailed as emancipation. Peter had penetrated to grasp the full meaning and wondrous novelty of that universality, when on Pentecost he pointed to 'that which had been spoken by the prophet Joel' as fulfilled on that day, 'I will pour forth of my Spirit upon all flesh ... Yea, and on my servants and handmaidens ... will I pour forth of my Spirit.' The rushing, mighty wind of that day soon dropped. The fiery tongues ceased to quiver on the disciples' heads, and the many voices that spoke were silenced, but the gift was permanent, and is poured out now as it was then, and now, as then, it is true that the whole company of believers receive the Spirit, though alas! by their own faults it is not true that 'they are all filled with the Holy Spirit.'

Christ is the giver. He has 'power over the Spirit of Holiness' and as the Evangelist has said in his comment on our Lord's great words, when 'He stood and cried,' 'If any man thirst let him come unto Me and drink,' 'This spake He of the Spirit which they that believed on Him were to receive.' We cannot pierce into the depth of the mutual relations of the three divine Persons mentioned in the context, but we can discern that Christ is for us the self-revealing activity of the divine nature, the right arm of the Father, or, to use another metaphor, the channel through which the else 'closed sea' of God flows into the world of creatures. Through that channel is poured into believing hearts the river of the water of life, which proceeds out of the one 'throne of God and of the Lamb.' This gift of the Spirit of Holiness to all believers is the deepest and truest conception of Christ's gifts to His Church. His past work of sacrifice for the sins of the world was finished, as with a parting cry He proclaimed on Calvary, and the power of that sacrifice will never be exhausted, but the taking away of the sins of the world is but the initial stage of the work of Christ, and its further stages are carried on through all the ages. He 'worketh hitherto,' and His present work, in so far as believers are concerned, is not only the forthputting of divine energy in regard to outward circumstances, but the imparting to them of the Divine Spirit to be the very life of their lives and the Lord of their spirits. Christian people are but too apt to give undue prominence to what Christ did for them when He died, and to lose sight, in the overwhelming lustre of His unspeakable sacrifice, of what He is doing for them whilst He lives. It would tend to restore the proportions of Christian truth and to touch our hearts into a deeper and more continuous love to Him, if we more habitually thought of Him, not only as the Christ who died, but also as the Christ who rather is risen again, who is even at the right hand of God, who also maketh intercession for us.

II. The gift of this grace is in itself unlimited.

Our text speaks of it as being according to the measure of the gift of Christ, and that phrase may either mean the gift which Christ receives or that which He gives. Probably the latter is the Apostle's meaning here, as seems to be indicated by the following words that 'when He ascended on high, He gave gifts unto men,' but what He gives is what He possesses, and the Apostle goes on to point out that the ultimate issue of His giving to the Church is that it attains to the measure of the stature of the fulness of Christ.

It may cast some light on this point if we note the remarkable variety of expressions in this epistle for the norm or standard or limit of the gift. In one place the Apostle speaks of the gift bestowed upon believers as being according to the riches of the Father's glory; then it has no limit short of a participation in the divine fulness. God's glory is the transcendent lustre of His own infinite character in its self-manifestation. The Apostle labours to flash through the dim medium of words the glory of that light by blending incongruously, but effectively, the other metaphor of riches, and the two together suggest a wonderful, though vague thought of the infinite wealth and the exhaustless brightness which we call Abba, Father. The humblest child may lift longing and confident eyes and believe that he has received in very deed, through his faith in Jesus Christ, a gift which will increase in riches and in light until it makes him perfect as his Father in heaven was perfect. It was an old faith, based upon insight far inferior to ours, which proclaimed with triumph over the frowns of death. 'I shall be satisfied when I awake with Thy likeness.' Would that those who have so much more for faith to build on, built as nobly as did these!

The gift has in itself no limit short of participation in the likeness of Christ. In another place in this letter the measure of that might which is the guarantee of Christian hope is set forth with an abundance of expression which might almost sound as an unmeaning accumulation of synonyms, as being 'according to the working of the strength of His might which He wrought in Christ'; and what is the range of the working of that might is disclosed to our faith in the Resurrection of Jesus, and the setting of Him high above all rule and authority and power and lordship and every creature in the present or in any future. Paul's continual teaching is that the Resurrection of Jesus Christ was wrought in Him, not as a mere human individual but as our head and representative. Through Him we rise, not only from an ethical death of sin and separation from God, but we shall rise from physical death, and in Him the humblest believer possessing a vital union with the Lord of life has a share in His dominion, and, as His own faithful word has promised, sits with Him on His throne, even as He is set down with the Father on His throne.

That gift has in itself no limit short of its own energy. In another part of this epistle the Apostle indicates the measure up to which our being filled is to take effect, as being 'all the fulness of God' and in such an overwhelming vision breaks forth into fervent praise of Him who is able to do exceeding abundantly above all that we ask or think, and then supplies us with a measure which may widen and heighten our petitions and expectations when He tells us that we are to find the measure of God's working for us, not in the impoverishment of our present possessions, but in the exceeding riches of the power that worketh in us- that is to say, that we are to look for the limit of the limitless gift in nothing short of the boundless energy of God Himself. In the Epistle to the Colossians Paul uses the same illustration with an individual reference to his own labours. In our text he associates with himself all believers, as being conscious of a power working in them, which is really the limitless power of God, and heartens them to anticipate that whatever limitless power can effect in them will certainly be theirs. God does not leave off till He has done and till He can look upon His completed work and pronounce it very good.

III. This boundless grace is in each individual case bounded for the time by our own faith.

When I lived near the New Forest I used to hear much of what they called 'rolling fences.' A man received or took a little piece of Crown land on which he built a house and put round it a fence which could be judiciously and silently pushed outwards by slow degrees and enclosed, year by year, a wider area. We Christian people have, as it were, our own small, cultivated plot on the boundless prairie, the extent of which we measure for ourselves and which we can enlarge as we will. We have been speaking of the various aspects under which the boundlessness of the gift is presented by the Apostle, but there is another 'according to' in Christ's own words, 'According to your faith be it unto you,' and that statement lays down the practical limits of our present possession of the boundless gift. We have as much as we desire; we have as much as we take; we have as much as we use; we have as much as we can hold. We are admitted into the treasure house, and all around us lie ingots of gold and vessels full of coins; we ourselves determine how much of the treasure should be ours, and if at any time we feel like empty-handed paupers rather than like possible millionaires, the reason lies in our own slowness to take that which is freely given to us of God. His word to us all is, 'Ye are not straitened in Me, ye are straitened in yourselves.' It is well for us to keep ever before us the boundlessness of the gift in itself and the working limit in ourselves which conditions our actual possession of the riches. For so, on the one hand, should we be encouraged to expect great things from God, and, on the other hand, be humbled by the contrast between what we might be and what we are. The river that rushes full of water from the throne can send but a narrow and shallow trickle through the narrow channel choked with much rubbish, which we provide for it. It is of little avail that the sun in the heavens pours down its flood of light and warmth if the windows of our hearts are by our own faults so darkened that but a stray beam, shorn of its brightness and warmth, can find its way into our darkness. The first lesson which we have to draw from the contrast between the boundlessness of the gift and the narrow limits of our individual possession and experience of it, is the lesson of penitent recognition and confession of the unbelief which lurks in our strongest faith. 'Lord I believe, help Thou mine unbelief,' should be the prayer of every Christian soul.

Not less surely will the recognition that the form and amount of the grace of God, which is possessed by each, is determined by the faith of each, lead to tolerance of the diversity of gifts. We have received our own proper gift of God, that which the strength and purity of our faith is capable of possessing, and it is not for us to carp at our brethren, either at those in advance of us or at those behind us. We have to remember that as it takes all sorts of people to make up a world, so it takes all varieties of Christian character to make a church. It is the body and not the individual members which represents Christ to the world. The firmest adherence to our own form of the universal gift will combine with the widest toleration of the gifts of others. The white light appears when red, green, and blue blend together, not when each tries to be the other. 'Every man hath his own proper gift of God, one after this fashion and another after that,' and we shall be true to the boundlessness of the gift and to the limitations of our own possession of it, in the measure of which we combine obedience to the light which shines in us, with thankful recognition of that which is granted to others.

The contrast between these two must be kept vivid if we would live in the freedom of the hope of the glory of God, for in the contrast lies the assurance of endless growth. A process is begun in every Christian soul of which the only natural end is the full possession of God in Christ, and that full possession can never be reached by a finite creature, but that does not mean that the ideal mocks us and retreats before us like the pot of gold, which the children fancy is at the end of the rainbow. Rather it means a continuous succession of our realisations of the ideal in ever fuller and more blessed reality. In this life we may, on condition of our growth in faith, grow in the possession of the fulness of God, and yet at each moment that possession will be greater, though at all moments we may be filled. In the Christian life to-morrow may be safely reckoned as destined to be 'as yesterday and much more abundant,' and when we pass from the imperfections of the most perfect earthly life, there will still remain ever before us the glory, which, according to the measure of our capacity, is also in us, and we shall draw nearer and nearer to it, and be for ever receiving into our expanding spirits more and more of the infinite fulness of God.

THE GOAL OF PROGRESS

Ephesians 4:13

The thought of the unity of the Church is much in the Apostle's mind in this epistle. It is set forth in many places by his two favourite metaphors of the body and the temple, by the relation of husband and wife and by the family. It is contemplated in its great historical realisation by the union of Jew and Gentile in one whole. In the preceding context it is set forth as already existing, but also as lying far-off in the future. The chapter begins with an earnest exhortation to preserve this unity and with an exhibition of the oneness which does really exist in body, spirit, hope, lord, faith, baptism. But the Apostle swiftly passes to the corresponding thought of diversity. There are varieties in the gifts of the one Spirit; whilst each individual in the one whole receives his due portion, there are broad differences in spiritual gifts. These differences do not break the oneness, but they may tend to do so; they are not causes of separation and do not necessarily interfere with unity, but they may be made so. Their existence leaves room for brotherly helpfulness, and creates a necessity for it. The wiser are to teach; the more advanced are to lead; the more largely gifted are to encourage and stimulate the less richly endowed. Such outward helps and brotherly impartations of gifts is, on the one hand, a result of the one gift to the whole body, and is on the other a sign of, because a necessity arising from, the imperfect degree in which each individual has received of Christ's fulness; and these helps of teaching and guidance have for their sole object to make Christian men able to do without them, and are, as the text tells us, to cease when, and to last till, we all attain to the fulness of Christ. To Paul, then, the manifest unity of the Church was to be the end of its earthly course, but it also was real, though incomplete, in the present, and the emphasis of our text is not so much laid on telling us when this oneness was to be manifested as in showing us in what it consists. We have here a threefold expression of the true unity, as consisting in a oneness of relation to Christ, a consequent maturity of manhood and a perfect possession of all which is in Christ.

I. The true unity is oneness of relation to Christ.

The Revised Version is here to be preferred, and its 'attain unto' brings out the idea which the Authorised Version fails to express, that the text is intended to point to the period at which Christ's provision of helpful gifts to the growing Church is to cease, when the individuals composing it have come to their destined unity and maturity in Him. The three clauses of our text are each introduced by the same preposition, and there is no reason why in the second and third it should be rendered 'unto' and in the first should be watered down to 'in.'

There are then two regions in which this unity is to be realised. These are expressed by the great words, 'the unity of the faith and knowledge of the Son of God.' These words are open to a misunderstanding, as if they referred to a unity as between faith and knowledge; but it is obvious to the slightest reflection that what is meant is the unity of all believers in regard to their faith, and in regard to their knowledge. It is to be noted that the Apostle has just said that there is one faith, now he points to the realisation of that oneness as the very end and goal of all discipline and growth. I suppose that we have to think here of the manifold and sad differences existing in Christian men, in regard to the depth and constancy and formative power of their faith. There are some who have it so strong and vigorous that it is a vision rather than a faith, a trust, deep and firm and settled, to which the present is but the fleeting shadow, and the unseen the eternal and only reality; but, alas! there are others in whom the light of faith burns feebly and flickers. Nor are these differences the attributes of different men, but the same man varies in the power of his faith, and we all of us know what it is to have it sometimes dominant over our whole selves, and sometimes weak and crushed under the weight of earthly passions. To-day we may be all flame, to-morrow all ice. Our faith may seem to us to be strong enough to move mountains, and before an hour is past we may find it, by experience, to be less than a grain of mustard seed. 'Action and reaction are always equal and contrary,' and that law is as true in reference to our present spiritual life as it is true in regard to physical objects. We have, then, the encouragement of such a word as that of our text for looking forward to and straining towards the reversal of these sad alterations in a fixed and continuous faith which should grasp the whole Christ and should always hold Him. There may still be diversities and degrees, but each should have his measure always full. 'Thy Sun shall no more go down'; there will no longer be the contrast between the flashing waters of a flood-tide and the dreary mud-banks disclosed at low water. We shall stand at different points, but the faces of all will be turned to Him who is the Light of all, and every face will shine with the likeness of His, when we see Him as He is.

But our text points us to another form of unity-the oneness of the knowledge of the Son of God.

The Apostle uses an emphatic term which is very familiar on his lips to designate this knowledge. It means not a mere intellectual apprehension, but a profound and vital acquaintance, dependent indeed upon faith, and realised in experience. It is the knowledge for which Paul was ready to 'count all things but loss' that he might know Jesus, and winning which he would count himself to 'have apprehended.' The unity in this deep and blessed knowledge has nothing to do with identity of opinion on the points which have separated Christians. It is not to be sought by outward unanimity, nor by aggregation in external communities. The Apostle's great thought is made small and the truth of it is falsified when it is over-hastily embodied in institutions. It has been sought in a uniformity which resembles unity as much as a bundle of faggots, all cut to the same length, and tied together with a rope, resemble the tree from which they were chopped, waving in the wind and living one life to the tips of its furthest branches. Men have made out of the Apostle's divine vision of a unity in the faith and knowledge of the Son of God 'a staunch and solid piece of framework as any January could freeze together,' and few things have stood more in the way of the realisation of his glowing anticipations than the formation of the great Corporation, imposing from its bulk and antiquity, to part from which was branded as breaking the unity of the spirit.

Paul gives no clear definition here of the time when the one body of Christian believers should have attained to the unity of the faith and knowledge of the Son of God, and the question may not have presented itself to him. It may appear that in view of the immediate context he regards the goal as one to be reached in our present life, or it may be that he is thinking rather of the Future, when the Master 'should bring together every joint and member and mould them into an immortal feature of loveliness and perfection.' But the time at which this great ideal should be attained is altogether apart from the obligation pressing upon us all, at all times, to work towards it. Whensoever it is reached it will only be by our drawing 'nearer, day by day, each to his brethren, all to God,' or rather, each to God and so all to his brethren. Take twenty points in a great circle and let each be advanced by one half of its distance to the centre, how much nearer will each be to each? Christ is our unity, not dogmas, not polities, not rituals: our oneness is a oneness of life. We need for our centre no tower with a top reaching to heaven, we have a living Lord who is with us, and in Him, we being many, are one.

II. Oneness in faith and knowledge knits all into a 'perfect man.'

'Perfect,' the Apostle here uses in opposition to the immediately following expression in the next verse, of 'children.' It therefore means not so much moral perfection as maturity or fulness of growth. So long as we fall short of the state of unity we are in the stage of immaturity. When we come to be one in faith and knowledge we have reached full-grown manhood. The existence of differences belongs to the infancy and boyhood of the Church, and as we grow one we are putting away childish things. What a contrast there is between Paul's vision here and the tendency which has been too common among Christians to magnify their differences, and to regard their obstinate adherence to these as being 'steadfastness in the faith'! How different would be the relations between the various communities into which the one body has been severed, if they all fully believed that their respective shibboleths were signs that they had not yet attained, neither were already perfect! When we began to be ashamed of these instead of glorying in them we should be beginning to grow into the maturity of our Christian life.

But the Apostle speaks of 'a perfect man' in the singular and not of 'men' in the plural, as he has already described the result of the union of Jew and Gentile as being the making 'of twain one new man.' This remarkable expression sets forth, in the strongest terms, the vital unity which connects all members of the one body so closely that there is but one life in them all. There are many members, but one body. Their functions differ, but the life in them all is identical. The eye cannot say to the hand, 'I have no need of thee,' nor again the head to the feet, 'I have no need of you.' Each is necessary to the completeness of the whole, and all are necessary to make up the one body of Christ. It is His life which manifests itself in every member and which gives clearness of vision to the eye, strength and deftness to the hand. He needs us all for His work on the world and for His revelation to the world of the fulness of His life. In some parts of England there are bell-ringers who stand at a table on which are set bells, each tuned to one note, and they can perform most elaborate pieces of music by swiftly catching up and sounding each of these in the right place. All Christian souls are needed for the Master's hand to bring out the note of each in its place. In the lowest forms of life all vital functions are performed by one simple sac, and the higher the creature is in the scale the more are its organs differentiated. In the highest form of all, 'as the body is one, and hath many members, and all the members of the body, being many, are one body, so also is Christ.'

III. This perfect manhood is the possession of all who are in Christ.

The fulness of Christ is the fulness which belongs to Him, or that of which He is full. All which He is and has is to be poured into His servants, and when all this is communicated to them the goal will be reached. We shall be full-grown men, and more wonderful still, we all shall make one perfect man, and individual completenesses will blend into that which is more complete than any of these, the one body, which corresponds to the measure of the stature of the fulness of Christ.

This is the goal of humanity in which, and in which alone, the dreams of thinkers about perfectibility will become facts, and the longings that are deeply rooted in every soul will find their fulfilment. By our personal union with Jesus Christ through faith, our individual perfection, both in the sense of maturity and in that of the realisation of ideal manhood, is assured, and in Him the race, as well as the individual, is redeemed, and will one day be glorified. The Utopias of many thinkers are but partial and distorted copies of the kingdom of Christ. The reality which He brings and imparts is greater than all these, and when the New Jerusalem comes down out of heaven, and is planted on the common earth, it will outvie in lustre and outlast in permanence all forms of human association. The city of wisdom which was Athens, the city of power which was Rome, the city of commerce which is London, the city of pleasure which is Paris, 'pale their ineffectual fires' before the city in the light whereof the nations should walk.

The beginning of the process, of which the end is this inconceivable participation in the glory of Jesus, is simple trust in Him. 'He that is joined to the Lord is one spirit,' and he who trusts in Him, loves Him, and obeys Him, is joined to Him, and thereby is started on a course which never halts nor stays so long as the faith which started him abides, till he 'grows up into Him in all things which is the head, even Christ.' The experience of the Christian life as God means it to be, and by the communication of His grace makes it possible for it to become, is like that of men embarked on some sun-lit ocean, sailing past shining headlands, and ever onwards, over the boundless blue, beneath a calm sky and happy stars. The blissful voyagers are in full possession at every moment of all which they need and of all of His fulness which they can contain, but the full possession at every moment increases as they, by it, become capable of fuller possession. Increasing capacity brings with it increasing participation in the boundless fulness of Him who filleth all in all.

CHRIST OUR LESSON AND OUR TEACHER

Ephesians 4:20-21

The Apostle has been describing in very severe terms the godlessness and corruption of heathenism. He reckons on the assent of the Ephesian Christians when he paints the society in which they lived as alienated from God, insensible to the restraints of conscience, and foul with all uncleanness. That was a picture of heathenism drawn from the life and submitted to the judgment of those who knew the original only too well. It has been reserved for modern eulogists to regard such statements as exaggerations. Those who knew heathenism from the inside knew that they were sober truth. The colonnades of the stately temple of Ephesus stank with proofs of their correctness.

Out of that mass of moral putridity these Ephesian Christians had been dragged. But its effects still lingered in them, and it was all about them with its pestilential miasma. So the first thing that they needed was to be guarded against it. The Apostle, in the subsequent context, with great earnestness gives a series of moral injunctions of the most elementary kind. Their very simplicity is eloquent. What sort of people must they have formerly been who needed to be bade not to steal and not to lie?

But before he comes to the specific duties, he lays down the broad general principle of which all these are to be but manifestations-viz. that they and we need, as the foundation of all noble conduct and of all theoretical ethics, the suppression and crucifixion of the old self and the investiture with a new self. And this double necessity, says the Apostle in my text, is the plain teaching of Jesus Christ to all His disciples.

Now the words which I have selected as my text are but a fragment of a closely concatenated whole, but I may deal with them separately at this time. They are very remarkable. They lay, as it seems to me, the basis for all Christian conduct; and they teach us how there is no real knowledge of Jesus Christ which does not effloresce into the practice of these virtues and graces which the Apostle goes on to describe.

I. First, Christ our Lesson and Christ our Teacher.

Mark the singular expression with which this text begins. 'Ye have not so learned Christ.' Now, we generally talk about learning a subject, a language, a science, or an art; but we do not talk about learning people. But Paul says we are Christ's disciples, not only in the sense that we learn of Him as Teacher-which follows in the next clause-but that we learn Him as the theme of our study.

That is to say, the relation of the person of Jesus Christ to all that He has to teach and reveal to the world is altogether different from that of all other teachers of all sorts of truth, to the truth which they proclaim. You can accept the truths and dismiss into oblivion the men from whom you got them. But you cannot reject Christ and take Christianity. The two are inseparably united. For, in regard to all spiritual and to all moral truth-truth about conduct and character-Jesus Christ is what He teaches. So we may say, turning well-known words of a poet in another direction: 'My lesson is in Thee.'

But that is not all. My text goes on to speak about another thing: 'Ye have learned Christ if so be that ye have heard Him and been taught.' Now that 'If so be' is not the 'if' of uncertainty or doubt, but it is equivalent to 'if, as I know to be the case,' or 'since ye have heard Him.' Away there in Ephesus, years and years after the crucifixion, these people who had never seen Christ in the flesh, nor heard a word from the lips 'into which grace was poured,' are yet addressed by the Apostle as those who had listened to Him and heard Him speak. They had 'heard Him and been taught.' So He was Lesson and He was Teacher. And that is as true about us as it was about them. Let me say only a word or two about each of these two thoughts.

I have already suggested that the underlying truth which warrants the first of them is that Jesus Christ's relation to His message and revelation

180

is altogether different from that of other teachers to what they have to communicate to the world. Of course we all know that, in regard to the wider sphere of religious and Christian truth, it is not only what Christ said, but even more what He did and was, that makes His revelation of the Father's heart. Precious as are the words which drop from His lips, which are spirit and are life, His life itself is more than all His teachings; and it is when we learn, not from Him, but when we learn Him, that we see the Father. But my text has solely reference to conduct, and in that aspect it just implies this thought, that the sum of all duty, the height of all moral perfectness, the realised ideal of humanity, is in Christ, and that the true way to know what a man or a nation ought to do is to study Him.

How strange it is, when one comes to consider it, that the impression of absolute perfection, free from all limitations of race or country or epoch or individual character-and yet not a vague abstraction but a true living Person-has been printed upon the minds and hearts of the world by these four little pamphlets which we call gospels! I do not think that there is anything in the whole history of literature to compare with the impression of veracity and historical reality and individual personality which is made by these fragmentary narratives. And although it has nothing to do with my present subject, I may just say in a sentence that it seems to me that the character of Jesus Christ as painted in the Gospels, in its incomparable vividness and vitality, is one of the strongest evidences for the simple faithfulness as biographies, of these books. Nothing else but the Man seen could have resulted in such compositions.

But apart altogether from that, how blessed it is that we have not to enter upon any lengthened investigations, far beyond the power of average minds, in order to get hold of the fundamental laws of moral conduct! How blessed it is that all the harshness of 'Obey this law or die' is by His life changed into 'Look at Me, and, for My love's sake, study Me and be like Me!' This is the blessed peculiarity which gives all its power and distinctive characteristic to the morality of the Gospel, that law is changed from a statuesque white ideal, pure as marble and cold and lifeless as it, into a living Person with a throbbing heart of love, and an outstretched hand of help, whose word is, 'If ye love Me, keep My commandments, and be like Me.'

Christian men and women! study Jesus Christ. That is the Alpha and Omega of all right knowledge of duty and of all right practice of it. Learn Him, His self-suppression, His self-command, His untroubled calmness, His immovable patience, His continual gentleness, His constant reference of all things to the Father's will. Study these. To imitate Him is blessedness; to resemble Him is perfection. 'Ye have learned Christ' if you are Christians at all. You have at least begun the alphabet, but oh! in Him 'are hid all the treasures,' not only 'of wisdom and knowledge,' but of 'whatsoever things are lovely and of good report'; and 'if there is any virtue, and if there is any praise,' we shall find them in Him who is our Lesson, our perfect Lesson.

But that is not all. Lessons are very well, but-dear me!-the world wants something besides lessons. It has had plenty of teaching. The trouble is not that we are not instructed, but that we do not take the lessons that are laid before us. And so my text suggests another thing besides the wholly inadequate conception, as it would be if it stood alone, of a mere exhibition of what we ought to be.

'If so be that ye have heard Him.' As I said, these Ephesian Christians, far away in Asia Minor, with seas and years between them and the plains of Galilee and the Cross of Calvary, are yet regarded by the Apostle as having listened to Jesus Christ. We, far away down the ages, and in another corner of the world, as really, without metaphor, in plain fact, may have Jesus Christ speaking to us, and may hear His voice. These Ephesians had heard Him, not only because they had heard about Him, nor because they had heard Him speaking through His servant Paul and others, but because, as Paul believed, that Lord, who had spoken with human lips words which it was possible for a man to utter when He was here on earth, when caught up into the third heaven was still speaking to men, even according to His own promise, which He gave at the very close of His career, 'I have declared Thy name unto My brethren, and will declare it.' So, though 'He began both to do and to teach' before He was taken up, after His Ascension He continues both the doing and the tuition. And, in verity, we all may hear His voice speaking in the depths of our hearts; speaking through the renewed conscience; speaking by that Spirit who will guide us into all the truth that we need; speaking through the ages to all who will listen to His voice.

The conception of Christ as a Teacher, which is held by many who deny His redeeming work and dismiss as incredible His divinity, seems to me altogether inadequate, unless it be supplemented by the belief that He now has and exercises the power of communicating wisdom and knowledge and warning and stimulus to waiting hearts; and that when we hear within the depth of our souls the voice saying to us, 'This is the way, walk ye in it,' or saying to us, 'Pass not by, enter not into it,' if we have waited for Him, and studied His example and character, and sought, not to please ourselves, but to be led by His wisdom, we may be sure that it is Christ Himself who speaks. Reverence the inward monitor, and when He within thy heart, by His Spirit, calls thee, do thou answer, 'Speak, Lord! Thy servant heareth.' 'Ye have learned Christ if so be that ye have hearkened to Him.'

II. Secondly, mark the condition of learning the Lesson and hearing the Teacher.

Our Authorised Version, in accordance with its very frequent practice, has evacuated the last words of my text of their true force by the substitution of the more intelligible 'by Him' for what the Apostle writes- 'in Him.' The true rendering gives us the condition on which we learn our Lesson and hear our Teacher. 'In Him,' is no mere surplusage, and is not to be weakened down, as this translation of ours does, into a mere 'by Him' but it declares that, unless we keep ourselves in union with Jesus Christ, His voice will not be heard in our hearts, and the lesson will pass unlearned.

You know, dear brother, how emphatically and continually in the New Testament this doctrine of the dwelling of the believing soul in Christ, and the reciprocal dwelling of Christ in the believing soul, is insisted upon. And I, for my part, believe that one great cause of the unsatisfactory condition of the average Christianity of this day is the slurring over and minimising of these twin great and solemn truths. I would fain bring you back to the Master's words, as declaring the deepest truths in relation to the connection between the believing soul and the Christ in whom it believes:-'Abide in Me, and I in you.' I wish you would go home and take this Epistle to the Ephesians and read it over, putting a pencil mark below each place in which occurs the words 'in Christ Jesus.' I think you would learn something if you would do it.

But all that I have to say at present is that, if we would keep ourselves, by faith, by love, by meditation, by aspiration, by the submission of the will, and by practical obedience, in Jesus Christ, enclosed in Him as it were-then, and then only, should we learn His lesson, and then, and then only, should we hear Him speak. Why! if you never think about Him, how can you learn Him? If you seldom, or sleepily, take up your Bibles and read the Gospels, of what good is His example to you? If you wander away into all manner of regions of thought and enjoyment instead of keeping near to Him, how can you expect that He will communicate Himself to you? If we keep ourselves in touch with that Lord, if we bring all our actions to Him, and measure our conduct by His pattern, then we shall learn His lesson. What does a student in a school of design do? He puts his feeble copy of some great picture beside the original, and compares it touch for touch, line for line, shade for shade, and so corrects its errors. Take your lives to the Exemplar in that fashion, and go over them bit by bit. Is this like Jesus Christ; is that what He would have done? Then 'in Him,' thus in contact with Him, thus correcting our daubs by the perfect picture, we shall learn our lesson and listen to our Teacher.

Still your passions, muzzle your inclinations, clap a bridle on your will, and, as some tumultuous crowd would be hushed into silence that they might listen to the king speaking to them, make a great silence in your hearts, and you will 'hear Him' and be taught 'in Him'.

III. Lastly, the test and result of having learned the Lesson and listened to the Teacher is unlikeness to surrounding corruption.

'Ye have not so learned Christ.' Of course the hideous immoralities of Ephesus are largely, but by no means altogether, gone from Manchester. Of course, nineteen centuries of Christianity have to a very large extent changed the tone of society and influenced the moral judgments and practices even of persons who are not Christians. But there still remains a world, and there still remains unfilled up the gulf between the worldly and the godly life. And I believe it is just as needful as ever it was, though in different ways, for Christians to exhibit unlikeness to the world. 'Not so,' must be our motto; or, as the Jewish patriot said, 'So did not I, because of the fear of the Lord.'

I do not wish you to make yourselves singular; I do not wish you to wear conventional badges of unlikeness to certain selected evil habits. A Christian man's unlikeness to the world consists a great deal more in doing or being what it does not do and is not than in not doing or being what it does and is. It is easy to abstain from conventional things; it is a great deal harder to put in practice the unworldly virtues of the Christian character.

There are wide regions of life in which all men must act alike, be they saints or sinners, be they believers, Agnostics, Mohammedans, Turks, Jews, or anything else. There are two ways of doing the same thing. If two women were sitting at a grindstone, one of them a Christian and the other not, the one that pushed her handle half round the circle for Christ's sake would do it in a different fashion from the other one who took it from her hand and brought it round to the other side of the stone, and did it without reference to God.

Brethren, be sure of this, that if you and I do not find in ourselves the impulse to abstain from coarse enjoyments, to put our feet upon passions and desires, appetites and aims, which godless men recognise and obey without qualm or restraint, we need to ask ourselves: 'In what sense am I a Christian, or in what sense have I heard Christ?' It is a poor affair to fling away our faithful protest against the world's evils for the sake of receiving the world's smile. Modern Christianity is often not vital enough to be hated by a godless world; and it is not hated because it only deserves to be scorned. Keep near Jesus Christ, live in the light of His face, drink in the inspiration and instruction of His example, and the unlikeness will come, and no mistake. Dwell near Him, keep in Him, and the likeness will come, as it always comes to lovers, who grow to resemble that or those whom they love. 'It is enough for the disciple to be as his Teacher, and for the slave to be like his Lord.'

A DARK PICTURE AND A BRIGHT HOPE

Ephesians 4:22

If a doctor knows that he can cure a disease he can afford to give full weight to its gravest symptoms. If he knows he cannot he is sorely tempted to say it is of slight importance, and, though it cannot be cured, can be endured without much discomfort.

And so the Scripture teachings about man's real moral condition are characterised by two peculiarities which, at first sight, seem somewhat opposed, but are really harmonious and closely connected. There is no book and no system in the whole world that takes such a dark view of what you and I are; there is none animated with so bright and confident a hope of what you and I may become. And, on the other hand, the common run of thought amongst men minimises the fact of sin, but when you say, 'Well, be it big or little, can I get rid of it anyhow?' there is no answer to give that is worth listening to. Christ alone can venture to tell men what they are, because Christ alone can radically change their whole nature and being. There are certain diseases of which a constant symptom is unconsciousness that there is anything the matter. A deep-seated wound does not hurt much. The question is not whether Christian thoughts about a man's condition are gloomy or not, but whether they are true. As to their being gloomy, it seems to me that the people who complain of our doctrine of human nature, as giving a melancholy view of men, do really take a far more melancholy one. We believe in a fall, and we believe in a possible and actual restoration. The man to whom evil is not an intrusive usurper can have no confidence that it will ever be expelled. Which is the gloomy system-that which paints in undisguised blackness the facts of life, and over against their blackest darkness, the radiant light of a great hope shining bright and glorious, or one that paints humanity in a uniform monotone of indistinguishable grey involving the past, the present, and the future-which, believing in no disease, hopes for no cure? My text, taken in conjunction with the grand words which follow, about 'The new man, which, after God, is created in righteousness and true holiness,' brings before us some very solemn views {which the men that want them most realise the least} with regard to what we are, what we ought to be and cannot be, and what, by God's help, we may become. The old man is 'corrupt according to the deceitful lusts,' says Paul. There are a set of characteristics, then, of the universal sinful human self. Then there comes a hopeless commandment-a mockery-if we are to stop with it, 'put it off.' And then there dawns on us the blessed hope and possibility of the fulfilment of the injunction, when we learn that 'the truth in Jesus' is, that we put off the old man with his deeds. Such is a general outline of the few thoughts I have to suggest to you.

I. I wish to fix, first of all, upon the very significant, though brief, outline sketch of the facts of universal sinful human nature which the Apostle gives here.

These are three, upon which I dilate for a moment or two. 'The old man' is a Pauline expression, about which I need only say here that we may take it as meaning that form of character and life which is common to us all, apart from the great change operated through faith in Jesus Christ. It is universal, it is sinful. There is a very remarkable contrast, which you will notice, between the verse upon which I am now commenting and the following one. The old man is set over against the new. One is created, the other is corrupted, as the word might be properly rendered. The one is created after God, the other is rotting to pieces under the influence of its lusts. The one consists of righteousness and holiness, which have their root in truth; the other is under the dominion of passions and desires, which, in themselves evil, are the instruments of and are characterised by deceit.

The first of the characteristics, then, of this sinful self, to which I wish to point for a moment is, that every Christless life, whatsoever the superficial differences in it, is really a life shaped according to and under the influence of passionate desires. You see I venture to alter one word of my text, and that for this simple reason; the word 'lusts' has, in modern English, assumed a very much narrower signification than either that of the original has, or than itself had in English when this translation was made. It is a very remarkable testimony, by the by, to the weak point in the bulk of men-to the side of their nature which is most exposed to assaults-that this word, which originally meant strong desire of any kind, should, by the observation of the desires that are strongest in the mass of people, have come to be restricted and confined to the one specific meaning of strong animal, fleshly, sensuous desires. It may point a lesson to some of my congregation, and especially to the younger portion of the men in it. Remember, my brother, that the part of your nature which is closest to the material is likewise closest to the animal, and is least under dominion {without a strong and constant effort} of the power which will save the flesh from corruption, and make the material the vehicle of the spiritual and divine. Many a young man comes into Manchester with the atmosphere of a mother's prayers and a father's teaching round about him; with holy thoughts and good resolutions beginning to sway his heart and spirit; and flaunting profligacy and seducing tongues beside him in the counting-house, in the warehouse, and at the shop counter, lead him away into excesses that banish all these, and, after a year or two of riot and sowing to the flesh, he 'of the flesh reaps corruption,' and that very literally-in sunken eye, and trembling hand, and hacking cough, and a grave opened for him before his time. Ah, my dear young friends! 'they promise them liberty.' It is a fine thing to get out of your father's house, and away from the restrictions of the society where you are known, and loving eyes-or unloving ones-are watching you. It is a fine thing to get into the freedom and irresponsibility of a big city! 'They promise them liberty,' and 'they themselves become the bond slaves of corruption.'

But, then, that is only the grossest and the lowest form of the truth that is here. Paul's indictment against us is not anything so exaggerated and extreme as that the animal nature predominates in all who are not Christ's. That is not true, and is not what my text says. But what it says is just this: that, given the immense varieties of tastes and likings and desires which men have, the point and characteristic feature of every godless life is that, be these what they may, they become the dominant power in that life. Paul does not, of course, deny that the sway and tyranny of such lusts and desires are sometimes broken by remonstrances of conscience; sometimes suppressed by considerations of prudence; sometimes by habit, by business, by circumstances that force people into channels into which they would not naturally let their lives run. He does not deny that often and often in such a life there will be a dim desire for something better-that high above the black and tumbling ocean of that life of corruption and disorder, there lies a calm heaven with great stars of duty shining in it. He does not deny that men are a law to themselves, as well as a bundle of desires which they obey; but what he charges upon us, and what I venture to bring as an indictment against you, and myself too, is this: that apart from Christ it is not conscience that rules our lives; that apart from Christ it is not sense of duty that is strongest; that apart from Christ the real directing impulse to which the inward proclivities, if not the outward activities, do yield in the main and on the whole, is, as this text says, the things that we like, the passionate desires of nature, the sensuous and godless heart.

And you say, 'Well, if it is so, what harm is it? Did not God make me with these desires, and am not I meant to gratify them?' Yes, certainly. The harm of it is, first of all, this, that it is an inversion of the true order. The passionate desires about which I am speaking, be they for money, be they for fame, or be they for any other of the gilded baits of worldly joys- these passionate dislikes and likings, as well as the purely animal ones- the longing for food, for drink, for any other physical gratification-these were never meant to be men's guides. They are meant to be impulses. They have motive power, but no directing power. Do you start engines out of a railway station without drivers or rails to run upon? It would be as reasonable as that course of life which men pursue who say, 'Thus I wish; thus I command; let my desire stand in the place of other argumentation and reason.' They take that part of their nature that is meant to be under the guidance of reason and conscience looking up to God, and put it in the supreme place, and so, setting a beggar on horseback, ride where we know such equestrians are said in the end to go! The desires are meant to be impelling powers. It is absurdity and the destruction of true manhood to make them, as we so often do, directing powers, and to put the reins into their hand. They are the wind, not the helm; the steam, not the driver. Let us keep things in their right places. Remember that the constitution of human nature, as God has meant it, is this: down there, under hatches, under control, the strong impulses; above them, the enlightened understanding; above that, the conscience, which has a loftier region than that of thought to move in, the moral region; and above that, the God, whose face, shining down upon the apex of the nature thus constituted, irradiates it with light which filters through all the darkness, down to the very base of the being; and sanctifies the animal, and subdues the impulses, and enlightens the understanding, and calms and quickens the conscience, and makes ductile and pliable the will, and fills the heart with fruition and tranquillity, and orders the life after the image of Him that created it.

I cannot dwell any longer on this first point; but I hope that I have said enough, not to show that the words are true-that is a very poor thing to do, if that were all that I aimed at-but to bring them home to some of our hearts and consciences. I pray God to impress the conviction that, although there be in us all the voice of conscience, which all of us more or less have tried at intervals to follow; yet in the main it abides for ever true-and it is true, my dear brethren, about you-a Christless life is a life under the dominion of tyrannous desires. Ask yourself what I cannot ask for you, Is it I? My hand fumbles about the hinges and handle of the door of the heart. You yourself must open it and let conviction come in!

Still further, the words before us add another touch to this picture. They not only represent the various passionate desires as being the real guides of 'the old man' but they give this other characteristic-that these desires are in their very nature the instruments of deceit and lies.

The words of my text are, perhaps, rather enfeebled by the form of rendering which our translators have here, as in many cases, thought proper to adopt. If, instead of reading 'corrupt according to the deceitful lusts,' we read 'corrupt according to the desires of deceit,' we should have got not only the contrast between the old man and the new man, 'created in righteousness and holiness of truth'-but we should have had, perhaps, a clearer notion of the characteristic of these lusts, which the Apostle meant to bring into prominence. These desires are, as it were, the tools and instruments by which deceit betrays and mocks men; the weapons used by illusions and lies to corrupt and mar the soul. They are strong, and their nature is to pursue after their objects without regard to any consequences beyond their own gratification; but, strong as they are, they are like the blinded Samson, and will pull the house down on themselves if they be not watched. Their strength is excited on false pretences. They are stirred to grasp what is after all a lie. They are 'desires of deceit.'

That just points to the truth of all such life being hollow and profitless. If regard be had to the whole scope of our nature and necessities, and to the true aim of life as deduced therefrom, nothing is more certain than that no man will get the satisfaction that his ruling passions promise him, by indulging them. It is very sure that the way never to get what you need and desire is always to do what you like.

And that for very plain reasons. Because, for one thing, the object only satisfies for a time. Yesterday's food appeased our hunger for the day, but we wake hungry again. And the desires which are not so purely animal have the same characteristic of being stilled for the moment, and of waking more ravenous than ever. 'He that drinketh of this water shall thirst again.' Because, further, the desire grows and the object of it does not. The fierce longing increases, and, of course, the power of the thing that we pursue to satisfy it decreases in the same proportion. It is a fixed quantity; the appetite is indefinitely expansible. And so, the longer I go on feeding my desire, the more I long for the food; and the more I long for it, the less taste it has when I get it. It must be more strongly spiced to titillate a jaded palate. And there soon comes to be an end of the possibilities in that direction. A man scarcely tastes his brandy, and has little pleasure in drinking it, but he cannot do without it, and so he gulps it down in bigger and bigger draughts till delirium tremens comes in to finish all. Because, for another thing, after all, these desires are each but a fragment of one's whole nature, and when one is satisfied another is baying to be fed. The grim brute, like the watchdog of the old mythology, has three heads, and each gaping for honey cakes. And if they were all gorged, there are other longings in men's nature that will not let them rest, and for which all the leeks and onions of Egypt are not food. So long as these are unmet, you 'spend your money for that which is not bread, and your labour for that which satisfieth not.'

So we may lay it down as a universal truth, that whoever takes it for his law to do as he likes will not for long like what he does; or, as George Herbert says,

'Shadows well mounted, dreams in a career,
Embroider'd lies, nothing between two dishes-
These are the pleasures here.'

Do any of you remember the mournful words with which one of our greatest modern writers of fiction closes his saddest, truest book: 'Ah! vanitas vanitatum! Which of us is happy in this world? which of us has his desire? or, having it, is satisfied?' No wonder that with such a view of human life as that the next and last sentence should be, 'Come, children, let us shut up the box and the puppets, for the play is played out.' Yes! if there be nothing more to follow than the desires which deceive, man's life, with all its bustle and emotion, is a subject for cynical and yet sad regard, and all the men and women that toil and fret are 'merely players.'

Then, again, one more point in this portraiture of 'the old man,' is that these deceiving desires corrupt. The language of our text conveys a delicate shade of meaning which is somewhat blurred in our version. Properly, it speaks of 'the old man which is growing corrupt,' rather than 'which is corrupt,' and expresses the steady advance of that inward process of decay and deterioration which is ever the fate of a life subordinated to these desires. And this growing evil, or rather inward eating corruption which disintegrates and destroys a soul, is contrasted in the subsequent verse with the 'new man which is created in righteousness.' There is in the one the working of life, in the other the working of death. The one is formed and fashioned by the loving hands and quickening breath of God; the other is gradually and surely rotting away by the eating leprosy of sin. For the former the end is eternal life; for the latter, the second death.

And the truth that underlies that awful representation is the familiar one to which I have already referred in another connection, that, by the very laws of our nature, by the plain necessities of the case, all our moral qualities, be they good or bad, tend to increase by exercise. In whatever direction we move, the rate of progress tends to accelerate itself. And this is preeminently the case when the motion is downwards. Every day that a bad man lives he is a worse man. My friend! you are on a sloping descent. Imperceptibly-because you will not look at the landmarks-but really, and not so very slowly either; convictions are dying out, impulses to good are becoming feeble, habits of neglect of conscience are becoming fixed, special forms of sin-avarice, or pride, or lust-are striking their claws deeper into your soul, and holding their bleeding booty firmer. In all regions of life exercise strengthens capacity. The wrestler, according to the old Greek parable, who began by carrying a calf on his shoulders, got to carry an ox by and by.

It is a solemn thought this of the steady continuous aggravation of sin in the individual character. Surely nothing can be small which goes to make up that rapidly growing total. Beware of the little beginnings which 'eat as doth a canker.' Beware of the slightest deflection from the straight line of right. If there be two lines, one straight and the other going off at the sharpest angle, you have only to produce both far enough, and there will be room between them for all the space that separates hell from heaven! Beware of lading your souls with the weight of small single sins. We heap upon ourselves, by slow, steady accretion through a lifetime, the weight that, though it is gathered by grains, crushes the soul. There is nothing heavier than sand. You may lift it by particles. It drifts in atoms, but heaped upon a man it will break his bones, and blown over the land it buries pyramid and sphynx, the temples of gods and the homes of men beneath its barren solid waves. The leprosy gnaws the flesh off a man's bones, and joints and limbs drop off-he is a living death. So with every soul that is under the dominion of these lying desires-it is slowly rotting away piecemeal, 'waxing corrupt according to the lusts of deceit.'

II. Note how, this being so, we have here the hopeless command to put off the old man.

That command 'put it off' is the plain dictate of conscience and of common sense. But it seems as hopeless as it is imperative. I suppose everybody feels sometimes, more or less distinctly, that they ought to make an effort and get rid of these beggarly usurpers that tyrannise over will, and conscience, and life. Attempts enough are made to shake off the yoke. We have all tried some time or other. Our days are full of foiled resolutions, attempts that have broken down, unsuccessful rebellions, ending like the struggles of some snared wild creature, in wrapping the meshes tighter round us. How many times, since you were a boy or a girl, have you said-'Now I am determined that I will never do that again. I have flung away opportunities. I have played the fool and erred exceedingly-but I now turn over a new leaf!' Yes, and you have turned it-and, if I might go on with the metaphor, the first gust of passion or temptation has blown the leaf back again, and the old page has been spread before you once more just as it used to be. The history of individual souls and the tragedy of the world's history recurring in every age, in which the noblest beginnings lead to disastrous ends, and each new star of promise that rises on the horizon leads men into quagmires and sets in blood, sufficiently show how futile the attempt in our own strength to overcome and expel the evils that are rooted in our nature.

Moralists may preach, 'Unless above himself he can erect himself, how mean a thing is man'; but all the preaching in the world is of no avail. The task is an impossibility. The stream cannot rise above its source, nor be purified in its flow if bitter waters come from the fountain. 'Who can bring a clean thing out of an unclean?' There is no power in human nature to cast off this clinging self. As in the awful vision of the poet, the serpent is grown into the man. The will is feeble for good, the conscience sits like a discrowned king issuing empty mandates, while all his realm is up in rebellion and treats his proclamations as so much waste paper. How can a man re-make himself? how cast off his own nature? The means at his disposal themselves need to be cleansed, for themselves are tainted. It is the old story-who will keep the keepers?-who will heal the sick physicians? You will sometimes see a wounded animal licking its wounds with its own tongue. How much more hopeless still is our effort by our own power to stanch and heal the gashes which sin has made! 'Put off the old man'-yes-and if it but clung to the limbs like the hero's poisoned vest, it might be possible. But it is not a case of throwing aside clothing, it is stripping oneself of the very skin and flesh-and if there is nothing more to be said than such vain commonplaces of impossible duty, then we must needs abandon hope, and wear the rotting evil till we die.

But that is not all. 'What the law could not do, in that it was weak through the flesh,' God sending His own Son did-He condemned sin in the flesh. So we come to

III. The possibility of fulfilling the command.

The context tells us how this is possible. The law, the pattern, and the power for complete victory over the old sinful self, are to be found, 'as the truth is-in Jesus.' Union with Christ gives us a real possession of a new principle of life, derived from Him, and like His own. That real, perfect, immortal life, which hath no kindred with evil, and flings off pollution and decay from its pure surface, will wrestle with and finally overcome the living death of obedience to the deceitful lusts. Our weakness will be made rigorous by His inbreathed power. Our gravitation to earth and sin will be overcome by the yearning of that life to its source. An all-constraining motive will be found in love to Him who has given Himself for us. A new hope will spring as to what may be possible for us, when we see Jesus, and in Him recognise the true Man, whose image we may bear. We shall die with Him to sin, when, resting by faith on Him who has died for sin, we are made conformable to His death, that we may walk in newness of life. Faith in Jesus gives us a share in the working of that mighty power by which He makes all things new. The renovation blots out the past, and changes the direction of the future. The fountain in our hearts sends forth bitter waters that cannot be healed. 'And the Lord showed him a tree,' even that Cross whereon Christ was crucified for us, 'which, when he had cast into the waters, the waters were made sweet.'

I remember a rough parable of Luther's, grafted on an older legend, on this matter, which runs somewhat in this fashion: A man's heart is like a foul stable. Wheelbarrows and shovels are of little use, except to remove some of the surface filth, and to litter all the passages in the process. What is to be done with it? 'Turn the Elbe into it,' says he. The flood will sweep away all the pollution. Not my own efforts, but the influx of that pardoning, cleansing grace which is in Christ will wash away the accumulations of years, and the ingrained evil which has stained every part of my being. We cannot cleanse ourselves, we cannot 'put off' this old nature which has struck its roots so deep into our being; but if we turn to Him with faith and say-Forgive me, and cleanse, and strip from me the foul and ragged robe fit only for the swine-troughs in the far-off land of disobedience, He will receive us and answer all our desires, and cast around us the pure garment of His own righteousness. 'The law of the spirit of life in Christ Jesus shall make us free from the law of sin and death.'

THE NEW MAN

Ephesians 4:24

We had occasion to remark in a former sermon that Paul regards this and the preceding clauses as the summing up of 'the truth in Jesus'; or, in other words, he considers the radical transformation and renovation of the whole moral nature as being the purpose of the revelation of God in Christ. To this end they have 'heard Him.' To this end they have 'learned Him.' To this end they have been 'taught in Him,' receiving, by union with Him, all the various processes of His patient discipline. This is the inmost meaning of all the lessons in that great school in which all Christians are scholars, and Christ is the teacher and the theme, and union to Him the condition of entrance, and the manifold workings of His providence and His grace the instruments of training, and heaven the home when school time is over-that we should become new men in Christ Jesus.

This great practical issue is set forth here under three aspects-one negative, two positive. The negative process is single and simple-'put off the old man.' The positive is double-a spiritual 'renewal' effected in our spirits, in the deep centre of our personal being, by that Divine Spirit who, dwelling in us, is 'the spirit of our minds'; and then, consequent upon that inward renewal, a renovation of life and character, which is described as being the 'putting on,' as if it were a garment, of 'the new man,' created by a divine act, and consisting in moral and spiritual likeness to God. It is not necessary to deal, except incidentally, with the two former, but I desire to consider the last of these-the putting on of the new man-a little more closely, and to try to bring out the wealth and depth of the Apostle's words in this wonderful text.

The ideas contained seem to me in brief to be these-the great purpose of the Gospel is our moral renewal; that moral renewal is a creation after God's image; that new creation has to be put on or appropriated by us;

the great means of appropriating it is contact with God's truth. Let us consider these points in order.

I. The great purpose of the Gospel is our moral renewal; 'the new man ... created in righteousness and ... holiness.'

Now, of course, there are other ways of stating the end of the Gospel. This is by no means an exhaustive setting forth of its purpose. We may say that Christ has come in order that men may know God. We may say that He comes in order that the Divine Love, which ever delights to communicate, may bestow itself, and may conceive of the whole majestic series of acts of self-revelation from the beginning as being-if I may so say-for the gratification of that impulse to impart itself, which is the characteristic of love in God and man. We may say that the purpose of the whole is the deliverance of men from the burden and guilt of sin. But whether we speak of the end of the Gospel as the glory of God, or the blessedness of man, or as here, as being the moral perfection of the individual or of the race, they are all but various phrases of the one complete truth. The Gospel is the consequence and the manifestation of the love of God, which delights to be known and possessed by loving souls, and being known, changes them into its own likeness, which to know is to be happy, which to resemble is to be pure.

The first thing that strikes me about this representation of our text is the profound sense of human sinfulness which underlies it.

The language is utterly unmeaning-or at all events grossly exaggerated-unless all have sinned, and the nature which belongs to men universally, apart from the transforming power of Christ's Spirit, be corrupt and evil. And that it is so is the constant view of Scripture. The Bible notion of what men need in order to be pure and good is very different from the superficial notions of worldly moralists and philanthropists. We hear a great deal about 'culture,' as if all that were needed were the training and strengthening of the nature, as if what was mainly needed was the development of the understanding. We hear about 'reformation' from some who look rather deeper than the superficial apostles of culture.

And how singularly the very word proclaims the insufficiency of the remedy which it suggests! 'Re-formation' affects form and not substance. It puts the old materials into a new shape. Exactly so-and much good may be expected from that! They are the old materials still, and it matters comparatively little how they are arranged. It is not re-formation, but re-novation, or, to go deeper still, re-generation, that the world needs; not new forms, but a new life; not the culture and development of what it has in itself, but extirpation of the old by the infusion of something now and pure that has no taint of corruption, nor any contact with evil. 'Verily, I say unto you, ye must be born again.'

All slighter notions of the need and more superficial diagnoses of the disease lead to a treatment with palliatives which never touch the true seat of the mischief, The poison flowers may be plucked, but the roots live on. It is useless to build dykes to keep out the wild waters. Somewhere or other they will find a way through. The only real cure is that which only the Creating hand can effect, who, by slow operation of some inward agency, can raise the level of the low lands, and lift them above the threatening waves. What is needed is a radical transformation, going down to the very roots of the being; and that necessity is clearly implied in the language of this text, which declares that a nature possessing righteousness and holiness is 'a new man' to be 'put on' as from without, not to be evolved as from within.

It is to be further noticed what the Apostle specifies as the elements, or characteristics of this new nature-righteousness and holiness.

The proclamation of a new nature in Christ Jesus, great and precious truth as it is, has often been connected with teaching which has been mystical in the bad sense of that word, and has been made the stalking horse of practical immorality. But here we have it distinctly defined in what that new nature consists. There is no vague mystery about it, no tampering with the idea of personality. The people who put on the new man are the same people after as before. The newness consists in moral and spiritual characteristics. And these are all summed up in the two-righteousness and holiness. To which is added in the substantially parallel passage in Colossians, 'Renewed in knowledge after the image of Him that created Him,' where, I suppose, we must regard the 'knowledge' as meaning that personal knowledge and acquaintance which has its condition in love, and is the foundation of the more purely moral qualities of which our text speaks.

Is there, then, any distinction between these two? I think there is very obviously so. 'Righteousness' is, I suppose, to be understood here in its narrower meaning of observance of what is right, the squaring of conduct according to a solemn sovereign law of duty. Substantially it is equivalent to the somewhat heathenish word 'morality,' and refers human conduct and character to a law or standard. What, then, is 'holiness'? It is the same general conduct and character, considered, however, under another aspect, and in another relation. It involves the reference of life and self to God, consecration to, and service of Him. It is not a mere equivalent of purity, but distinctly carries the higher reference. The obedience now is not to a law but to a Lord. The perfection now does not consist in conformity to an ideal standard, but in likeness and devotion to God. That which I ought to do is that which my Father in heaven wills. Or, if the one word may roughly represent the more secular word 'morality,' the other may roughly represent the less devout phrase, 'practical religion.'

These are 'new,' as actually realised in human nature. Paul thinks that we shall not possess them except as a consequence of renovation. But they are not 'new' in the sense that the contents of Christian morality are different from the contents of the law written on men's hearts. The Gospel proclaims and produces no fantastic ethics of its own. The actions which it stamps in its mint are those which pass current in all lands-not a provincial coinage, but recognised as true in ring, and of full weight everywhere. Do not fancy that Christian righteousness is different from ordinary 'goodness,' except as being broader and deeper, more thorough-going, more imperative. Divergences there are, for our law is more than a republication of the law written on men's hearts. Though the one agrees with the other, yet the area which they cover is not the same. The precepts of the one, like some rock-hewn inscriptions by forgotten kings, are weathered and indistinct, often illegible, often misread, often neglected. The other is written in living characters in a perfect life. It includes all that the former attempts to enjoin, and much more besides. It alters the perspective, so to speak, of heathen morals, and brings into prominence graces overlooked or despised by them. It breathes a deeper meaning and a tenderer beauty into the words which express human conceptions of virtue, but it does take up these into itself. And instead of setting up a 'righteousness' which is peculiar to itself, and has nothing to do with the world's morality, Christianity says, as Christ has taught us, 'Except your righteousness exceed the righteousness of the scribes and Pharisees, ye shall not enter into the kingdom of God.' The same apostle who here declares that actual righteousness and holiness are new things on the earth, allows full force to whatsoever weight may be in the heathen notion of 'virtue,' and adopts the words and ideas which he found ready made to his hands, in that notion-as fitly describing the Christian graces which he enjoined. Grecian moralists supplied him with the names true, honest, just, and pure. His 'righteousness' accepted these as included within its scope. And we have to remember that we are not invested with that new nature, unless we are living in the exercise of these common and familiar graces which the consciences and hearts of all the world recognise for 'lovely' and 'of good report,' hail as 'virtue,' and crown with 'praise.'

So, then, let me pause here for a moment to urge you to take these thoughts as a very sharp and salutary test. You call yourselves Christian people. The purpose of your Christianity is your growth and perfecting in simple purity, and devotion to, and dependence on, our loving Father. Our religion is nothing unless it leads to these. Otherwise it is like a plant that never seeds, but may bear some feeble blossoms that drop shrunken to the ground before they mature. To very many of us the old solemn remonstrance should come with awakening force-'Ye did run well, what did hinder you?' You have apprehended Christ as the revealer and bringer of the great mercy of God, and have so been led in some measure to put your confidence in Him for your salvation and deliverance. But have you apprehended Him as the mould into which your life is to be poured, that life having been made fluent and plastic by the warmth of His love? You have apprehended Him as your refuge; have you apprehended Him as your inward sanctity? You have gone to Him as the source of salvation from the guilt and penalties of sin; have you gone to Him, and are you daily growing in the conscious possession of Him, as the means of salvation from the corruption and evil of sin? He comes to make us good. What has He made you? Anything different from what you were twenty years ago? Then, if not, and in so far as you are unchanged and unbettered, the Gospel is a failure for you, and you are untrue to it. The great purpose of all the work of Christ-His life, His sorrows, His passion, His resurrection, His glory, His continuous operation by the Spirit and the word is to make new men who shall be just and devout, righteous and holy.

II. A second principle contained in these words, is that this moral Renewal is a Creation in the image of God.

The new man is 'created after the image of God'-that is, of course, according to or in the likeness of God. There is evident reference here to the account of man's creation in Genesis, and the idea is involved that this new man is the restoration and completion of that earlier likeness, which, in some sense, has faded out of the features and form of our sinful souls. It is to be remembered, however, that there is an image of God inseparable from human nature, and not effaceable by any obscuring or disturbance caused by sin. Man's likeness to God consists in his being a person, possessed of a will and self-consciousness, and that mysterious gift of personality abides whatever perishes. But beyond that natural image of God, as we may call it, there is something else which fades wholly with the first breath of evil, like the reflexion of the sky on some windless sea. The natural likeness remains, and without it no comparison would be possible. We should not think of saying that a stone or an eagle were unlike God. But while the personal being makes comparison fitting, what makes the true contrast? In what respect is man unlike God? In moral antagonism. What is the true likeness? Moral harmony. What separates men from their Father in heaven? Is it that His 'years are throughout all generations,' and 'my days are as an handbreadth'? Is it that His power is infinite, and mine all thwarted by other might and over tending to weakness and extinction? Is it that His wisdom, sunlike, waxes not nor wanes, and there is nothing hid from its beams, while my knowledge, like the lesser light, shines by reflected radiance, serves but to make the night visible, and is crescent and decaying, changeful and wandering? No. All such distinctions based upon what people call the sovereign attributes of God-the distinctions of creator and created, infinite and finite, omnipotent and weak, eternal and transient-make no real gulf between God and man. If we have only to say, 'As the heavens are higher than the earth, so are' His 'ways higher than' our 'ways,' that difference is not unlikeness, and establishes no separation; for low and flat though the dull earth be, does not heaven bend down round it, and send rain and sun, dew and blessing? But it is because 'your ways are not as my ways'-because there is actual opposition, because the directions are different-that there is unlikeness. The image of God lies not only in that personality which the 'Father of Lies' too possesses, but in 'righteousness and holiness.'

But besides this reference to the original creation of man, there is another reason for the representation of the new nature as being a work of divine creative power. It is in order to give the most emphatic expression possible to the truth that we do not make our righteousness for ourselves, but receive it as from Him. The new man is not our work, it is God's creation. As at the beginning, the first human life is represented as not originated in the line of natural cause and effect, but as a new and supernatural commencement, so in every Christian soul the life which is derived from God, and will unfold itself in His likeness, comes from His own breath inbreathed into the nostrils. It too is out of the line of natural causes. It too is a direct gift from God. It too is a true supernatural being-a real and new creation.

May I venture a step further? 'The new man' is spoken of here as if it had existence ere we 'put it on.' I do not press that, as if it necessarily involved the idea which I am going to suggest, for the peculiar form of expression is probably only due to the exigencies of the metaphor. Still it may not be altogether foreign to the whole scope of the passage, if I remind you that the new man, the true likeness of God, has, indeed, a real existence apart from our assumption of it. Of course, the righteousness and holiness which make that new nature in me have no being till they become mine. But we believe that the righteousness and holiness which we make ours come from another, who bestows them on us. 'The new man' is not a mere ideal, but has a historical and a present existence. The ideal has lived and lives, is a human person, even Jesus Christ the express image of the Father, who is the beginning of the new creation, who of God is made unto us wisdom and righteousness. That fair vision of a humanity detached from all consequences of sin, renewed in perfect beauty, stainless and Godlike, is no unsubstantial dream, but a simple fact. He ever liveth. His word to us is, 'I counsel thee to buy of me-white raiment.' And a full parallel to the words of our text, which bid us 'put on the new man, created after God in righteousness and holiness,' is found in the other words of the same Apostle-'Let us cast off the works of darkness, and let us put on the armour of light. Put ye on the Lord Jesus Christ.'

In accordance with this-

III. It is further to be noticed that this new creation has to be put on and appropriated by us.

The same idea which, as I have already remarked, is conveyed by the image of a new creation, is reiterated in this metaphor of putting on the new nature, as if it were a garment. Our task is not to weave it, but to wear it. It is made and ready.

And that process of assumption or putting on has two parts. We are clothed upon with Christ in a double way, or rather in a double sense. We are 'found in Him not having our own righteousness,' but invested with His for our pardon and acceptance. We are clothed with His righteousness for our purifying and sanctifying.

Both are the conditions of our being like God. Both are the gifts of God. The one, however, is an act; the other a process. Both are received. The one is received on condition of simple faith; the other is received by the medium of faithful effort. Both are included in the wide conception of salvation, but the law for the one is 'Not by works of righteousness which we have done, but by His mercy He saved us'; and the law for the other is-'Work out your own salvation with fear and trembling.' Both come from Christ, but for the one we have the invitation, 'Buy of Me white raiment that thou mayest be clothed'; and for the other we have the command, 'Put on the Lord Jesus Christ, and make not provision for the flesh.' There is the assumption of His righteousness which makes a man a Christian, and has for its condition simple faith. There is the assumption of His righteousness sanctifying and transforming us which follows in a Christian course, as its indispensable accompaniment and characteristic, and that is realised by daily and continuous effort.

And one word about the manner, the effort as set forth here; twofold, as I have already pointed out-a negative and positive. We are not concerned here with the relations of these amongst themselves, but I may remark that there is no growth in holiness possible without the constant accompanying process of excision and crucifixion of the old. If you want to grow purer and liker Christ, you must slay yourselves. You cannot gird on 'righteousness' above the old self, as some beggar might buckle to himself royal velvet with its ermine over his filthy tatters. There must be a putting off in order to and accompanying the putting on. Strip yourselves of yourselves, and then you 'shall not be found naked,' but clothed with the garments of salvation, as the bride with the robe which is the token of the bridegroom's love, and the pledge of her espousals to him.

And let nobody wonder that the Apostle here commands us, as by our own efforts, to put on and make ours what is in many other places of Scripture treated as God's gift. These earnest exhortations are perfectly consistent with the belief that all comes from God. Our faithful adherence to our Lord and Master, our honest efforts in His strength to secure more and more of His likeness, determine the extent to which we shall possess that likeness. The new nature is God's gift, and it is given to us according to His own fulness indeed, but also according to the measure of our faith. Blessed be His name! we have nothing to do but to accept His gift. The garment with which He clothes our nakedness and hides our filth is woven in no earthly looms. As with the first sinful pair, so with all their children since, 'the Lord God made them' the covering which they cannot make for themselves. But we have to accept it, and we have by daily toil, all our lives long, to gather it more and more closely around us, to wrap ourselves more and more completely in its ample folds. We have by effort and longing, by self-abnegation and aspiration, by prayer and work, by communion and service, to increase our possession of that likeness to God which lives in Jesus Christ, and from Him is stamped ever more and more deeply on the heart. For the strengthening of our confidence and our gratitude, we have to remember with lowly trust that it is true of us, 'If any man be in Christ he is a new creature.' For the quickening of our energy and faithful efforts we have to give heed to the command, and fulfil it in ourselves-'Be ye renewed in the Spirit of your minds, and put on the new man.'

IV. And, finally, the text contains the principle that the means of appropriating this new nature is contact with the truth.

If you will look at the margins of some Bibles you will see that our translators have placed there a rendering, which, as is not unfrequently the case, is decidedly better than that adopted by them in the text. Instead of 'true holiness,' the literal rendering is 'holiness of truth'-and the Apostle's purpose in the expression is not to particularise the quality, but the origin of the 'holiness.' It is 'of truth,' that is, produced by the holiness which flows from the truth as it is in Jesus, of which he has been speaking a moment before.

And we come, therefore, to this practical conclusion, that whilst the agent of renovation is the Divine Spirit, and the condition of renovation is our cleaving to Christ, the medium of renovation and the weapon which transforming grace employs is 'the word of the truth of the Gospel' whereby we are sanctified. There we get the law, and there we get the motive and the impulse. There we get the encouragement and the hope. In it, in the grand simple message-'God was in Christ, reconciling the world unto Himself, not imputing their trespasses unto them,' lie the germs of all moral progress. And in proportion as we believe that-not with the cold belief of our understandings, but with the loving affiance of our hearts and our whole spiritual being-in proportion as we believe that, in that proportion shall we grow in 'knowledge,' shall we grow in 'righteousness,' in the 'image of Him that created us.' The Gospel is the great means of this change, because it is the great means by which He who works the change comes near to our understandings and our hearts.

So let us learn how impossible are righteousness and holiness, morality and religion in men, unless they flow from this source. It is the truth that sanctifies. It is the Spirit who wields that truth who sanctifies. It is Christ who sends the Spirit who sanctifies. But, brethren, beyond the range of this light is only darkness, and that nature which is not cleansed by His priestly hand laid upon it remains leprous, and he who is clothed with any other garment than His righteousness will find 'the covering narrower than that he can wrap himself in it.' And let us learn, on the other hand, the incompleteness and monstrosity of a professed belief in 'the truth' which does not produce this righteousness and holiness. It may be real-God forbid that we should step into His place and assume His office of discerning the thoughts of the heart, and the genuineness of Christian professions! But, at any rate, it is no exaggeration nor presumption to say that a professed faith which is not making us daily better, gentler, simpler, purer, more truthful, more tender, more brave, more self-oblivious, more loving, more strong-more like Christ-is wofully deficient either in reality or in power-is, if genuine, ready to perish-if lit at all, smouldering to extinction. Christian men and women! is 'the truth' moulding you into Christ's likeness? If not, see to it whether it be the truth which you are holding, and whether you are holding the truth or have unconsciously let it slip from a grasp numbed by the freezing coldness of the world.

And for us all, let us see that we lay to heart the large truths of this text, and give them that personal bearing without which they are of no avail. I need renovation in my inmost nature. Nothing can renew my soul but the power of Christ, who is my life. I am naked and foul. Nothing can cleanse and clothe me but He. The blessed truth which reveals Him calls for my individual faith. And if I put my confidence in that Lord, He will dwell in my inmost spirit, and so sway my affections and mould my will that I shall be transformed unto His perfect likeness. He begins with each one of us by bringing the best robe to cast over the rags of the returning prodigal. He ends not with any who trust Him, until they stand amid the hosts of the heavens who follow Him, clothed with fine linen clean and white, which is the righteousness of His Holy ones.

GRIEVING THE SPIRIT

Ephesians 4:30

The miracle of Christianity is the Incarnation. It is not a link in a chain, but a new beginning, the entrance into the cosmic order of a Divine Power. The sequel of Bethlehem and Calvary and Olivet is the upper room and the Pentecost. There is the issue of the whole mission and work of Christ-the planting in the heart of humanity of a new and divine life. All Christendom is professing to commemorate that fact to-day, [Preached on Whitsunday] but a large portion of us forget that it was but a transient sign of a perpetual reality. The rushing mighty wind has died down into a calm; the fiery tongues have ceased to flicker on the disciples' heads, but the miracle, which is permanent, and is being repeated from day to day, in the experience of every believing soul, is the inrush of the very breath of God into their lives, and the plunging of them into a fiery baptism which melts their coldness and refines away their dross. Now, my text brings before us some very remarkable thoughts as to the permanent working of the Divine Spirit upon Christian souls, and upon this it bases a very tender and persuasive exhortation to conduct. And I desire simply to try to bring out the fourfold aspect in those words. There is, first, a wondrous revelation; second, a plain lesson as to what that Divine Spirit chiefly does; third, a solemn warning as to man's power and freedom to thwart it; and, lastly, a tender motive for conduct. 'Grieve not the Holy Spirit, whereby ye are sealed unto the day of redemption.'

Now let us look briefly at these four thoughts: Here we have-

I. A wonderful revelation.

Wonderful to all, startling to some. If you can speak of grief, you must be speaking of a person. An influence cannot be sorry, whatever may happen to it. And that word of my text is no more violent metaphor or exaggeratedly strong way of suggesting a motive, but it keeps rigidly

210

within the New Testament limits, in reference to that Divine Spirit, when to Him it attributes this personal emotion of sorrow with its correlation of possible joy.

Now, I do not need to dwell upon the thought here, but I do desire to emphasise it, especially in view of the strangely hazy and defective conceptions which so many Christian people have upon this matter. And I desire to remind you that the implied assumption of a personal Spirit, capable of being 'grieved,' which is in this text, is in accordance with all the rest of the New Testament teaching.

What did Jesus Christ mean when He spoke of one who 'will guide you into all truth'; of one who 'whatsoever He shall hear, those things shall He speak'? What does the book of the Acts mean when it says that the Spirit said to the believers in Antioch, 'Separate me Barnabas and Saul for the work whereunto I have called them'? What did Paul mean when he said, 'In every city the Holy Ghost testifieth that bonds and afflictions await me'? What does the minister officiating in baptism mean when he says, 'I baptize thee in the name of the Father, and of the Son, and of the Holy Ghost'? That form presents, according to many interpretations, a Divine Person, a Man, and an Influence. Why are these bracketed together? And what do we mean when, at the end of every Christian service, we invoke 'The grace of our Lord Jesus Christ, and the love of God the Father, and the fellowship of the Holy Spirit'? A Man, and God, and an Influence-is that the interpretation? You cannot get rid from the New Testament teaching, whether you accept it or not-you cannot eliminate from it this, that the divine causality of our salvation is threefold and one, the Father, the Son, and the Holy Ghost.

Now, brethren, I do not think I am exaggerating when I say that practically the average orthodox believer believes in a duality, and not a Trinity, in the divine nature. I do not care about the scholastic words, but what I would insist upon is that the course of Christian thinking has been roughly this. First of all, in the early Church, the question of the Divine nature came into play, mainly in reference to the relation of the Eternal Word to the Eternal Father, and of the Incarnation to both. And then, when that was roughly settled, there came down through many ages, and there still subsists, the endeavour to cast into complete and intelligible forms the doctrine, if I must use the word, of Christ's nature and work. And now, as I believe, to a very large extent, the foremost and best thinking of the Christian Church is being occupied with that last problem, the nature and work of that Divine Spirit. I believe that we stand on the verge of a far clearer perception of, and of a far more fervent and realising faith in, the Spirit of God, than ever the Churches have seen before. And I pray you to remember that however much your Christian thought and Christian faith may be centred upon, and may be drawing its nourishment and its joy from, the work of Jesus Christ who died on the Cross for our salvation, and lives to be our King and Defender, there is a gap-not only in your Christian Creed, but also in your Christian experiences and joys and power, unless you have risen to this thought, that the Divine Spirit is not only an influence, a wind, a fire, an oil, a dove, a dew, but a Divine Person. We have to go back to the old creed-'I believe in God the Father Almighty ... and in Jesus Christ His only Son our Lord ... I believe in the Holy Ghost.'

But further, this same revelation carries with it another, and to some of us a startling thought. 'Grieve not the Holy Spirit': that Divine Person is capable of grief. I do not believe that is rhetorical exaggeration. Of course I know that we should think of God as the ever-blessed God, but we also in these last days begin to think more boldly, and I believe more truly, that if man is in the image of God, and there is a divine element in humanity, there must be a human element in divinity. And though I know that it is perilous to make affirmations about a matter so far beyond our possibility of verification by experience, I venture to think that perhaps the doctrine that God is lifted up high above all human weaknesses and emotions does not mean that there can be no shadow cast on the divine blessedness by the dark substance of human sin. I do not venture to assert: I only suggest; and this I know, that He who said to us, 'He that hath seen Me hath seen the Father,' had His eyes filled with tears, even in His hour of triumph, as He looked across the valley and saw the city sparkling in the rays of the morning sun. May we venture to see there an unveiling of the divine heart? Love has an infinite capacity of sorrow as of joy. But I leave these perhaps too presumptuous and lofty thoughts, to turn to the other points involved in the words before us.

I said, in the second place, there was-

II. A plain lesson here, as to the great purpose for which the Divine Spirit has been lodged in the heart of humanity.

I find that in the two words of my text, 'the Holy Spirit,' and 'ye were thereby sealed unto the day of redemption.' If the central characteristic which it imports us to know and to keep in mind is that implied by the name, 'the Holy Spirit' then, of course, the great work that He has to perform upon earth is to make men like Himself. And that is further confirmed by the emblem of the seal which is here; for the seal comes in contact with the thing sealed, and leaves the impression of its own likeness there. And whatever else-and there is a great deal else that I cannot touch now-may be included in that great thought of the sealing by the Divine Spirit, these things are inseparably connected with, and suggested by it, viz. the actual contact of the Spirit of God with our spirits, which is expressed, as you may remember, in the other metaphors of being baptized in and anointed with, and yet more important, the result purposed by that contact being mainly to make us holy.

Now, I pray you to think of how different that is from all other notions of inspiration that the world has ever known, and how different it is from a great many ideas that have had influence within the Christian Church. People say there are not any miracles now, and say we are worse off than when there used to be. That Divine Spirit does not come to give gifts of healing, interpretations of tongues, and all the other abnormal and temporary results which attended the first manifestations. These, when they were given, were but means to an end, and the end subsists whilst the means are swept away. It is better to be made good than to be filled with all manner of miraculous power. 'In this rejoice, not that the spirits are subject to you, but rather rejoice because your names are written in heaven.' All the rest is transient. It is gone; let it go, we are not a bit the poorer for want of it. This remains-not tongues, nor gifts of healing, nor any other of these miraculous and extraordinary and external powers-but the continual operation of a divine influence, moulding men into its own likeness.

Christianity is intensely ethical, and it sets forth, as the ultimate result of all its machinery, changing men into the likeness of God. Holiness is that for which Christ died, that for which the Divine Spirit works. Unless we Christian people recognise the true perspective of the Spirit's gifts, and put at the base the extraordinary, and higher than these, but still subordinate, the intellectual, and on top of all the spiritual and moral, we do not understand the meaning of the central gift and possible blessing of Christianity, to make us holy, or, if you do not like the theological word, let us put it into still plainer and more modern English, to make you and me good men and women, like God. That is the mightiest work of that Divine Spirit.

We have here-

III. A plain warning as to the possibility of thwarting these influences.

Nothing here about irresistible grace; nothing here about a power that lays hold upon a man, and makes him good, he lying passive in its hands like clay in the hands of the potter! You will not be made holy without the Divine Spirit, but you will not be made holy without your working along with it. There is a possibility of resisting, and there is a possibility of co-operating. Man is left free. God does not lay hold of any one by the hair of his head, and drag him into paths of righteousness whether he will or no. But whilst there is the necessity for co-operation, which involves the possibility of resistance, we must also remember that that new life which comes into a man, and moulds his will as well as the rest of his nature, is itself the gift of God. We do not get into a contradiction when we thus speak, we only touch the edge of a great ocean in which our plummets can find no bottom. The same unravellable knot as to the co-operation of the divine and the creatural is found in the natural world, as in the experiences of the Christian soul. You have to work, and your work largely consists in yielding yourselves to the work of God upon you. 'Work out your own salvation with fear and trembling, for it is God that worketh in you.' Brethren! If you and I are Christian people, we have put into our hearts and spirits the talent. It depends on us whether we wrap it in a napkin, and stow it away underground somewhere, or whether we use it, and fructify and increase it. If you wrap it in a napkin and put it away underground, when you come to take it out, and want to say, 'Lo! there Thou hast that is Thine,' you will find that it was not solid gold, which could not rust or diminish, but that it has been like some volatile essence, put away in an unventilated place, and imperfectly secured: the napkin is there, but the talent has vanished. We have to work with God, and we can resist. Ay, and there is a deeper and a sadder word than that applied by the same Apostle in another letter to the same subject. We can 'quench' the light and extinguish the fire.

What extinguishes it? Look at the catalogue of sins that lie side by side with this exhortation of my text! They are all small matters-bitterness, wrath, anger, clamour, evil-speaking, malice, stealing, lying, and the like; very 'homely' transgressions, if I may so say. Yes, and if you pile enough of them upon the spark that is in your hearts you will smother it out. Sin, the wrenching of myself away from the influences, not attending to the whispers and suggestions, being blind to the teaching of the Spirit through the Word and through Providence: these are the things that 'grieve the Holy Spirit of God.'

And so, lastly, we have here-

IV. A Tender Motive, a dissuasive from sin, a persuasive to yielding and to righteousness.

Many a man has been kept from doing wrong things by thinking of a sad pale face sitting at home waiting for him. Many a boy has been kept from youthful transgressions which war against his soul here, on the streets of Manchester, full as they are of temptations, by thinking that it would grieve the poor old mother in her cottage, away down in the country somewhere. We can bring that same motive to bear, with infinitely increased force, in regard to our conduct as Christian people. 'Grieve not the Holy Spirit of God.' A father feels a pang if he sees that his child makes no account of some precious gift that he has bestowed upon him, and leaves it lying about anywhere. A loving friend, standing on the margin of the stream, and calling to his friends in a boat when they are drifting to the rapids, turns away sad if they do not attend to his voice. That Divine Spirit pleads with us, and proffers its gifts to us, and turns away-I was going to use too strong a word, perhaps-sick at heart, not because of wounded authority, but because of wounded love and baffled desire to help, when we, in spite of It, will take our own way, neglect the call that warns us of our peril, and leave untouched the gifts that would have made us safe.

Dear brethren, surely such a dissuasive from evil, and such a persuasive to good, is mightier than all abstractions about duty and conscience and right, and the like. 'Do it rightly' says Paul, 'and you will please Him that hath called you'; leave the evil thing undone, 'and my heart shall be glad, even mine.' You and I can grieve the Christ whose Spirit is given to us. You and I can add something to 'the joy of our Lord.'

EPHESIANS 5

EPHESIANS CHAPTER 5 CONTENTS

GOD'S IMITATORS

Ephesians 5:1

The Revised Version gives a more literal and more energetic rendering of this verse by reading, 'Be ye, therefore, imitators of God, as beloved children.' It is the only place in the Bible where that bold word 'imitate' is applied to the Christian relation to God. But, though the expression is unique, the idea underlies the whole teaching of the New Testament on the subject of Christian character and conduct. To be like God, and to set ourselves to resemble Him, is the sum of all duty; and in the measure in which we approximate thereto, we come to perfection. So, then, there are here just two points that I would briefly touch upon now- the one is the sublime precept of the text, and the other the all-sufficient motive enforcing it. 'Be ye imitators of God as'-because you are, and know yourselves to be-'beloved children,' and it therefore behoves you to be like your Father.

I. First, then, this sublime precept.

Now notice that, broad as this precept is, and all-inclusive of every kind of excellence and duty as it may be, the Apostle has a very definite and specific meaning in it. There is one feature, and only one, in which, accurately speaking, a man may be like God. Our limited knowledge can never be like the ungrowing perfect wisdom of God. Our holiness cannot be like His, for there are many points in our nature and character which have no relation or correspondence to anything in the divine nature. But what is left? Love is left. Our other graces are not like the God to whom they cleave. My faith is not like His faithfulness. My obedience is not like His authority. My submission is not like His autocratic power. My emptiness is not like His fulness. My aspirations are not like His gratifying of them. They correspond to God, but correspondence is not similarity; rather it presupposes unlikeness. Just as a concavity will fit into a convexity, for the very reason that it is concave and not convex, so the human unlikenesses, which are correspondent to God, are the characteristics by which it becomes possible that we should cleave to Him and inhere in Him. But whilst there is much in which He stands alone and incomparable, and whilst we have all to say, 'Who is like unto Thee, O Lord?' or what likeness shall we compare unto Him? we yet can obey in reference to one thing,-and to one thing only, as it seems to me-the commandment of my text, 'Be ye imitators of God.' We can be like Him in nothing else, but our love not only corresponds to His, but is of the same quality and nature as His, howsoever different it may be in sweep and in fervour and in degree. The tiniest drop that hangs upon the tip of a thorn will be as perfect a sphere as the sun, and it will have its little rainbow on its round, with all the prismatic colours, the same in tint and order and loveliness, as when the bow spans the heavens. The dew-drop may imitate the sun, and we are to be imitators of God; knit to Him by the one thing in us which is kindred to Him in the deepest sense-the love that is the life of God and the perfecting of man.

Well, then, notice how the Apostle in the context fastens upon a certain characteristic of that divine love which we are to imitate in our lives; and thereby makes the precept a very practical and a very difficult one. Godlike love will be love that gives as liberally as His does. What is the very essence of all love? Longing to be like. And the purest and deepest love is love which desires to impart itself, and that is God's love. The Bible seems to teach us that in a very mysterious sense, about which the less we say the less likely we are to err, there is a quality of giving up, as well as of giving, in God's love; for we read of the Father that 'spared not His Son,' by which is meant, not that He did not shrink from inflicting something upon the Son, but that He did not grudgingly keep that Son for Himself. 'He spared not His own Son, but delivered Him up to the death for us all.' And if we can say but little about that surrender on the part of the infinite Fountain of all love, we can say that Jesus Christ, who is the activity of the Father's love, spared not Himself, but, as the context puts it, 'gave Himself up for us.'

And that is the pattern for us. That thought is not a subject to be decorated with tawdry finery of eloquence, or to be dealt with as if it were a sentimental prettiness very fit to be spoken of, but impossible to be practised. It is the duty of every Christian man and woman, and they have not done their duty unless they have learned that the bond which unites them to men is, in its nature, the very same as the bond which unites men to God; and that they will not have lived righteously unless they learn to be 'imitators of God,' in the surrender of themselves for their brother's good.

Ah, friend, that grips us very tight-and if there were a little more reality and prose brought into our sentimental talk about Christian love, and that love were more often shown in action, in all the self-suppression and taking a lift of a world's burdens, which its great Pattern demands, the world would be less likely to curl a scornful lip at the Church's talk about brotherly love.

You say that you are a Christian-that is to say a child of God. Do you know anything, and would anybody looking at you see that you knew anything, about the love which counts no cost and no sacrifice too great to be lavished on the unworthy and the sinful?

But that brings me to another point. The Apostle here, in the context, not for the sake of saying pretty things, but for the sake of putting sharp points on Christian duty, emphasises another thought, that Godlike love will be a forgiving love. Why should we be always waiting for the other man to determine our relations to him, and consider that if he does not like us we are absolved from the duty of loving him? Why should we leave him to settle the terms upon which we are to stand? God has love, as the Sermon on the Mount puts it, 'to the unthankful and the evil,' and we shall not be imitating His example unless we carry the same temper into all our relationships with our fellows.

People sit complacently and hear all that I am now trying to enforce, and think it is the right thing for me to say, but do you think it is the right thing for you to do? When a man obviously does not like you, or perhaps tries to harm you, what then? How do you meet him? 'He maketh His sun to shine, and sendeth His rain, on the unthankful and the evil.' 'Be ye imitators of God, as beloved children.'

Now note the all-sufficient motive for this great precept.

The sense of being loved will make loving, and nothing else will. The only power that will eradicate, or break without eradicating, our natural tendency to make ourselves our centres, is the recognition that there, at the heart, and on the central throne of the universe, and the divinest thing in it, there sits perfect and self-sacrificing Love, whose beams warm even us. The only flame that kindles love in a man's heart, whether it be to God or to man, is the recognition that he himself stands in the full sunshine of that blaze from above, and that God has loved him. Our hearts are like reverberating furnaces, and when the fire of the consciousness of the divine love is lit in them, then from sides and roof the genial heat is reflected back again to intensify the central flame. Love begets love, and according to Paul, and according to John, and according to the Master of both of them, if a man loves God, then that glowing beam will glow whether it is turned to earth or turned to heaven.

The Bible does not cut love into two, and keep love to God in one division of the heart and love to man in another, but regards them as one and the same; the same sentiment, the same temper, the same attitude of heart and mind, only that in the one case the love soars, and in the other it lives along the level. The two are indissolubly tied together.

It is because a man knows himself to be beloved that therefore he is stimulated and encouraged to be an 'imitator of God' and, on the other hand, the sense of being God's child underlies all real imitation of Him. Imitation is natural to the child. It is a miserable home where a boy does not imitate his father, and it is the father's fault in nine cases out of ten if he does not. Whoever feels himself to be a beloved child is thereby necessarily drawn to model himself on the Father that he loves, because he knows that the Father loves him.

So I come to the blessed truth that Christian morality does not say to us, 'Now begin, and work, and tinker away at yourselves, and try to get up some kind of excellence of character, and then come to God, and pray

Him to accept you.' That is putting the cart before the horse. The order is reversed. We are to begin with taking our personal salvation and God's love to us for granted, and to work from that. Realise that you are beloved children, and then set to work to live accordingly. If we are ever to do what is our bounden duty to do, in all the various relations of life, we must begin with recognising, with faithful and grateful hearts, the love wherewith God has loved us. We are to think much and confidently of ourselves as beloved of God, and that, and only that, will make us loving to men.

The Nile floods the fields of Egypt and brings greenness and abundance wherever its waters are carried, because thousands of miles away, close up to the Equator, the snows have melted and filled the watercourses in the far-off wilderness. And so, if we are to go out into life, living illustrations and messengers of a love that has redeemed even us, we must, in many a solitary moment, and in the depths of our quiet hearts, realise and keep fast the conviction that God hath loved us, and Christ hath died for us.

But a solemn consideration has to be pressed on all our consciences, and that is that there is something wrong with a man's Christian confidence whose assurance that he himself possesses a share in the love of God in Christ, is not ever moving him to imitation of the love in which he trusts. It is a shame that any one without Christian faith and love should be as charitable, as open to pity and to help, as earnest in any sort of philanthropic work, as Christian men and women are. But godless and perfectly secular philanthropy treads hard on the heels of Christian charity to-day. The more shame to us if we have been eating our morsels alone, and hugging ourselves in the possession of the love which has redeemed us; and if it has not quickened us to the necessity of copying it in our relations to our fellows. There is something dreadfully wrong about such a Christian character. 'He that loveth not his brother whom he hath seen, how shall he love God whom he hath not seen?'

Take these plain principles, and honestly fit them to your characters and lives, and you will revolutionise both.

223

WHAT CHILDREN OF LIGHT SHOULD BE

Ephesians 5:8

It was our Lord who coined this great name for His disciples. Paul's use of it is probably a reminiscence of the Master's, and so is a hint of the existence of the same teachings as we now find in the existing Gospels, long before their day. Jesus Christ said, 'Believe in the light, that ye may be the children of light'; and Paul gives substantially the same account of the way by which a man becomes a Son of the Light when he says, in the words preceding my text, 'Ye were sometimes darkness, but now are ye light in the Lord.'

Union with Him makes light, just as the bit of carbon will glow as long as it is in contact with the electric force, and subsides again into darkness when that is switched off. To be in Christ is to be a child of light, and to believe in Christ is to be in Him.

But the intense moral earnestness of our Apostle is indicated by the fact that on both occasions in which he uses this designation he does so, not for the purpose of heightening the sense of the honour and prerogative attached to it, but for the sake of deducing from it plain and stringent moral duties, and heightening the sense of obligation to holy living.

'Walk as children of light.' Be true to your truest, deepest self. Manifest what you are. Let the sweet, sacred secrets of inward communion come out in the trivialities of ordinary conduct; make of your every thought a deed, and see to it that every deed be vitalised and purified by its contact with the great truths and thoughts that lie in this name. These are various ways of putting this one all-sufficient directory of conduct.

Now, in the context, the Apostle expands this concentrated exhortation in three or four different directions, and perhaps we may best set forth its meaning if we shape our remarks by these, I venture to cast them, for the sake of emphasis, into a hortatory form.

I. Aim at an all-round productiveness of the natural fruits of the light.

The true reading is, 'Walk as children of light, for the fruit of the light' {not spirit, as the Authorised Version reads it} 'is in all goodness and righteousness and truth.' Now, it is obvious that the alteration of 'light' instead of 'spirit' brings the words into connection with the preceding and the following. The reference to the 'fruits of the spirit' would be entirely irrelevant in this place; a reference to the 'fruit of the light,' as being every form of goodness and righteousness and truth, is altogether in place.

There is, then, a natural tendency in the light to blossom out into all forms and types of goodness. 'Fruit' suggests the idea of natural, silent, spontaneous, effortless growth. And, although that is by no means a sufficient account of the process by which bad men become good men, it is an inseparable element, in all true moral renovation, that it be the natural outcome and manifestation of an inward principle; otherwise it is mere hypocritical adornment, or superficial appearance. If we are to do good we must first of all be good. If from us there are to come righteousness and truth, and all other graces of character, there must, first of all, be the radical change which is involved in passing from separateness in the darkness to union with Jesus Christ in the light. The Apostle's theory of moral renovation is that you must begin with the implantation in the spirit of the source of all moral goodness-viz. Jesus Christ-brought into the heart by the uniting power of humble faith. And then there will be lodged in our being a vital power, of which the natural outcome will be all manner of fair and pure things. Effort is needed, as I shall have to say; but prior to effort there must be union with Jesus Christ.

This wide, general commandment of our text is sufficiently definite, thinks Paul; for if the light be in you it will naturally effloresce into all forms of beauty. Light is the condition of fruitfulness. Everywhere the vital germ is only acted upon by the light. No sunshine, no flowers; darkness produces thin, etiolated, whitened, and feeble shoots at the best. Let the light blaze in, and the blanched feebleness becomes vigorous and unfolds itself. How much more will light be the condition of fruitfulness when the very light itself is the seed from which all fruit is developed.

But, still further, mark how there must be an all-round completeness in order that we shall fairly set forth the glory and power of the light of which our faith makes us children and partakers. The fruit 'is in all goodness and righteousness and truth.' These three aspects-the good, the right, the true-may not be a scientific, ethical classification, but they give a sufficiently plain and practical distinction. Goodness, in which the prevailing idea is beneficence and the kindlier virtues; righteousness, which refers to the sterner graces of justice; truth, in which the prevalent idea is conformity in action with facts and the conditions of man's life and entire sincerity-these three do cover, with sufficient completeness, the whole ground of possible human excellence. But the Apostle widens them still further by that little word all.

We all tend to cultivate those virtues which are in accordance with our natural dispositions, or are made most easy to us by our circumstances. And there is nothing in which we more need to seek comprehensiveness than in the effort to educate ourselves into, and to educe from ourselves, kinds of goodness and forms of excellence which are not naturally in accordance with our dispositions, or facilitated by our circumstances. The tree planted in the shrubbery will grow all lopsided; the bushes on the edge of the cliff will be shorn away on the windward side by the teeth of the south-western gale, and will lean over northwards, on the side of least resistance. And so we all are apt to content ourselves with doing the good things that are easiest for us, or that fit into our temperament and character. Jesus Christ would have us to be all-round men, and would that we should seek to aim after and possess the kinds of excellence that are least cognate to our characters. Are you strong, and do you pride yourself upon your firmness? Cultivate gentleness. Are you amiable, and pride yourself, perhaps, upon your sympathetic tenderness? Try to get a little iron and quinine into your constitution. Seek to be the man that you are least likely to be, and aim at a comprehensive development of 'all righteousness and goodness and truth.'

Further, remember that this all-round completeness is not attained as the result of an effortless growth. True, these things are the fruits of the light, but also true, they are the prizes of struggle and the trophies of warfare. No man will ever attain to the comprehensive moral excellence which it is in his own power to win; no Christian will ever be as all-round a good man as he has the opportunities of being, unless he makes it his business, day by day, to aim after the conscious increase of gifts that he possesses, and the conscious appropriation and possession of those of which he is still lacking. 'Nothing of itself will come,' or very little. True, the light will shine out in variously tinted ray if it be in a man, as surely as from the seed come the blade and the ear and the full corn in the ear, but you will not have nor keep the light which thus will unfold itself unless you put forth appropriate effort. Christ comes into our hearts, but we have to bring Him there. Christ dwells in our hearts, but we have to work into our nature, and work out in action, the gifts that He bestows. They will advance but little in the divine life who trust to the natural unfolding of the supernatural life within them, and do not help its unfolding by their own resolute activity. 'Walk as children of the light.' There is your duty, for 'the fruit of the light is all righteousness.' One might have supposed that the commandments would be, 'Be passive as children of the light, for the light will grow.' But the Apostle binds together, as always, the two things, the divine working and the human effort at reception, retention, and application of that divine work, just as he does in the great classical passage, 'Work out your own salvation, for it is God that worketh in you.'

II. Secondly, the general exhortation of my text widens out itself into this-test all things by Christ's approval of them.

'Proving what is well pleasing unto the Lord.' That, according to the natural construction of the Greek, is the main way by which the Apostle conceives that his general commandment of 'walking as children of the light' is to be carried out. You do it if, step by step, and moment by moment, and to every action of life, you apply this standard-Does Christ like it? Does it please Him? When that test is rigidly applied, then, and only then, will you walk as becomes the children of the light.

So, then, there is a standard-not what men approve, not what my conscience, partially illuminated, may say is permissible, not what is recognised as allowable by the common maxims of the world round about us, but Christ's approval. How different the hard, stern, and often unwelcome prescriptions of law and rigidity of some standards of right become when they are changed into that which pleases the Divine Lord and Lover! Surely it is something blessed that the hard, cold, and to such a large extent powerless conceptions of duty or obligation shall be changed into pleasing Jesus Christ; and that so our hearts shall be enlisted in the service of our consciences, and love shall be glad to do the Beloved's will. There are many ways by which the burden of life's obligations is lightened to the Christian. I do not know that any of them is more precious than the fact that law is changed into His will, and that we seek to do what is right because it pleases the Master. There is the standard.

It will be easy for us to come to the right appreciation of individual actions when we are living in the light. Union with Jesus Christ will make us quick to discern His will. We have a conscience;-well, that needs educating and enlightening, and very often correcting. We have the Word of God;-well, that needs explanation, and needs to be brought close to our hearts. If we have Christ dwelling in us, in the measure in which we are in sympathy with Him, we shall be gifted with clear eyes, not indeed to discern the expedient-that belongs to another region altogether-but we shall be gifted with very clear eyes to discern right from wrong, and there will be an instinctive recoil from the evil, and an instinctive attachment of ourselves to the good. If we are in the Lord we shall easily be able to prove what is acceptable and well-pleasing to Him.

We shall never walk as the children of the light, unless we have the habit of referring everything, trifles and great things, to His arbitrament, and seeking in them all to do what is pleasing in His sight. The smallest deed may be brought under the operation of the largest principles. Gravitation influences the microscopic grain of sand as well as planets and sun. There is nothing so small but you can bring it into this category-it either pleases or displeases Jesus Christ. And the faults into which Christian men fall and in which they continue are very largely owing to their carelessness in applying this standard to the small things of their daily lives. The sleepy Custom House officers let the contraband article in because it seems to be of small bulk. There are old stories about how strong castles were taken by armed men hidden in an innocent-looking cart of forage. Do you keep up a rigid inspection at the frontier, and see to it that everything vindicates its right to enter because it is pleasing to Jesus Christ.

III. Thirdly, we have here another expansion of the general command, and that is-keep well separate from the darkness.

Have no fellowship with the unfruitful works of darkness, but rather reprove them.' Now, your time will not allow me to dwell, as I had hoped to do, upon the considerations to be suggested here. The very briefest possible mention of them is all that I can afford.

'The unfruitful works of darkness';-well, then, the darkness has its works, but though they be works they are not worth calling fruit. That is to say, nothing except the conduct which flows from union with Jesus Christ so corresponds to the man's nature and relations, or has any such permanence about it as to entitle it to be called fruit. Other acts may be 'works' but Paul will not dishonour the great word 'fruit' by applying it to such rubbish as these, and so he brands them as 'unfruitful works of darkness.'

Keep well clear of them, says the Apostle. He is not talking here about the relations between Christians and others, but about the relations between Christian men and the works of darkness. Only, of course, in order to avoid fellowship with the works you will sometimes have to keep yourselves well separate from their doers. Much association with such men is forced upon us by circumstances, and much is the imperative duty of Christian beneficence and charity. But I venture to express the strong and growing conviction that there are few exhortations that the secularised Church of this generation needs more than this commandment of my text: 'Have no fellowship with the unfruitful works of darkness' 'What communion hath light with darkness?' Ah! we see plenty of it, unnatural as it is, in the so-called Church of to-day. 'What concord hath Christ with Belial? What part hath he that believeth with an infidel? Come ye out from among them, and be ye separate.'

And, brethren, remember, a part of the separation is that your light shall be a constant condemnation of the darkness. 'But rather reprove them,' says my text; that is a work that devolves upon all Christians. It is to be done, no doubt, by the silent condemnation of evil which ever comes from the quiet doing of good. As an old preacher has it, 'The presence of a saint hinders the devil of elbow-room for doing his tricks.' The old legend told us that the fire-darting Apollo shot his radiant arrows against the pythons and 'dragons of the slime.' The sons of light have the same office-by their light of life to make the darkness aware of itself, and ashamed of itself; and to change it into light.

But silent reproving is not all our duty. The Christian Church has wofully fallen beneath its duty, not only in regard to its complicity with the social crimes of each generation, but in regard to its cowardly silence towards them; especially when they flaunt and boast themselves in high places. What has the Church said worthy of itself in regard to war? What has the Church said worthy of itself in regard to impurity? What has the Church said worthy of itself in regard to drunkenness? What has the Church said worthy of itself in regard to the social vices that are honeycombing society and this city to-day? If you are the sons of light, walk as the sons of light, and have 'no fellowship with the unfruitful works of darkness'; but set the trumpet to your lips, and 'declare unto My people their transgressions, and to the house of Israel their sin.'

THE FRUIT OF THE LIGHT

Ephesians 5:9

This is one of the cases in which the Revised Version has done service by giving currency to an unmistakably accurate and improved reading. That which stands in our Authorised Version, 'the fruit of the Spirit' seems to have been a correction made by some one who took offence at the violent metaphor, as he conceived it, that 'light' should bear 'fruit' and desired to tinker the text so as to bring it into verbal correspondence with another passage in the Epistle to the Galatians, where 'the fruits of the Spirit' are enumerated. But the reading, 'the fruit of the light,' has not only the preponderance of manuscript authority in its favour, but is preferable because it preserves a striking image, and is in harmony with the whole context.

The Apostle has just been exhorting his Ephesian friends to walk as 'children of the light' and before he goes on to expand and explain that injunction he interjects this parenthetical remark, as if he would say, To be true to the light that is in you is the sum of duty, and the condition of perfectness, 'for the fruit of the light is in all goodness and righteousness and truth' That connection is entirely destroyed by the substitution of 'spirit.' The whole context, both before and after my text, is full of references to the light as working in the life; and a couple of verses after it we read about 'the unfruitful works of darkness' an expression which evidently looks back to my text.

So please do understand that our text in this sermon is-'The fruit of the light consists in all goodness and righteousness and truth.'

I. Now, first of all, I have just a word to say about this light which is fruitful.

Note-for it is, I think, not without significance-a minute variation in the Apostle's language in this verse and in the context. He has been speaking of 'light,' now he speaks of 'the light'; and that, I think, is not accidental. The expression, 'walk as children of light,' is more general and vague. The expression, 'the fruit of the light,' points to some specific source from which all light flows. And observe, also, that we have in the previous context, 'Ye were sometime darkness, but now are ye light in the Lord,' which evidently implies that the light of which my text speaks is not natural to men, but is the result of the entrance into their darkness of a new element.

Now I do not suppose that we should be entitled to say that Paul here is formally anticipating the deep teaching of the Apostle John that Jesus Christ is 'the Light of men,' and especially of Christian men. But he is distinctly asserting, I think, that the light which blesses and hallows humanity is no diffused glow, but is all gathered and concentrated into one blazing centre, from which it floods the hearts of men. Or, to put away the metaphor, he is here asserting that the only way by which any man can cease to be, in the doleful depths of his nature, darkness in its saddest sense is by opening his heart through faith, that into it there may rush, as the light ever does where an opening-be it only a single tiny cranny-is made, the light which is Christ, and without whom is darkness.

I know, of course, that, apart altogether from the exercise of faith in Jesus Christ, there do shine in men's hearts rays of the light of knowledge and of purity; but if we believe the teaching of Scripture, these, too, are from Christ, in His universally-diffused work, by which, apart altogether from individual faith, or from a knowledge of revelation, He is 'the light that lighteth every man coming into the world.' And I hold that, wheresoever there is conscience, wheresoever there is judgment and reason, wheresoever there are sensitive desires after excellence and nobleness, there is a flickering of a light which I believe to be from Christ Himself. But that light, as widely diffused as humanity, fights with, and is immersed in, darkness. In the physical world, light and darkness are mutually exclusive: where the one is the other comes not; but in the spiritual world the paradox is true that the two co-exist. Apart from revelation and the acceptance of Jesus Christ's person and work by our humble faith, the light struggles with the darkness, and the darkness obstinately refuses to admit its entrance, and 'comprehendeth it not.' And so, ineffectual but to make restless and to urge to vain efforts and to lay up material for righteous judgment, is the light that shines in men whose hearts are shut against Christ. The fruitful light is Christ within us, and, unless we know and possess it by the opening of heart and mind and will, the solemn words preceding my text are true of us: 'Ye were sometime darkness.' Oh, brother! do you see to it that the subsequent words are true of you: 'Now are ye light in the Lord.' Only if you are in Christ are you truly light.

II. Now, secondly, notice the fruitfulness of this indwelling light.

Of course the metaphor that light, like a tree, grows and blossoms and puts forth fruit, is a very strong one. And its very violence and incongruity help its force. Fruit is generally used in Scripture in a good sense. It conveys the notion of something which is the natural outcome of a vital power, and so, when we talk about the light being fruitful, we are setting, in a striking image, the great Christian thought that, if you want to get right conduct, you must have renewed character; and that if you have renewed character you will get right conduct. This is the principle of my text. The light has in it a productive power; and the true way to adorn a life with all things beautiful, solemn, lovely, is to open the heart to the entrance of Jesus Christ.

God's way is-first, new life, then better conduct. Men's way is, 'cultivate morality, seek after purity, try to be good.' And surely conscience and experience alike tell us that that is a hopeless effort. To begin with what should be second is an anachronism in morals, and will be sure to result in failure in practice. He is not a wise man that tries to build a house from the chimneys downwards. And to talk about making a man's doings good before you have secured a radical change in the doer, by the infusion into him of the very life of Jesus Christ Himself, is to begin at the top story, instead of at the foundation. Many of us are trying to put the cart before the horse in that fashion. Many of us have made the attempt over and over again, and the attempt always has failed and always will fail. You may do much for the mending of your characters and for the incorporation in your lives of virtues and graces which do not grow there naturally and without effort. I do not want to cut the nerves of any man's stragglings, I do not want to darken the brightness of any man's aspirations, but I do say that the people who, apart from Jesus Christ, and the entrance into their souls by faith of His quickening power, are seeking, some of them nobly, some of them sadly, and all of them vainly, to cure their faults of character, will never attain anything but a superficial and fragmentary goodness, because they have begun at the wrong end.

But 'make the tree good' and its fruit will be good. Get Christ into your heart, and all fair things will grow as the natural outcome of His indwelling. The fruitfulness of the light is not put upon its right basis until we come to understand that the light is Christ Himself, who, dwelling in our hearts by faith, is made in us as well as 'unto us wisdom, and righteousness, and salvation, and redemption.' The beam that is reflected from the mirror is the very beam that falls on the mirror, and the fair things in life and conduct which Christian people bring forth are in very deed the outcome of the vital power of Jesus Christ which has entered into them. 'I live, yet not I, but Christ liveth in me,' is the Apostle's declaration in the midst of his struggles; and the perfected saints before the throne cast their crowns at His feet, and say, 'Not unto us! not unto us, but unto Thy name be the glory.' The talent is the Lord's, only the spending of it is the servant's. And so the order of the Divine appointment is, first, the entrance of the light, and then the conduct that flows from it.

Note, too, how this same principle of the fruitfulness of the light gives instruction as to the true place of effort in the Christian life. The main effort ought to be to get more of the light into ourselves. 'Abide in Me, and I in you.' And so, and only so, will fruit come.

And such an effort has to take in hand all the circumference of our being, and to fix thoughts that wander, and to still wishes that clamour, and to empty hearts that are full of earthly loves, and to clear a space in minds that are crammed with thoughts about the transient and the near, in order that the mind may keep in steadfast contemplation of Jesus, and the heart may be bound to Him by cords of love that are not capable of being snapped, and scarcely of being stretched, and the will may in patience stand saying, 'Speak, Lord! for Thy servant heareth'; and the whole tremulous nature may be rooted and built up in and on Him. Ah, brother! if we understand all that goes to the fulfilment of that one sweet and merciful injunction, 'Abide in Me,' we shall recognise that there is the field on which Christian effort is mainly to be occupied.

But that is not all. For there must be likewise the effort to appropriate, and still more to manifest in conduct, the fruit-bringing properties of that indwelling light. 'Giving all diligence add to your faith.' 'Having these promises, let us cleanse ourselves from all filthiness of flesh and spirit, perfecting holiness in the fear of the Lord.' We are often told that just as we trust Christ for our forgiveness and acceptance, so we are to trust Him for our sanctifying and perfecting. It is true, and yet it is not true. We are to trust Him for our sanctifying and our perfecting. But the faith which trusts Him for these is not a substitute for effort, but it is the foundation of effort. And the more we rely on His power to cleanse us from all evil, the more are we bound to make the effort in His power and in dependence on Him, to cleanse ourselves from all evil, and to secure as our own the natural outcomes of His dwelling within us, which are 'the fruits of the light.'

III. And so, lastly, notice the specific fruits which the Apostle here dwells upon.

They consist, says he, in all goodness and righteousness and truth. Now 'goodness' here seems to me to be used in its narrower sense, just as the same Apostle uses it in the Epistle to the Romans, in contrast with 'righteousness,' where he says, 'for a good man some would even dare to die.' There he means by 'good,' as he does here by 'goodness,' not the general expression for all forms of virtue and gracious conduct, but the specific excellence of kindliness, amiability, or the like. 'Righteousness' again, is that which rigidly adheres to the strict law of duty, and carefully desires to give to every man what belongs to him, and to every relation of life what it requires. And 'truth' is rather the truth of sincerity, as opposed to hypocrisy and lies and shams, than the intellectual truth as opposed to error.

Now, all these three types of excellence-kindliness, righteousness, truthfulness-are apt to be separated. For the first of them-amiability, kindliness, gentleness-is apt to become too soft, to lose its grip of righteousness, and it needs the tonic of the addition of those other graces, just as you need lime in water if it is to make bone. Righteousness, on the other hand, is apt to become stern, and needs the softening of goodness to make it human and attractive. The rock is grim when it is bare; it wants verdure to drape it if it is to be lovely. Truth needs kindliness and righteousness, and they need truth. For there are men who pride themselves on 'speaking out,' and take rudeness and want of regard for other people's sensitive feelings to be sincerity. And, on the other hand, it is possible that amiability may be sweeter than truth is, and that righteousness may be hypocritical and insincere. So Paul says, 'Let this white light be resolved in the prism of your characters into the threefold rays of kindliness, righteousness, truthfulness.'

And then, again, he desires that each of us should try to make our own a fully developed, all-round perfection-all goodness and righteousness and truth; of every sort, that is, and in every degree. We are all apt to cultivate graces of character which correspond to our natural disposition and make. We are all apt to become torsos, fragmentary, one-sided, like the trees that grow against a brick wall, or those which stand exposed to the prevailing blasts from one quarter of the sky. But we should seek to appropriate types of excellence to which we are least inclined, as well as those which are most in harmony with our natural dispositions. If you incline to kindliness, try to brace yourselves with righteousness; if you incline to righteousness, to take the stern, strict view of duty, and to give to every man what he deserves, remember that you do not give men their dues unless you give them a great deal more than their deserts, and that righteousness does not perfectly allot to our fellows what they ought to receive from us, unless we give them pity and indulgence and forbearance and forgiveness when it is needed. The one light breaks into all colours-green in the grass, purple and red in the flowers, flame-coloured in the morning sky, blue in the deep sea. The light that is in us ought, in like manner, to be analysed into, and manifested in, 'whatsoever things are lovely and of good report.'

And so, dear friends, here is a test for us all. Devout emotion, orthodox creed, practical diligence in certain forms of benevolence and philanthropic work, are all very well; but Jesus Christ came to make us like Himself, and to turn our darkness into light that betrays its source by its resemblance, though it be a weakened one, to the sun from which it came. We have no right to call ourselves Christ's followers unless we are, in some measure, Christ's pictures.

Here is a message of cheer and hope for us all. We have all tried, and tried, and tried, over and over again, to purge and mend these poor characters of ours. How long the toil, how miserable and poor the results! A million candles will not light the night; but when God's mercy of sunrise comes above the hills, beasts of prey slink to their dens and birds begin to sing, and flowers open, and growth resumes again. We cannot mend ourselves except partially and superficially; but we can open will, heart, and mind, by faith, for His entrance; and where He comes, there He slays the evil creatures that live in and love the dark, and all gracious things will blossom into beauty. If we are in the Lord we shall be light; and if the Lord, who is the Light, is in us, we, too, shall bear fruits of 'all righteousness and goodness and truth.'

PLEASING CHRIST

Ephesians 5:10

These words are closely connected with those which precede them in the 8th verse-'Walk as children of light.' They further explain the mode by which that commandment is to be fulfilled. They who, as children of light, mindful of their obligations and penetrated by its brightness, seek to conform their active life to the light to which they belong, are to do so by making experiment of, or investigating and determining, what is 'acceptable to the Lord.' It is the sum of all Christian duty, a brief compendium of conduct, an all-sufficient directory of life.

There need only be two remarks made by way of explanation of my text. One is that the expression rendered 'acceptable' is more accurately and forcibly given, as in the Revised Version, by the plainer word 'well-pleasing.' And the other is that 'the Lord' here, as always in the New Testament-unless the context distinctly forbids it-means Jesus Christ. Here the context distinctly demands it. For only a sentence or two before, the Apostle has been speaking about 'those who were sometime darkness having been made light in the Lord'-which is obviously in Jesus Christ.

And here, therefore, what pleases Christ is the Christian's highest duty, and the one prescription which is required to be obeyed in order to walk in the light is, to do that which pleases Him.

I. So, then, in these brief words, so comprehensive, and going so deep into the secrets of holy and noble living, I want you to notice that we have, first, the only attitude which corresponds to our relations to Christ.

How remarkable it is that this Apostle should go on the presumption that our conduct affects Him, that it is possible for us to please, or to displease Jesus Christ now. We often wonder whether the beloved dead are cognisant of what we do; and whether any emotions of something

238

like either our earthly complacency or displeasure, can pass across the undisturbed calm of their hearts, if they are aware of what their loved ones here are doing. That question has to be left very much in the dark, however our hearts may sometimes seek to enforce answers. But this we know, that that loving Lord, not merely by the omniscience of His divinity, but by the perpetual knowledge and sympathy of His perfect manhood, is not only cognizant of, but is affected by, the conduct of His professed followers here on earth. And since it is true that He now is not swept away into some oblivious region where the dead are, but is close beside us all, cognizant of every act, watching every thought, and capable of having something like a shadow of a pang passing across the Divine depth of His eternal joy and repose at the right hand of God, then, surely, the only thing that corresponds to such a relationship as at present subsists between the Christian soul and the Lord is that we should take as our supreme and continual aim that, 'whether present or absent, we should be well-pleasing to Him.' Nor does that demand rest only upon the realities of our present relation to that Lord, but it goes back to the past facts on which our present relation rests. And the only fitting response to what He has been and done for us is that we should, each of us, in the depth of our hearts, and in the widest circumference of the surface of our lives, enthrone Him as absolute Lord, and take His good pleasure as our supreme law. Jesus Christ is King because He is Redeemer. The only adequate response to what He has done for me is that I should absolutely submit myself to Him, and say to Him, 'O Lord! truly I am Thy servant! Thou hast loosed my bonds.' The one fitting return to make for that Cross and Passion is to enthrone His will upon my will, and to set Him as absolute Monarch over the whole of my nature. Thoughts, affections, purposes, efforts, and all should crown Him King, because He has died for me. The conduct which corresponds to the relations which we bear to Christ as the present Judge of our work, and the Redeemer of our souls by His mighty deed in the past, is this of my text, to make my one law His will, and to please Him that hath called me to be His soldier.

The meaning of being a Christian is that, in return for the gift of a whole Christ, I give my whole self to Him. 'Why call ye me Lord! Lord! and do not the things which I say?' If He is what He assuredly is to every one of us, nothing can be plainer than that we are thereby bound by obligations which are not iron, but are more binding than if they were, because they were woven out of the cords of love and the bands of a man, bound to serve Him supremely, Him only, Him always, Him by the suppression of self, and the making His pleasure our law.

II. Now, secondly, let me ask you to notice that we have here the all-sufficient guide for practical life.

It sounds very mystical, and a trifle vague, to say, Do everything to please Jesus Christ. It is all-comprehensive; it is mystical in the sense that it goes down below the mere surface of prescriptions about conduct. But it is not vague, and it is capable of immediate application to every part, and to every act, of every man's life.

For what is it that pleases Jesus Christ? His own likeness; as, according to the old figure-which is, I suppose, true to spiritual facts, whether to external facts or not-the refiner knows that the metal is ready to flow when he can see his own face in it. Jesus Christ desires most that we should all be like Him. That we are to bear His image is as comprehensive, and at the same time as specific, a way of setting forth the sum of Christian duty, as are the words of my text. The two phrases mean the same thing.

And what is the likeness to Jesus Christ which it is thus our supreme obligation and our truest wisdom and perfection to bear? Well! we can put it all into two words-self-suppression and continual consciousness of obedience to the Divine will. The life of Jesus Christ, in its brief records in Scripture, is felt by every thoughtful man to contain within its narrow compass adequate direction for, and to set forth the ideal of, human life. That is not because He went through all varieties of earthly experience, for He did not. The life of a Jewish peasant nineteen centuries ago was extremely unlike the life of a Manchester merchant, of a college professor, of a successful barrister, of a struggling mother, in this present day. But in the narrow compass of that life there are set forth these two things, which are the basis of all human perfection-the absolute annihilation of self-regard, and the perpetual recognition of a Divine will. These are the things which every Christian man and woman is bound by the power of Christ's Cross to translate into the actions correspondent with their particular circumstances. And so the student at his desk and the sailor on his deck, the miner in his pit, the merchant on 'Change, the worker in various handicrafts, may each be sure that they are doing what is pleasing to Christ if, in their widely different ways, they seek to do what they can do in all the varieties of life-crucify self, and commune with God.

That is not easy. Whatever may be the objections to be brought against this summary of Christian duty, the objection that it is vague is the last that can be sustained. Try it, and you will find out that it is anything but vague. It will grip tight enough, depend upon it. It will go deep enough down into all the complexities of our varying circumstances. If it has a fault {which it has not} it is in the direction of too great stringency for unaided human nature. But the stringency is not too great when we depend upon Him to help us, and an impossible ideal is a certain prophet of its own fulfilment some day.

So, brethren, here is the sufficient guide, not because it cumbers us with a mass of wretched little prescriptions such as a martinet might give, about all sorts of details of conduct. That is left to profitless casuists like the ancient rabbis. But the broad principles will effloresce into all manner of perfectnesses and all fruits. He that has in his heart these thoughts, that the definition of virtue is pleasing Jesus Christ, that the concrete form of goodness is likeness to Him, and that the elements of likeness to Him are these two, that I should never think about myself, and always think about God, needs no other guide or instructor to fill his life with 'whatsoever things are lovely and of good report,' and to make his own all that the world calls virtue, and all which the consciences of good men have conspired to praise.

But not only does this guide prove its sufficiency by reason of its comprehensiveness, but also because there is no difficulty in ascertaining what at each moment it prescribes. Of course, I know that such a precept as this cannot contain in itself guidance in matters of mere practical expediency. But, apart from these-which are to be determined by the ordinary exercise of prudence and common sense-in regard to the right and the wrong of our actions, I believe that if a man wants to know Christ's will, and takes the way of knowing it which Christ has appointed, he shall not be left in darkness, but shall have the light of life.

For love has a strange power of divining love's wishes, as we all know, and as many a sweetness in the hearts and lives of many of us has shown us. If we cherish sympathy with Jesus Christ we shall look on things as He looks on them, and we shall not be left without the knowledge of what His pleasure is. If we keep near enough to Him the glance of His eye will do for guidance, as the old psalm has it. They are rough animal natures that do not understand how to go, unless their instructors be the crack of the whip or the tug of the bridle. 'I will guide thee with Mine eye.' A glance is enough where there are mutual understanding and love. Two musical instruments in adjoining rooms, tuned to the same pitch, have a singular affinity, and if a note be struck on the one the other will vibrate to the sound. And so hearts here that love Jesus Christ and keep in unison with Him, and are sympathetic with His desires, will learn to know His will, and will re-echo the music that comes from Him. And if our supreme desire is to know what pleases Jesus Christ, depend upon it the desire will not be in vain, 'If any man wills to do His will he shall know of the doctrine.' Ninety per cent. of all our perplexities as to conduct come from our not having a pure and simple wish to do what is right in His sight, clearly supreme above all others. When we have that wish it is never left unsatisfied.

And even if sometimes we do make a mistake as to what is Christ's pleasure, if our supreme wish and honest aim in the mistake have been to do His pleasure, we may be sure that He will be pleased with the deed. Even though its body is not that which He willed us to do, its spirit is that which He does desire. And if we do a wrong thing, a thing in itself displeasing to Him, whilst all the while we desired to please Him, we shall please Him in the deed which would otherwise have displeased Him. And so two Christian men, for instance, who take opposite sides in a controversy, may both of them be doing what is well-pleasing in His sight, whilst they are contradicting one another, if they are doing it for His sake. And it is possible that the inquisitor and his victim may both have been serving Christ. At all events, let us be sure of this, that whensoever we desire to please Him, He will help us to do it, and ordinarily will help us by making clear to us the path on which His smile rests.

III. Again, notice that we have here an all-powerful motive for Christian life.

The one thing which all other summaries of duty lack is motive power to get themselves carried into practice. But we all know, from our own happy human experience, that no motive which can be brought to bear upon men is stronger, when there are loving hearts concerned, than this simple one, 'Do it to please me.' And that is what Jesus Christ really says. That is no piece of mere sentiment, brethren, nor of mere pulpit rhetoric. That is the deepest thought of Christian morality, and is the distinctive peculiarity which gives the morality of the New Testament its clear supremacy over all other. There are precepts in it far nobler and loftier than can be found elsewhere. The perspective of virtues and graces in it is different from that which ordinarily prevails amongst men. But I do not think that it is in the details of its precepts so much as in the communication of power to obey them, and in the suggestion of the motive which makes them all easy, that the difference of Christ's ethics from all the teaching of the world beside is most truly to be found.

And here lies the excellence thereof. It is a poor, cold thing to say to a man, 'Do this because it is right.' It is a still more powerless thing to say to him, 'Do this because it is expedient' 'Do this because, in the long run, it leads to happiness.' It is all different when you say, 'Do this to please Jesus Christ, to please that Christ who pleased not Himself but gave Himself for you.' That is the fire that melts the ore. That is the heat that makes flexible the hard, stiff material. That is the motive which makes duty delight, which makes 'the rough places plain' and 'the crooked things straight.' It does not abolish natural tastes, it does not supersede natural disinclinations, but it does smooth and soften unwelcome and hard tasks, and it invests service with a halo of glory, and changes the coldness of duty into rosy light; as when the sunrise strikes on the peaks of the frozen mountains. The one motive which impels men, and can be trusted to secure in them whatsoever things are noble, is to please Him.

So we have the secret of blessedness in these words. For self-submission and suppression are blessedness. Our miseries come from our unbridled wills, far more than from our sensitive organisations. It is because we do not accept providences that providences hurt. It is because we do not accept the commandments that the commandments are burdensome. Those who have no will, except as it is vitalised by God's will, have found the secret of blessedness, and have entered into rest. In the measure in which we approximate to that condition, our wills will be strengthened as well as our hearts set at ease.

And blessedness comes, too, because the approbation of the Master, which is the aim of the servant, is reflected in the satisfaction of an approving conscience, which points onwards to the time when the Master's approval shall be revealed in the servant's glory.

I was reading the other day about a religious reformer who arose in Eastern lands a few years since, and gathered many disciples. He and his principal follower were seized and about to be martyred. They were suspended by cords from a gibbet, to be fired at by a platoon of soldiers. And as they hung there, the disciple turned to his teacher, and as his last word on earth said, 'Master! are you satisfied with me?' His answer was a silent smile; and the next minute a bullet was in his heart. Dear brethren, do you turn to Jesus Christ with the same question, 'Master! art Thou satisfied with me?' and you will get His smile here; and hereafter, 'Well done, good and faithful servant.'

UNFRUITFUL WORKS OF DARKNESS

Ephesians 5:11

We have seen in a former sermon that 'the fruit,' or outcome, 'of the Light' is a comprehensive perfection, consisting in all sorts and degrees of goodness and righteousness and truth. Therefore, the commandment, 'Walk as children of the light,' sums up all Christian morality. Is there need, then, for any additional precept? Yes; for Christian people do not live in an empty world. If there were no evil round them, and no proclivity to evil within them, it would be amply sufficient to say to them, 'Be true to the light which you behold.' But since both these things are, the commandment of my text is further necessary. We do not work in vacuo, and therefore friction and atmosphere have to be taken account of; and an essential part of 'walking as children of the light' is to know how to behave ourselves when confronted with 'the works of darkness.'

These Ephesian Christians lived in a state of society honeycombed with hideous immorality, the centre of which was the temple, which was their city's glory and shame. It was all but impossible for them to have nothing to do with the works of evil, unless, indeed, they went out of the world. But the difficulty of obedience does not affect the duty of obedience, nor slacken in the smallest degree the stringency of a command. This obligation lies upon us as fully as it did upon them, and the discharge of it by professing Christians would bring new life to moribund churches.

I. Let me ask you to note with me, first, the fruitlessness inherent in all the works of darkness.

You may remember that I pointed out, in a former discourse on the context, that the Apostle, here and elsewhere, draws a very significant distinction between 'works' and 'fruit,' and that distinction is put very strikingly in the words of my text. There are works which are barren. It is a grim thought that there may be abundant activity which, in the eyes of God, comes to just nothing; and that pages and pages of laborious calculations, when all summed up, have for result a great round 0. Men are busy, and hosts of them are doing what the old fairy stories tell us that evil spirits were condemned to do-spinning ropes out of sea-sand; and their life-work is nought when they come to reckon it up.

I have no time to dwell upon this thought, but I wish, just for a moment or two, to illustrate it.

All godless life is fruitless, inasmuch as it has no permanent results. Permanent results of a sort, indeed, follow everything that men do, for all our actions tend to make character, and they all have a share in fixing that which depends upon character-viz. destiny, both here and yonder. And thus the most fleeting of our deeds, which in one aspect is as transitory as the snow upon the great plains when the sun rises, leaves everlasting traces upon ourselves and upon our condition. But yet acts concerned with transitory things may have permanent fruit, or may be as transient as the things with which they are concerned. And the difference depends on the spirit in which they are done. If the roots are only in the surface-skin of soil, when that is pared off the plant goes. A life that is to be eternal must strike its roots through all the superficial humus down to the very heart of things. When its roots twine themselves round God then the deeds which blossom from them will blossom unfading for ever.

Think of men going empty-handed into another world, and saying, 'O Lord! I made a big fortune in Manchester when I lived there, and I left it all behind me'; or, 'I mastered a science, and one gleam of the light of eternity has antiquated it'; or, 'I gained prizes, won my aims, and they have all dropped from my hands, and here I stand, having to say in the most tragic sense: Nothing in my hands I bring.' And another man dies in the Lord, and his 'works do follow' him. It is not every vintage that bears exportation. Some wines are mellowed by crossing the ocean; some are turned into vinegar. The works of darkness are unfruitful because they are transient.

And they are unfruitful because, whilst they last, they yield no real satisfaction. The Apostle could say to another Church with a certainty as to what the answer would be, 'What fruit had ye then'-when ye were doing them-'in the things whereof ye are now ashamed?' And the answer is 'None!' Of course, it is true that men do bad things because they like them better than good. Of course, it is true that the misery of mankind is that they have no appetite in the general for the only real satisfaction. But it is also true that no man who feeds his heart and mind on anything short of God is really at rest in anything that he does or possesses. Occasional twinges of conscience, dim perceptions that after all they are walking in a vain show; glimpses of nobler possibilities, a vague unrest, an unwillingness to reflect and look the facts of their condition in the face, like men that will not take stock because they half suspect that they are insolvent-these are the conditions that attach to all godless men's lives. There is no real fruit for their thirsty lips to feed upon. The smallest man is too large to be satisfied with anything short of Infinity, The human heart is like some narrow opening on a hill-side, so narrow that it looks as if a glassful of water would fill it. But it goes away down, down, down into the depths of the mountain, and you may pour in hogsheads and no effect is visible. God, and God alone, brings to the thirsty heart the fruit that it needs.

Another solemn thought illustrates the unfruitfulness of a godless life. There is no correspondence between what such a man does and what he is intended to do. Think of what the most degraded and sensuous wretch that shambles about the slums of a city, sodden with beer and rotten with profligacy, could be. Think of the raptures of devout contemplation and the energies of holy work which are possible for that soul, and then say-though it is an extreme case, the principle holds in less extreme cases-Are these things that men do apart from God, however shining, noble, illustrious they may be in the eyes of the world, and trumpeted forth by the mouthpieces of popular opinion, are these things worth calling fruits fit to be borne by such a tree? No more than the cankers on a rose-bush or the galls on an oak-tree are worthy of being called fruit are these works that some of you have as the only products of a life's activity. 'Wherefore, when I looked that it should bring forth grapes, brought it forth wild grapes?'

II. And now, secondly, notice the plain Christian duty of abstinence.

'Have no fellowship with the unfruitful works of darkness.' Now, the text, as it stands in our version, seems to suggest that these dark works are personified as companions whom a good man ought to avoid; and that, therefore, the bearing of the exhortation is, 'Have nothing to do, in your own individual lives, with evil things that one man can commit.' But I take it that, important as that injunction and prohibition is, the Apostle's meaning is somewhat different, and that my text would perhaps be more accurately translated if another word were substituted for 'have no fellowship with.' The original expression seems rather to mean, 'Do not go partners with other people in works of darkness, which it takes more than one to commit.' Or, to put it into another language, the Apostle is regarding Christian people here as members of society, and exhorting them to a certain course of conduct in reference to plain and palpable existing evils around them. And such an exhortation to the duty of plain abstinence from things that the opinion of the world around us has no objection to, but which are contrary to the light, is addressed to all Christian people.

The need of it I do not require to illustrate at any length. But let me remind you that the devil has no more cunning way of securing a long lease of life for any evil than getting Christian people and Christian Churches to give it their sanction. What was it that kept slavery alive for centuries? Largely, that Christian men solemnly declared that it was a divine institution. What is it that has kept war alive for all these centuries? Largely, that bishops and preachers have always been ready to bless colours, and to read a Christening service over a man-of-war- and, I suppose, to ask God that an eighty-ton gun might be blessed to smash our enemies to pieces, and not to blow our sailors to bits. And what is it that preserves the crying evils of our community, the immoralities, the drunkenness, the trade dishonesty, and all the other things that I do not need to remind you of in the pulpit? Largely this, that professing Christians are mixed up with them. If only the whole body of those who profess and call themselves Christians would shake their hands clear of all complicity with such things, they could not last.

Individual responsibility for collective action needs to be far more solemnly laid to heart by professing Christians than ever it has been.

Nor need I remind you, I suppose, with what fatal effects on the Gospel and the Church itself all such complicity is attended. Even the companions of wrongdoers despise, whilst they fraternise with, the professing Christian who has no higher standard than their own. What was it that made the Church victorious over the combined forces of imperial persecution, pagan superstition, and philosophic speculation? I believe that among all the causes that a well-known historian has laid down for the triumph of Christianity, what was as powerful as-I was going to say even more than-the Gospel of peace and love which the Church proclaimed was the standard of austere morality which it held up to a world rotting in its own filth. And sure I am that wherever the Church says, 'So do not I, because of the fear of the Lord,' it will gain a power, and will be regarded with a possibly reluctant, but a very real, respect which no easy-going coming down to the level of popular moralities will ever secure for a silver-slippered Christianity. And so, brethren, I would say to you, Do not be afraid of the old name Puritan. Ignorant people use it as a scoff. It should be a crown of glory. 'Have no fellowship with the unfruitful works of darkness.'

But how is this to be done? Well, of course, there is only one way of abstaining, and that is, to abstain. But there are a great many different ways of abstaining. Light is not fire. And the more that Christian people feel themselves bound to stand aloof from common evils, the more are they bound to see that they do it in the spirit of the Master, which is meekness. It is always an invidious position to take up. And if we take it up with any heat and temper, with any lack of moderation, with any look of ostentation of superior righteousness, or with any trace of the Boanerges spirit which says, 'Let us call down fire from heaven and consume them,' our testimony will be weakened, and the world will have a right to say to us, 'Jesus we know, and Paul we know; but who are ye?' 'Who made this man a judge and a divider over us?' 'In meekness instructing them that oppose themselves.'

III. Lastly, note the still harder Christian duty of vigorous protest.

The further duty beyond abstinence which the text enjoins is inadequately represented by our version, 'but rather reprove them.' For the word rendered in our version 'reprove' is the same which our Lord employed when He spoke of the mission of the Comforter as being to 'convince {or convict} the world of sin.' And it does not merely mean 'reprove,' but so to reprove as to produce the conviction which is the object of the reproof.

This task is laid on the shoulders of all professing Christians. A silent abstinence is not enough. No doubt, the best way, in some circumstances, to convict the darkness is to shine. Our holiness will convict sin of its ugliness. Our light will reveal the gloom. The presentation of a Christian life is the Christian man's mightiest weapon in his conflict with the world's evil. But that is not all. And if Christian people think that they have done all their duty, in regard to clamant and common iniquities, by simply abstaining from them and presenting a nobler example, they have yet to learn one very important chapter of their duty. A dumb Church is a dying Church, and it ought to be; for Christ has sent us here in order, amongst other things, that we may bring Christian principles to bear upon the actions of the community; and not be afraid to speak when we are called upon by conscience to do so.

Now I am not going to dwell upon this matter, but I want just to point out to you how, in the context here, there are two or three very important principles glanced at which bear upon it. And one of them is this, that one reason for speaking out is the very fact that the evils are so evil that a man is ashamed to speak about them. Did you ever notice this context, in which the Apostle, in the next verse to my text, gives the reason for his commandment to 'reprove' thus-'For it is a shame even to speak of those things which are done of them in secret'? Did you ever hear of a fantastic tenderness for morality so very sensitive that it is not at all shocked when the immoral things are done, but glows with virtuous indignation when a Christian man speaks out about them? There are plenty of people nowadays who tell us that it is 'indelicate' and 'indecent' and 'improper,' and I do not know how much else, for a Christian teacher or minister to say a word about certain moral scandals. But they do not say anything about the immorality and the indelicacy and the indecency of doing them. Let us have done with that hypocrisy, brethren. I am arguing for no disregard for proprieties; I want all fitting reticence observed, and I do not wish indiscriminate rebukes to be flung at foul things; but it is too much to require that, by reason of the very inky cloud of filth that they fling up like cuttlefish, they should escape censure. Let us remember Paul's exhortation, and reprove because the things are too bad to be spoken about.

Further, note in the context the thought that the conviction of the darkness comes from the flashing upon it of the light. 'All things when they are reproved are made manifest by the light.' Which, being translated into other words, is this:-Be strong in your brave protest, because it only needs that the thing should be seen as it is, and called by its right name, in order to be condemned.

The Assyrians had a belief that if ever, by any chance, a demon saw himself in a mirror, he was frightened at his own ugliness and incontinently fled. And if Christian people would only hold up the mirror of Christian principle to the hosts of evil things that afflict our city and our country, they would vanish like ghosts at sunrise. They cannot stand the light, therefore let us cast the light upon them.

And do not forget the other final principle here, which is imperfectly represented by our translation. We ought to read, 'Whatever is made manifest is light.' Yes. In the physical world when light falls upon a thing, you see it because there is on it a surface of light. And in the moral world the intention of all this conviction is that the thing disclosed to be darkness should, in the very disclosure, cease to be dark, should forsake its nature and be transformed into light. Such transformation is not always the case. Alas! There are evil deeds on which the light falls, and it does nothing. But the purpose in all cases should be, and the issue in many will be, that the merciful conviction by the light will be followed by the conversion of darkness into light.

251

And so, dear brethren, I bring this text to your hearts, and lay it upon your consciences. We may not all be called upon to speak; we are all called upon to be. You can shine, and by shining show how dark the darkness is. The obligation is laid upon us all; the commandment still comes to every Christian which was given to the old prophet, 'Declare unto My people their transgression, and to the house of Jacob their sin.' A quaint old writer says that the presence of a saint 'hinders the devil of elbow room to do his tricks.' We can all rebuke sin by our righteousness, and by our shining reveal the darkness to itself. We do not walk as children of the light unless we keep ourselves from all connivance with works of darkness, and by all means at our disposal reprove and convict them. 'Come out from among them, and be ye separate, and touch no unclean thing, saith the Lord.'

PAUL'S REASONS FOR TEMPERANCE

Ephesians 5:11-21

There are three groups of practical exhortations in this passage, of which the first deals with the Christian as a reproving light in darkness; the second, with the Christian life as wisdom in the midst of folly; and the third with Christian sobriety and inspiration as the true exhilaration in contrast with riotous drunkenness. Probably such intoxication was prevalent in Ephesus in connection with the worship of 'Diana of the Ephesians,' for Paul was not the man to preach vague warnings against vices to which his hearers were not tempted. An under-current of allusion to such orgies accompanying the popular cult may be discerned in his words.

These two preceding sets of precepts can only be briefly touched on now. They lead up to the third, and the second is built on the first by a 'therefore' {ver.15}. The Apostle has just been saying that Christians were 'darkness, but are now light in the Lord,' and thence drawing the law for their life, to walk as 'children of light.' A very important part of such walk is recoiling from all share in 'the unfruitful works of darkness,'- a significant expression branding such deeds as being both bad in their source and in their results. Dark doings have consequences tragic enough and certain enough, but they are barren of all such issues as correspond to men's obligations and capacities. Their outcome is like the growths on a tree, which are not fruit, but products of disease. There is no fruit grown in the dark; there is no worthy product from us unless Christ is our light. If He is, and we are therefore 'light in the Lord,' we shall 'reprove' or 'convict' the Christless life. Its sinfulness will be shown by the contrast with the Christ-life. A thunder-cloud never looks so lividly black as when smitten by sunshine.

Our lives ought to make evil things ashamed to show their ugly faces. Christians should be, as it were, the incarnate conscience of a community. The Apostle is not thinking so much of words as of deeds, though words are not to be withheld when needful. The agent of reproof is 'the light,' which here is the designation of character as transformed by Jesus, and the process of reproof or conviction is simply the manifestation of the evil in its true nature, which comes from setting it in the beams of the light. To show sin as it is, is to condemn it; 'for everything that is made manifest is light.' Observe that Paul here speaks of 'light,' not 'the light,'-that is, he is speaking now not of Christian character, which he had likened to light, but of physical light to which he had likened it, and is backing up his figurative statement as to the reproving and manifesting effects of the former, by the plain fact as to the latter, that, when daylight shines on anything, it is revealed, and, as it were, becomes light. He clenches his exhortation by quoting probably an early Christian hymn, which regards Christ as the great illuminator, ready to shine on all drowsy, dark souls as soon as they stir and rouse themselves from drugged and fatal sleep.

The second set of exhortations here is connected with the former by a 'therefore,' which refers to the whole preceding precept. Because the Christian is to shake himself free from complicity with works of darkness, and to be their living condemnation, he must take heed to his goings. A climber on a glacier has to look to his feet, or he will slip and fall down a crevasse, perhaps, from which he will never be drawn up. Heedlessness is folly in such a world as this. '"Don't care" comes to the gallows.' The temptation to 'go as you please' is strong in youth, and it is easy to scoff at 'cold-blooded folks who live by rule,' but they are the wise people, after all. A great element in that heedfulness is a quick insight into the special duty and opportunity of the moment, for life is not merely made up of hours, but each has its own particular errand for us, and has some possibility in it which, neglected, may be lost for ever.

The mystic solemnity of time is that it is made up of 'seasons.' We shall walk heedfully in the degree in which we are awake to the moment's meaning, and grasp opportunity by the forelock, or, as Paul says, 'buy up the opportunity.' But wise heed to our walk is not enough, unless we have a sure standard by which to regulate it. A man may take great care of his watch, but unless he can compare it with a chronometer, or, as they do in Edinburgh, pull out their watches when the one o'clock gun is fired on a signal from Greenwich, he may be far out and not know it. So the Apostle adds the one way to keep our lives right, and the one source of true, practical wisdom-the 'understanding what the will of the Lord is.' He will not go far wrong whose instinctive question, as each new moment, with its solemn, animating possibilities, meets him, is, 'What wilt Thou have me to do?' He will not be nearly right who does not first of all ask that.

Then Paul comes to his precept of temperance. It naturally flows from the preceding, inasmuch as a drunken man is as sure to be incapable of taking heed to his conduct as of walking straight. He reels in both. He is stone-blind to the meaning of the moments. He hears no call, though the 'voice of the trumpet' may be 'exceeding loud,' and as for understanding what the will of the Lord is, that is far beyond him. The intoxication of an hour or the habit of drinking makes obedience to the foregoing precepts impossible. This master vice carries all other vices in its pocket.

Paul makes a daring, and, as some would think, an irreverent, comparison, when he proposes being 'filled with the Spirit' as the Christian alternative or substitute to being 'drunken with wine.' But the daring comparison suggests deep truth. The spurious exhilaration, the loosening of the bonds of care, the elevation above the pettiness and monotony of daily life, which the drunkard seeks, and is degraded and deceived in proportion as he momentarily finds, are all ours, genuinely, nobly, and to our infinite profit, if we have our empty spirits filled with that Divine Life. That exhilaration does not froth away, leaving bitter dregs in the cup. That loosening of the bonds of care, and elevation above life's sorrows, does not flow from foolish oblivion of facts, nor end in their being again roughly forced on us. 'Riot' bellows itself hoarse, and is succeeded by corresponding depression; but the calm joys of the Spirit-filled spirit last, grow, and become calmer and more joyful every day.

The boisterous songs of boon companions are set in contrast with the Christian 'psalms and hymns and spiritual songs,' which were already in use, and a snatch from one of which Paul has just quoted. Good-fellowship tempts men to drink together, and a song is a shoeing-horn for a glass; but the camaraderie is apt to end in blows, and is a poor caricature of the bond knitting all who are filled with the Spirit to one another, and making them willing to serve one another. The roystering or maudlin geniality cemented by drink generally ends in quarrels, as everybody knows that the truculent stage of intoxication succeeds the effusively affectionate one. But they who have the Spirit in them, and not only 'live in the Spirit,' but 'walk in the Spirit,' esteem each the other better than themselves. In a word, to be filled with the Spirit is the way to possess all the highest forms of the good which men are tempted to intoxication to secure, and which in it they find only for a moment, and which is coarse and unreal.

SLEEPERS AT NOONDAY

Ephesians 5:14

This is the close of a short digression about 'light.' The 'wherefore' at the beginning of my text seems to refer to the whole of the verses that deal with that subject. It is as if the Apostle had said, 'I have been telling you about light and its blessed effects. Now I tell you how you may win it for yours. The condition on which it is to be received by men is that they awake and arise from the dead.'

'He saith.' Who? The speaker whose words are quoted is not named, but this is the common formula of quotation from the Old Testament. It is, therefore, probable that the word 'Creator' or 'God' is to be supplied. But there is no Old Testament passage which exactly corresponds to the words before us; the nearest approach to such being the ringing exhortation of the prophet to the Messianic Church, 'Arise! Shine, for thy light is come, and the glory of the Lord is risen upon thee.' And it is probable that the Apostle is here quoting, without much regard either to the original connection or the primary purpose of the word, a well-known old saying which seemed to him appropriately to fall in with the trend of his thoughts. Like other writers he often adorns his own words with the citation of those of others without being very careful as to whether he, in some measure, diverts these from their original intention. But the words of my text fairly represent the prophetic utterance, in so far as they echo the call to the sleepers to wake, and share the prophet's confidence that light is streaming out for all those whose eyes are opened.

The want of precise correspondence between our text and the prophetic passage has led some to suppose that we have here the earliest recorded fragment of a Christian hymn. It would be interesting if that were so, but the formula of citation seems to oblige us to look to Scripture for the source from which my text is taken. However, let us leave these thoughts, and come to the text itself. It is an earnest call from God. It describes a condition, peals forth a summons, and gives a promise. Let us listen to what 'He saith' in all these regards.

I. First of all, then, the condition of the persons addressed.

The two sad metaphors, slumberers and dead, are applied to the same persons. There must, therefore, be some latitude in the application of the figures and they must be confined in their interpretation to some one or more points in which sleep and death are alike.

Now we all know that, as the proverb says, 'sleep is the image of death.' And what is the point of comparison? Mainly this, that the sleeper and the corpse are alike unconscious of an external world, unable to receive impressions from it, or to put forth action on it; and there, as I take it, is especially the point which is in the Apostle's view.

The sleeper and the dead man alike are in the midst of an order of things of which they are all unaware. And you and I live in two worlds, one, this low, fleeting, material one; and the other the white, snowy peaks that girdle it as do the Alps the Lombard plains; and men live all unconscious of that which lies on their horizon. But the metaphor of a level ground encircled by mountains does not fully represent the closeness of the connection between these two worlds, of both of which every one of us is a denizen. For on all sides, pressing in upon us, enfolding us like an atmosphere, penetrating into all the material, underlying all which is visible, all of which has its roots in the unseen, is that world which the mass of men are in a conspiracy to ignore and forget. And just as the sleeper is unconscious of all around him in his chamber, and of all the stir and beauty of the world in which he lives, so the bulk of us go blind and darkling through life, absorbed in the things seen, and never lift even a momentary and lack-lustre glance to the august realities which lie behind these, and give them all their significance and beauty.

Yes; and just as in a dream men are busy with baseless phantoms that vanish and are forgotten, and seem to themselves to be occupied, whilst all the while they are lying prone and passive, so the mass of us are sleep-walkers. What are many men who will be hurrying on to the

Manchester Exchange on Tuesday? What are they but men who are dreaming that they are at work, but are only at work on dreams which will vanish when the eyes are opened? Practical men, who are busy and absorbed with affairs and with the things of this present, curl their lips about 'idealists' of all sorts, be they idealists of thought, or of art, or of benevolence, or of religion, and call them dreamers. The boot is on the other leg. It is the idealists that are awake, and it is you people that live for to-day, and have not learned that to-day is a little fragment and sliver of eternity-it is you who are dreamers, and all these things round about us-the solid-seeming realities-are illusions, and

'Like the bubbles on a river,
Sparkling, bursting, borne away,'

they will disappear. There is only one reality, and that is God, and the only lives that lay hold of the substance are those which grasp Him. The rest of you are shadows hunting for shadows.

The two metaphors of my text coincide in suggesting another thing, and that is the awful contrast in the average life between what is in a man and what comes out of him. 'Dormant power,' we talk about. Ah, how tragically the true man is dormant in all the work of worldly hearts! God has made a great mistake in making you what you are, if there is no place for you to exercise your powers in but this present world, and nothing to exercise them on except the things that pass and perish. Travellers in lands where civilisation used to be, and barbarism now is, find sculptured stones from temples turned into fences for cattle-sheds and walls round pigstyes. And that is something like what men do with the faculties that God has given them. Why, the best part of you, brother, if you are not a Christian, and living a Christian life-the best part of you is asleep, and it is only the lower nature of you that is awake! Sometimes the sleepers stir uneasily. It used to be said that earthquakes were caused by a giant rolling himself from side to side in his troubled slumber. And there are earthquakes in your heart and spirit caused by the half-waking of the dormant self, the true man, who is immersed and embruted in sense and the things of time. Some of you by earthly lusts, some of you by over-indulgence in fleshly appetites, eating and drinking and the like; some of you by absorption in the mere externals of trade and profession and occupation to the entire neglect of the inward thing which would glorify and exalt these-but all of us somehow, unless we are living for God, have lulled our best, true, central self into slumber, and lie as if dead.

Now, brethren, do not forget that this exhortation of my text, and therefore this description, is addressed to a community of professing Christians. I hope you will not misunderstand me as if I thought that such a picture as I have been trying to draw applies only to men that have no religion in them at all. It applies in varying degrees to men that have, as-I was going to say the bulk, but perhaps that is exaggeration, let me say a tragically large number-of professing Christians, and a proportionate number of the professing Christians in this audience have, a little life and a great circumference of death. Dear brethren, you may call yourselves, and may be Christian people, and have somewhat shaken off the torpor, and roused yourself from the slumbering death of which I have been speaking. Remember that it still hangs to you, and that it was of Christians that the Master said: 'Whilst the Lord was away they all slumbered and slept'; and that it was of a Christian Church, and not of a pagan world, that the same voice from heaven said: 'Thou hast a name that thou livest, and art dead.' And so I beseech you, bear with me, and do not think I am scolding, or flinging about wild words at random, when I make a very earnest appeal to each individual professing, and real, Christian in this congregation, and ask them to consider, each for themselves, how much of sleep is still in their drowsy eyes, and how far it is true that the quickening life of Jesus Christ has penetrated, as the sunbeams into the darkness, into the heavy mass of their natural death.

II. Secondly, let me ask you to look at the summons to awake.

It comes like the morning bugle to an army, 'Awake, thou that sleepest, and arise from the dead.' Now, I am not going to waste your time by talking about the old, well-worn, interminable, and unprofitable controversy as to God's part and man's in this awaking, but I do wish to insist upon this plain fact, that the command here presupposes upon our parts, whether we be Christian people or not, the ability to obey. God would not mock a man by telling him to do what he cannot do. And it is perfectly clear that the one attitude in which we may be sure of God's help to keep any of His commandments, and this amongst the rest, is when we are trying to keep them. 'Stretch out thy hand,' said Christ to the man whose disease was that he could not stretch it out. 'Arise and walk,' said Christ to the man whose lifelong sadness it was that his limbs had no power. 'Lazarus, come forth,' said Christ unto the dull, cold ear of death. And Lazarus heard, wherever he was, and, though his feet were tangled with the graveclothes, he came stumbling out, because the power to do what he was bid had come wrapped in the command to do it. And if these other two men had turned to Jesus and said, 'What is the use of telling me to stretch out my hand, or me to move my limbs? Thou knowest that I can not,' they would have lain there paralysed till they died. But when they heard the command there came a tingling sense of new ability into the withered limb. 'And he stretched forth his hand, and it was restored whole as the other.' Ay, but the process of restoration began when he willed to stretch it out in obedience to the command, which was a promise as much as a command. So we need not trouble ourselves with the question how the dead man can arise, or how the sleeper can wake himself.

This, at all events, is clear, that if what I have been saying is true as to the main point in view in both the metaphors, viz. the unconsciousness of the unseen world, and the slumbering powers that we have within us, then the remedy for that is in our own hands. There are scarcely any limits to be put to a man's capacity of determining for himself what shall be the object of his thought, his interest, his affection, or his pursuits. You can withdraw your desires and contemplations from the intrusive and absorbing present. You can coerce yourselves to concentrate more thought than you do, more interest, affection, and effort than you have ever done, upon the things that are unseen. You can turn your gaze thither. You cannot directly and immediately regulate your feelings, but you can settle the thoughts which shall guide the feelings, and you can, and you do, fix for yourselves, though not consciously, the things which shall be uppermost in your regard, and supreme in the ordering of your life.

And so the commandment of my text is but this, 'Wake from the illusions; rouse yourselves to the contemplation of the things unseen and eternal. Let the Lord always be before your face.' And you will be awake and alive.

III. And so my last point is the promise of the morning light which gladdens the wakeful eye. 'Christ shall give thee light.'

Now, if the words of my text are an allusion to the prophecy to which I have already referred, it is striking to observe, though I cannot dwell upon the thought, that Paul here unhesitatingly ascribes to Jesus Christ an action which, in the source of his quotation, is ascribed to Jehovah. 'Arise, shine, for thy light has come, and the glory of Jehovah is risen upon thee,' says the prophet. 'Arise! thou that sleepest,' says Paul, 'and Christ shall give thee light.' As always, he regards his Lord as possessed of fully divine attributes; and he has learned the depth of the Master's own saying, 'Whatsoever things the Father doeth, these also doeth the Son likewise.' But I turn from that to the main point to be insisted upon here, that the Apostle is setting forth this as a certainty, that if a man will open his eyes he will have light enough. The sunshine is flooding the world. It falls upon the closed eyelids of the sleepers, and would fain gently lift them, that it might enter. A man needs nothing more than to shake off the slumber, and bring himself into the conscious presence of the unseen glories that surround us, in order to get light enough and to spare-whether you mean by light knowledge for guidance on the path of life, or whether you mean by it purity that shall scatter the darkness of evil from the heart, or whether you mean by it the joy that comes in the morning, radiant and fresh as the sunrise over the Eastern hills. 'Awake, and Christ shall give thee light.'

The miracle of Goshen is reversed, in the case of many of us, the land is flashing in the sunshine, but within our houses there is midnight darkness, not because there is not light around, but because the shutters are shut. Oh, brethren, it is a solemn thing to choose the darkness rather than the light. And you do that-though not consciously, and in so many words, making your election-by indifference, by neglect, by the direction of the main current of your thoughts and desires and aims to perishable things, and by the deeds that follow from such a disposition. These choose for you, and you, in effect, choose by them.

I beseech you, do not let Christ's own trumpet-call fall upon your ears, as if faint and far away, like the unwelcome summons that comes to a drowsy man in the morning. You know that if, having been called, he makes up his mind to lie a little longer, he is almost sure to fall more dead asleep than he was before. And if you hear, however dim, distantly, and through my poor words, Christ's voice saying to you, 'Awake! thou that sleepest,' do not neglect it. The only safe course is to spring up at once. If thou dost, 'Christ shall give thee light,' never fear. The light is all about you. You only need to open your eyes, and it will pour in. If you do not, you surround yourself with darkness that may be felt here, and ensures for yourself a horror of great darkness in the death hereafter.

REDEEMING THE TIME

Ephesians 5:15-16

Some of us have, in all probability, very little more 'time' to 'redeem.' Some of us have, in all probability, the prospect of many years yet to live. For both classes my text presents the best motto for another year. The most frivolous among us, I suppose, have some thoughts when we step across the conventional boundary that seems to separate the unbroken sequence of moments into periods; and as you in your business take stock and see how your accounts stand, so I would fain, for you and myself, make this a moment in which we may see where we are going, what we are doing, and how we are using this great gift of life.

My text gives us the true Christian view of time. It tells us what to do with it, and urges by implication certain motives for the conduct.

I. We have, first, what we ought to think about 'the time.'

There are two words in the New Testament, both of which are translated time, but they mean very different things. One of them, the more common, simply implies the succession of moments or periods; the other, which is employed here, means rather a definite portion of time to which some definite work or occurrence belongs. It is translated sometimes season, sometimes opportunity. Both these renderings occur in immediate proximity in the Epistle to the Galatians, where the Apostle says: 'As we have therefore opportunity let us do good to all men, for in due season we shall reap, if we faint not....' And, again, it is employed side by side with the other word to which I have referred, in the Acts of the Apostles, where we read, 'It is not for you to know the times or the seasons'-the former word simply indicating the succession of moments, the latter word indicating epochs or crises to which special work or events belong.

And so here 'redeeming the time' does not merely mean making the most of moments, but means laying hold of, and understanding the special significance of, life as a whole, and of each succeeding instant of it as the season for some specific duty. It is not merely 'time,' it is 'the time'; not merely the empty succession of beats of the pendulum, but these moralised, as it were, heightened, and having significance, because each is apprehended as having a special mission, and affording an opportunity for a special work.

Now, there are two aspects of that general thought, on each of which I would touch. The Apostle here uses the singular number, and speaks not of the times, but of 'the time'; as if the whole of life were an opportunity, a season for some one clear duty which manifestly belongs to it, and is meant to be done in it.

What is that? There are a great many ways of answering that question, but even more important perhaps than the way of answering is the mood of mind which asks it. If we could only get into this, as our habitual temper and disposition, asking ourselves what life is for, then we should have conquered nine-tenths of our temptations, and all but secured that we shall aim at the purpose which thus clearly and constantly shines before us. Oh! if I could get some of my friends here this morning, who have never really looked this solemn question in the face, to rise above the mere accidents of their daily occupations, and to take their orders, not from circumstances, or from the people whom they admire and imitate, but at first hand from considering what they really are here for, and why their days in their whole sweep are given them, I should not have spoken in vain. The sensualist answers the question in one way, the busy Manchester man in another, the careful, burdened mother in another, the student in another, the moralist in another. But all that is good in each answer is included in the wider one, that the end of life, the purpose for which 'the season' is granted us, is that 'we should glorify God and enjoy Him for ever.'

I do not care whether you say that the end for which we live is the salvation of our souls, or whether you put it in other words, and say that it is the cultivation and perfecting of a Christ-like and God-pleasing character, or whether you admit still another aspect, and say that it is the intention of time to prepare us for that which lies beyond time. Time is the lackey of eternity, and the chamberlain that opens the gates of the Kingdom of God. All these various answers are at bottom one. Life is ours mainly in order that, by faith in Jesus Christ, we should struggle, and do, and by struggles, by sorrows, and by all that befalls us, should grow liker Him, and so fitter for the calm joys of that place where the throb of the pendulum has ceased, and the hours are stable and eternal. We live here in order to get ready for living yonder. And we get ready for living yonder, when here we understand that every moment of life is granted us for the one purpose, which can be pursued through all life- viz. the becoming liker our dear Lord, and the drinking in to our own hearts more of His Spirit, and moulding our characters more in conformity with His image. That is what my life and yours are given us for. If we succeed in that, we succeed all round. If we fail in that, whatever else we succeed in, we have failed altogether.

But then, remember, still further, the other aspect in which we can look at this thought. That ultimate, all-embracing end is reached through a multitude of nearer and intermediate ones. Whilst life, as a whole, is the season for learning to know and for possessing God, life is broken up into smaller portions and periods, each of which has some special duty appropriate to it and a 'lesson for the day.'

Now many of us, who entirely agree, theoretically, in saying that all life is granted for this highest purpose, go wrong here and fail to discern the significance of single moments. To-day is always commonplace; it is yesterday that is beautiful, and to-morrow that is full of possibilities, to the vulgar mind. But to-day is common and low. There are mountains ahead and mountains behind, purple with distance and radiant with sunshine, and the sky bends over them and seems to touch their crests. But here, on the spot where we stand, life seems flat and mean, and far away from the heavens. We admit the meaning of life taken altogether, but it is very hard to break up that recognition into fragments, and to feel the worth of these fleeting moments which, just because they are here, seem to be of small account. So we forget that life is only the aggregate of small present instants, and that the hour is sixty times sixty insignificant seconds, and the day twenty-four brief hours, and the year 365 commonplace days, and the life threescore years and ten. Brethren, carry your theoretical recognition of the greatness and solemnity of the purposes for which life has been given here into each of the moments of the passing day, and you will find that there is nothing so elastic as time; and that you can crowd into a day as much as a languid thousand years do sometimes hold, of sacrifice and service, of holy joys, and of likeness to Jesus Christ. He who has learned that all the moments are heavy with significance, and pregnant with immortal issues, he, too, in some measure may share in the prerogative of the timeless God, and to Him 'one day may be as a thousand years, and a thousand years as one day.' It is not the beat of the pendulum or the tick of the clock that measure time, but it is the deeds which we crowd into it, and the feelings and thoughts which it ministers to us. This passing life draws all its importance from the boundless eternal issues to which it leads. Every little puddle on the paving-stones this morning, a quarter of an inch broad and a film deep, will be mirroring bright sunshine, and blue with the reflected heaven. And so we may make the little drop of our lives radiant with the image of God, and bright with the certainties of immortality.

II. Now, note secondly, how to make the most of the season.

'Redeeming the time,' says the Apostle. The figure is very simple and natural, and has only been felt to be difficult and obscure, because people have tried to ride the metaphor further than it was meant. The questions of who is the seller and what is the price do not enter into the Apostle's mind at all. Metaphors are not to be driven so far as that. We have to confine ourselves to the simple thought that there is a need for making the opportunity which is given truly our own; and that that can only be done by giving something in exchange for it. That is the notion of purchase, is it not? Acquisition, by giving something else. Thus, says Paul, you have to buy the opportunity which time affords us.

That is to say, to begin with, life gives us opportunities and no more. We may, in and through it, become wise, good, pure, happy, noble, Christ-like, or we may not. The opportunity is there, swinging, as it were, in vacuo. Lay hold of it, says he, and turn it into more than an opportunity- even an actuality and a fact.

And how is that to be done? We have to give something away, if we get the opportunity for our very own. What have we to give away? Well, mainly the lower ends for which the moment might serve. These have to be surrendered-sometimes abandoned altogether, always rigidly restricted and kept in utter subordination to the highest purposes. To-day is given us mainly that we may learn to know God better, and to love Him more, and to serve Him more joyfully. Our daily duties are given us for the same purpose. But if we go about them without thinking of God or the highest ends which life is meant to serve, then we shall certainly lose the highest ends, and an opportunity will go past us unimproved. But if, on the other hand, whilst we follow our daily business for the sake of legitimate temporal gain, we see, above that, the aspect of daily life as educating in all Christian nobleness and lofty thoughts and purposes, then we shall have given away the lower ends for the sake of attaining the higher. You live, suppose, to found a business, to become masters of your trade, to gain wisdom and knowledge, to establish for yourselves a position amongst your fellow-men, to cultivate your character so as to grow in wisdom and purity, apart from God. Or you live in order to win affection and move thankfully in the heaven of loving associations in your home, amongst your children. Or you live for the sake of carrying some lower but real good amongst men. Many of these ends are beautiful and noble, and necessary for the cultivation and discharge of the various duties and relationships of life; but unless they are all kept secondary, and there towers above them this other, life is wasted. If life is not to be wasted, they must be bartered for the higher, and we must recognise that to give all things for the sake of Christ and His love is wise merchandise and good exchange. 'What things were gain to me, those I counted loss for Christ. Yea! doubtless, and I count all things but loss that I may win Him and be found of Him.' You must barter the lower if you are to secure the higher ends for which life is the appointed season.

And then, still more minutely, my text gives us another suggestion about this 'redeeming the time.' 'See, then,' says the Apostle, 'that ye walk circumspectly.' The word rendered circumspectly might better, perhaps, be translated in some such way as 'strictly,' 'rigidly,' 'accurately,' 'punctiliously.' As I take it, it is to be connected with the 'walk,' and not with the 'see, then,' as the Revised Version does.

So here is a practical direction, walk strictly, accurately, looking to your feet; as a man would do who was upon what they call in the Alps an arrete. Suppose a narrow ridge of snow piled on the top of a ledge of rock, with a precipice of 5000 feet on either side, and a cornice of snow hanging over empty space. The climber puts his alpenstock before his foot, he tests with his foot before he rests his weight, for a false step and down he goes!

'See that you walk circumspectly,' rigidly, accurately, punctiliously. Live by law-that is to say, live by principles which imply duties; for to live by inclination is ruin. The only safety is, look to your feet and look to your road, and restrain yourselves, 'and so redeem the time.'

There is something else to look to. Feet? Yes! Road? Yes! But also look to your guide. Tread in Christ's footsteps, 'follow the Lamb whithersoever He goeth.' Make Him the pattern and example, and then you shall walk safely; and the path will carry you right into 'His presence where there is fulness of joy.' No great, noble, right, blessed life is lived without rigid self-control, self-denial, and self-crucifixion. Do not fancy that that means the absence of joy and spontaneity. 'I will walk at liberty for I keep Thy precepts.' Hedges are blessings when, on the other side, there are bottomless swamps of poisonous miasma, into which if a man ventures he will either drown or be plague-stricken. The narrow way that leads to life is the way of peace, just because it is a way of restrictions. Better to walk on the narrowest path that leads to the City than to be chartered libertines, wandering anywhere at our own bitter wills, and finding 'no end, in devious mazes lost.' Freedom consists in obeying from the heart the restriction of love; and walking punctiliously.

III. Lastly, note the motives for this course.

The Apostle says, 'see that ye walk strictly, not as fools but as wise.' That is to say, such limitation, which buys the opportunity and uses it for the highest purposes, is the only true wisdom. If you take the mean, miserable, partial, fleeting purposes for which some of us, alas, are squandering our lives, and contrast these with the great, perfect, all-satisfying, blessed, and eternal end for which it was given us, how can we escape being convicted of folly? One day, dear friends, it will be found out that the virgins that were not ready when the Lord came were the foolish ones. One day it will be asked of you and of me, 'What did you do with the life which I gave you, that you might know Me?' And if we have only the answer, 'O Lord! I founded a big business in Manchester-I made a fortune-I wrote a clever book, that was most favourably reviewed-I brought up a family'-the only thing fit to be said to us is, 'Thou fool!' The only wisdom is the wisdom that secures the end for which life was given.

Then there is another motive here. 'Redeeming the time because the days are evil.' That is singular. 'The days' are 'the time,' and yet they are 'evil' days, which being translated into other words is just this-we are to make a definite effort to keep in view, and to effect, the purposes for which all the days of our lives are given us, because these days have in themselves a tendency to draw us away from the true path and to blind us as to their real meaning. The world is full of possibilities of good and evil, and the same day which, in one aspect, is the 'season' for serving God is, in another aspect, an 'evil' day which may draw us away from Him. And if we do not put out manly effort, it certainly will do so. The ocean is meant to bear the sailor to his port, but from the waves rise up fair forms, siren voices, with sweet harps and bright eyes that tempt the weary mariner to his destruction. And the days which may be occasions for our getting nearer God, if we let them work their will upon us, will be evil days which draw us away from Him.

Let me add one last motive which is not stated in my text, but is involved in the very idea of opportunity or season-viz. that the time for the high and noble purposes of which I have been speaking is rigidly limited and bounded; and once past is irrevocable. The old, wise mythological story tells us that Occasion is bald behind, and is to be grasped by the forelock. The moment that is past had in it wonderful possibilities for us. If we did not grasp them with promptitude and decision they have gone for ever. You may as well try to bring back the water that has been sucked over Niagara, and churned into white foam at its base, as to recall the wasted opportunities. They stand all along the course of our years, solemn monuments of our unfaithfulness, and none of them can ever return again. Life is full of too-lates; that sad sound that moans through the roofless ruins of the past, like the wind through some deserted temple. 'Too late, too late; ye cannot enter now.' 'The sluggard will not plough by reason of the cold, therefore he shall beg in harvest and have nothing.' Oh! let us see to it that we wring out of the passing moments their highest possibilities of noblest good. Let us begin to live; for only he who lives to God really lives. Life is given to us that we may know Jesus Christ-trust Him, love Him, serve Him, be like Him. That is the pearl which, if we bring up from the sea of time, we shall not have been cast in vain into its stormy waves. Do you take care that this new year which is dawning upon us go not to join the many wasted years that lie desolate behind us, but let us all see to it that the flood which sweeps us and it away bears us straight to God, Who is our home. 'Now is the accepted time, now is the day of salvation.'

EPHESIANS 6

EPHESIANS CHAPTER 6 CONTENTS

THE PANOPLY OF GOD

Ephesians 6:13

The military metaphor of which this verse is the beginning was obviously deeply imprinted on Paul's mind. It is found in a comparatively incomplete form in his earliest epistle, the first to the Thessalonians, in which the children of the day are exhorted to put on the breastplate of faith and love, and for a helmet the hope of salvation. It reappears, in a slightly varied form, in the Epistle to the Romans, where those whose salvation is nearer than when they believed, are exhorted, because the day is at hand, to cast off, as it were, their night-gear, and to put on the 'armour of light'; and here, in this Epistle of the Captivity, it is most fully developed. The Roman legionary, to whom Paul was chained, here sits all unconsciously for his portrait, every detail of which is pressed by Paul into the service of his vivid imagination; the virtues and graces of the Christian character, which are 'the armour of light,' are suggested to the Apostle by the weapon which the soldier by his side wore. The vulgarest and most murderous implements assume a new character when looked upon with the eyes of a poet and a Christian. Our present text constitutes the general introduction to the great picture which follows, of 'the panoply of God.'

I. We must be ready for times of special assaults from evil.

Most of us feel but little the stern reality underlying the metaphor, that the whole Christian life is warfare, but that in that warfare there are crises, seasons of special danger. The interpretation which makes the 'evil day' co-extensive with the time of life destroys the whole emphasis of the passage: whilst all days are days of warfare, there will be, as in some prolonged siege, periods of comparative quiet; and again, days when all the cannon belch at once, and scaling ladders are reared on every side of the fortress. In a long winter there are days sunny and calm followed, as they were preceded, by days when all the winds are let loose at once. For us, such times of special danger to Christian character may arise from temporal vicissitudes. Joy and prosperity are

274

as sure to occasion them as are sorrows, for to Paul the 'evil day' is that which especially threatens moral and spiritual character, and these may be as much damaged by the bright sunshine of prosperity as by the midwinter of adversity, just as fierce sunshine may be as fatal as killing frost. They may also arise, without any such change in circumstances, from some temptation coming with more than ordinary force, and directed with terrible accuracy to our weakest point.

These evil days are ever wont to come on us suddenly; they are heralded by no storm signals and no falling barometer. We may be like soldiers sitting securely round their camp fire, till all at once bullets begin to fall among them. The tiger's roar is the first signal of its leap from the jungle. Our position in the world, our ignorance of the future, the heaped-up magazines of combustibles within, needing only a spark, all lay us open to unexpected assaults, and the temptation comes stealthily, 'as a thief in the night.' Nothing is so certain as the unexpected. For these reasons, then, because the 'evil day' will certainly come, because it may come at any time, and because it is most likely to come 'when we look not for it,' it is the dictate of plain common sense to be prepared. If the good man of the house had known at what hour the thief would have come, he would have watched; but he would have been a wiser man if he had watched all the more, because he did not know at what hour the thief would come.

II. To withstand these we must be armed against them before they come.

The main point of the exhortation is this previous preparation. It is clear enough that it is no time to fly to our weapons when the enemy is upon us. Aldershot, not the battlefield, is the place for learning strategy. Belshazzar was sitting at his drunken feast while the Persians were marching on Babylon, and in the night he was slain. When great crises arise in a nation's history, some man whose whole life has been preparing him for the hour starts to the front and does the needed work. If a sailor put off learning navigation till the wind was howling and a reef lay ahead, his corpse would be cast on the cruel rocks. It is well not to be 'over-exquisite,' to cast the fashion of 'uncertain evils,' but certain ones cannot be too carefully anticipated, nor too sedulously prepared for.

The manner in which this preparation is to be carried out is distinctly marked here. The armour is to be put on before the conflict begins. Now, without anticipating what will more properly come in considering subsequent details, we may notice that such a previous assumption implies mainly two things-a previous familiarity with God's truth, and a previous exercise of Christian virtues. As to the former, the subsequent context speaks of taking the sword of the Spirit, which is the word of God, and of having the loins girt with truth, which may be objective truth. As to the latter, we need not elaborate the Apostle's main thought that resistance to sudden temptations is most vigorous when a man is accustomed to goodness. One of the prophets treats it as being all but impossible that they who have been accustomed to evil shall learn to do well, and it is at least not less impossible that they who have been accustomed to do well shall learn to do evil. Souls which habitually walk in the clear spaces of the bracing air on the mountains of God will less easily be tempted down to the shut-in valleys where malaria reigns. The positive exercise of Christian graces tends to weaken the force of temptation. A mind occupied with these has no room for it. Higher tastes are developed which makes the poison sweetness of evil unsavoury, and just as the Israelites hungered for the strong, coarse-smelling leeks and garlic of Egypt, and therefore loathed 'this light bread,' so they whose palates have been accustomed to manna will have little taste for leeks and garlic. The mental and spiritual activity involved in the habitual exercise of Christian virtues will go far to make the soul unassailable by evil. A man, busily occupied, as the Apostle would have us to be, may be tempted by the devil, though less frequently the more he is thus occupied; but one who has no such occupations and interests tempts the devil. If our lives are inwardly and secretly honeycombed with evil, only a breath will be needed to throw down the structure. It is possible to become so accustomed to the calm delights of goodness, that it would need a moral miracle to make a man fall into sin.

III. To be armed with this armour, we must get it from God.

Though it consists mainly of habitudes and dispositions of our own minds, none the less have we to receive these from above. It is 'the panoply of God,' therefore we are to be endued with it, not by exercises in our own strength, but by dependence on Him. In old days, before a squire was knighted, he had to keep a vigil in the chapel of the castle, and through the hours of darkness to watch his armour and lift his soul to God, and we shall never put on the armour of light unless in silence we draw near to Him who teaches our hands to war and our fingers to fight. Communion with Christ, and only communion with Christ, receives from Him the life which enables us to repel the diseases of our spirits. What He imparts to those who thus wait upon Him, and to them only, is the Spirit which helps their infirmities and clothes their undefended nakedness with a coat of mail. If we go forth to war with evil, clothed and armed only with what we can provide, we shall surely be worsted in the fray. If we go forth into the world of struggle from the secret place of the Most High, 'no weapon that is formed against us shall prosper,' and we shall be more than conquerors through Him that loved us.

But waiting on God to receive our weapons from Him is but part of what is needful for our equipment. It is we who have to gird our loins and put on the breastplate, and shoe our feet, and take the shield of faith, and the helmet of salvation, and the sword of the Spirit. The cumbrous armour of old days could only be put on by the help of another pulling straps, and fixing buckles, and lifting and bracing heavy shields on arms, and fastening helmets upon heads; but we have, by our own effort, to clothe ourselves with God's great gift, which is of no use to us, and is in no real sense ours, unless we do. It takes no small effort to keep ourselves in the attitude of dependence and receptivity, without which none of the great gifts of God come to us, and, least of all, the habitual practice of Christian virtues. The soldier who rushed into the fight, leaving armour and arms huddled together on the ground, would soon fall, and God's giving avails nothing for our defence unless there is also our taking. It is the woful want of taking the things that are freely given to us of God, and of making our own what by His gift is our own, that is mainly responsible for the defeats of which we are all conscious. Looking back on our own evil days, we must all be aware that our defeats have mainly come from one or other of the two errors which lie so near us all, and which are intimately connected with each other-the one being that of fighting in our own strength, and the other being that of leaving unused our God-given power.

IV. The issue of successful resistance is increased firmness of footing.

If we are able to 'withstand in the evil day,' we shall 'stand' more securely when the evil day has stormed itself away. If we keep erect in the shock of battle, we shall stand more secure when the wild charge has been beaten back. The sea hurls tons of water against the slender lighthouse on the rock, and if it stands, the smashing of the waves consolidates it. The reward of firm resistance is increased firmness. As the Red Indians used to believe that the strength of the slain enemies whom they had scalped passed into their arms, so we may have power developed by conflict, and we shall more fully understand, and more passionately believe in, the principles and truths which have served us in past fights. David would not wear Saul's armour because, as he said, 'I have not proved it,' and the Christian who has come victoriously through one struggle should be ready to say, 'I have proved it'; we have the word of the Lord, which is tried, to trust to, and not we only, but generations, have tested it, and it has stood the tests. Therefore, it is not for us to hesitate as to the worth of our weapons, or to doubt that they are more than sufficient for every conflict which we may be called upon to wage.

The text plainly implies that all our life long we shall be in danger of sudden assaults. It does contemplate victory in the evil day, but it also contemplates that after we have withstood, we have still to stand and be ready for another attack to-morrow. Our life here is, and must still be, a continual warfare. Peace is not bought by any victories; 'There is no discharge in that war.' Like the ten thousand Greeks who fought their way home through clouds of enemies from the heart of Asia, we are never safe till we come to the mountain-top, where we can cry, 'The Sea!' But though all our paths lead us through enemies, we have Jesus, who has conquered them all, with us, and our hearts should not fail so long as we can hear His brave voice encouraging us: 'In the world ye have tribulation, but be of good cheer, I have overcome the world.'

THE BREASTPLATE OF RIGHTEOUSNESS

Ephesians 6:14

There can be no doubt that in this whole context the Apostle has in mind the great passage in Isaiah 59 where the prophet, in a figure of extreme boldness, describes the Lord as arming Himself to deliver the oppressed faithful, and coming as a Redeemer to Zion. In that passage the Lord puts on righteousness as a breastplate-that is to say, God, in His manifestation of Himself for the deliverance of His people, comes forth as if arrayed in the glittering armour of righteousness. Paul does not shrink from applying the same metaphor to those who are to be 'imitators of God as beloved children,' and from urging upon them that, in their humble degree and lowly measure, they too are to be clothed in the bright armour of moral rectitude. This righteousness is manifested in character and in conduct, and as the breastplate guards the vital organs from assault, it will keep the heart unwounded.

We must note that Paul here gathers up the whole sum of Christian character and conduct into one word. All can be expressed, however diversified may be the manifestations, by the one sovereign term 'righteousness,' and that is not merely a hasty generalisation, or a too rapid synthesis. As all sin has one root and is genetically one, so all goodness is at bottom one. The germ of sin is living to oneself: the germ of goodness is living to God. Though the degrees of development of either opposite are infinite, and the forms of its expression innumerable, yet the root of each is one.

Paul thinks of righteousness as existent before the Christian soldier puts it on. In this thought we are not merely relying on the metaphor of our text, but bringing it into accord with the whole tone of New Testament teaching, which knows of only one way in which any soul that has been living to self, and therefore to sin, can attain to living to God, and therefore can be righteous. We must receive, if we are ever to possess, the righteousness which is of God, and which becomes ours through Jesus Christ. The righteousness which shines as a fair but unattainable vision before sinful men, has a real existence, and may be theirs. It is not to be self-elaborated, but to be received.

That existent righteousness is to be put on. Other places of Scripture figure it as the robe of righteousness; here it is conceived of as the breastplate, but the idea of assumption is the same. It is to be put on, primarily, by faith. It is given in Christ to simple belief. He that hath faith thereby has the righteousness which is through faith in Christ, for in his faith he has the one formative principle of reliance on God, which will gradually refine character and mould conduct into whatsoever things are lovely and of good report. That righteousness which faith receives is no mere forensic treating of the unjust as just, but whilst it does bring with it pardon and oblivion from past transgressions, it makes a man in the depths of his being righteous, however slowly it may afterwards transform his conduct. The faith which is a departure from all reliance on works of righteousness which we have done, and is a single-eyed reliance on the work of Jesus Christ, opens the heart in which it is planted to all the influences of that life which was in Jesus, that from Him it may be in us. If Christ be in us {and if He is not, we are none of His}, 'the spirit is life because of righteousness,' however the body may still be 'dead because of sin.'

But the putting on of the breastplate requires effort as well as faith, and effort will be vigorous in the measure in which faith is vivid, but it should follow, not precede or supplant, faith. There is no more hopeless and weary advice than would be the exhortation of our text if it stood alone. It is a counsel of despair to tell a man to put on that breastplate, and to leave him in doubt where he is to find it, or whether he has to hammer it together by his own efforts before he can put it on. There is no more unprofitable expenditure of breath than the cry to men, Be good! Be good! Moral teaching without Gospel preaching is little better than a waste of breath.

This injunction is continuously imperative upon all Christian soldiers. They are on the march through the enemy's country, and can never safely lay aside their armour. After all successes, and no less after all failures, we have still to arm ourselves for the fight, and it is to be remembered that the righteousness of which Paul speaks differs from common earthly moralities only as including and transcending them all. It is, alas, too true that Christian righteousness has been by Christians set forth as something fantastic and unreal, remote from ordinary life, and far too heavenly-minded to care for common virtues. Let us never forget that Jesus Himself has warned us, that except our righteousness exceed the righteousness of the Scribes and Pharisees, we shall in no wise enter the Kingdom of Heaven. The greater orbit encloses the lesser within itself.

The breastplate of righteousness is our defence against evil. The opposition to temptation is best carried on by the positive cultivation of good. A habit of righteous conduct is itself a defence against temptation. Untilled fields bear abundant weeds. The used tool does not rust, nor the running water gather scum. The robe of righteousness will guard the heart as effectually as a coat of mail. The positive employment with good weakens temptation, and arms us against evil. But so long as we are here our righteousness must be militant, and we must be content to live ever armed to meet the enemy which is always hanging round us, and watching for an opportunity to strike. The time will come when we shall put off the breastplate and put on the fine linen 'clean and white,' which is the heavenly and final form of the righteousness of Saints.

A SOLDIER'S SHOES

Ephesians 6:15

Paul drew the first draft of this picture of the Christian armour in his first letter. It is a finished picture here. One can fancy that the Roman soldier to whom he was chained in his captivity, whilst this letter was being written, unconsciously sat for his likeness, and that each piece of his accoutrements was seized in succession by the Apostle's imagination and turned to a Christian use. It is worth noticing that there is only one offensive weapon mentioned-'the sword of the Spirit.' All the rest are defensive-helmet, breastplate, shield, girdle, and shoes. That is to say, the main part of our warfare consists in defence, in resistance, and in keeping what we have, in spite of everybody, men and devils, who attempt to take it from us. 'Hold fast that thou hast; let no man take thy crown.'

Now, it seems to me that the ordinary reader does not quite grasp the meaning of our text, and that it would be more intelligible if, instead of 'preparation,' which means the process of getting a thing ready, we read 'preparedness,' which means the state of mind of the man who is ready. Then we have to notice that the little word 'of' does duty to express two different relations, in the two instances of its use here. In the first case-'the preparedness of the Gospel'-it states the origin of the thing in question. That condition of being ready comes from the good news of Christ. In the second case-'the Gospel of peace'-it states the result of the thing in question. The good news of Christ gives peace. So, taking the whole clause, we may paraphrase it by saying that the preparedness of spirit, the alacrity which comes from the possession of a Gospel that sheds a calm over the heart and brings a man into peace with God, is what the Apostle thinks is like the heavy hob-nailed boots that the legionaries wore, by which they could stand firm, whatever came against them.

I. The first thing that I would notice here is that the Gospel brings peace.

I suppose that there was ringing in Paul's head some echoes of the music of Isaiah's words, 'How beautiful upon the mountains are the feet of Him that bringeth good tidings, that publisheth peace, that bringeth good tidings of good!' But there is a great deal more than an unconscious quotation of ancient words here; for in Paul's thought, the one power which brings a man into harmony with the universe and to peace with himself, is the power which proclaims that God is at peace with him. And Jesus Christ is our peace, because He has swept away the root and bitter fountain of all the disquiet of men's hearts, and all their chafing at providences-the consciousness that there is discord between themselves and God. The Gospel brings peace in the deepest sense of that word, and, primarily, peace with God, from out of which all other kinds of tranquillity and heart-repose do come-and they come from nothing besides.

But what strikes me most here is not so much the allusion to the blessed truth that was believed and experienced by these Ephesian Christians, that the Gospel brought peace, and was the only thing that did, as the singular emergence of that idea that the Gospel was a peace-bringing power, in the midst of this picture of fighting. Yes, it brings both. It brings us peace first, and then it says to us, 'Now, having got peace in your heart, because peace with God, go out and fight to keep it.' For, if we are warring with the devil we are at peace with God; and if we are at peace with the devil we are warring with God. So the two states of peace and war go together. There is no real peace which has not conflict in it, and the Gospel is 'the Gospel of peace,' precisely because it enlists us in Christ's army and sends us out to fight Christ's battles.

So, then, dear brother, the only way to realise and preserve 'the peace of God which passes understanding' is to fling ourselves manfully into the fight to which all Christ's soldiers are pledged and bound. The two conditions, though they seem to be opposite, will unite; for this is the paradox of the Christian life, that in all regions it makes compatible apparently incompatible and contradictory emotions. 'As sorrowful'-and Paul might have said 'therefore' instead of 'yet'-'as sorrowful yet always rejoicing; as having nothing yet'-therefore-'possessing all things'; as in the thick of the fight, and yet kept in perfect peace, because the soul is stayed on God. The peace that comes from friendship with Him, the peace that fills a heart tranquil because satisfied, the peace that soothes a conscience emptied of all poison and robbed of all its sting, the peace that abides because, on all the horizon in front of us nothing can be seen that we need to be afraid of-that peace is the peace which the Gospel brings, and it is realised in warfare and is consistent with it. All the armies of the world may camp round the fortress, and the hurtling noise of battle may be loud in the plains, but up upon the impregnable cliff crowned by its battlements there is a central citadel, with a chapel in the heart of it; and to the worshippers there none of the noise ever penetrates. The Gospel which laps us in peace and puts it in our hearts makes us soldiers.

II. Further, this Gospel of peace will prepare us for the march.

A wise general looks after his soldiers' boots. If they give out, nothing else is of much use. The roads are very rough and very long, and there need to be strong soles and well-sewed uppers, and they will be none the worse for a bit of iron on the heels and the toes, in order that they may not wear out in the midst of the campaign. 'Thy shoes shall be iron and brass,' and these metals are harder than any of the rock that you will have to clamber over. Which being translated into plain fact is just this-a tranquil heart in amity with God is ready for all the road, is likely to make progress, and is fit for anything that it may be called to do.

A calm heart makes a light foot; and he who is living at peace with God, and with all disturbance within hushed to rest, will, for one thing, be able to see what his duty is. He will see his way as far as is needful for the moment. That is more than a good many of us can do when our eyes get confused, because our hearts are beating so loudly and fast, and our own wishes come in to hide from us God's will. But if we are weaned from ourselves, as we shall be if we are living in possession of the peace of God which passes understanding, the atmosphere will be transparent, as it is on some of the calm last days of autumn, and we shall see far ahead and know where we ought to go.

The quiet heart will be able to fling its whole strength into its work. And that is what troubled hearts never can do, for half their energy is taken up in steadying or quieting themselves, or is dissipated in going after a hundred other things. But when we are wholly engaged in quiet fellowship with Jesus Christ we have the whole of our energies at our command, and can fling ourselves wholly into our work for Him. The steam-engine is said to be a very imperfect machine which wastes more power than it utilises. That is true of a great many Christian people; they have the power, but they are so far away from that deep sense of tranquillity with God, of which my text speaks, that they waste much of the power that they have. And if we are to have for our motto 'Always Ready.' as an old Scottish family has, the only way to secure that is by having 'our feet shod with the preparedness' that comes from the Gospel that brings us peace. Brethren, duty that is done reluctantly, with hesitation, is not done. We must fling ourselves into the work gladly and be always 'ready for all Thy perfect will.'

There was an English commander, who died some years ago, who was sent for to the Horse Guards one day and asked, 'How long will it take for you to be ready to go to Scinde?' 'Half an hour,' said he; and in three-quarters he was in the train, on his road to reconquer a kingdom. That is how we ought to be; but we never shall be, unless we live habitually in tranquil communion with God, and in the full faith that we are at peace with Him through the blood of His Son. A quiet heart makes us ready for duty.

III. Again, the Gospel of peace prepares us for combat.

In ancient warfare battles were lost or won very largely according to the weight of the masses of men that were hurled against each other; and the heavier men, with the firmer footing, were likely to be the victors. Our modern scientific way of fighting is different from that. But in the old time the one thing needful was that a man should stand firm and resist the shock of the enemies as they rushed upon him. Unless our footing is good we shall be tumbled over by the onset of some unexpected antagonist. And for good footing there are two things necessary. One is a good, solid piece of ground to stand on, that is not slippery nor muddy, and the other is a good, strong pair of soldier's boots, that will take hold on the ground and help the wearer to steady himself. Christ has set our feet on the rock, and so the first requisite is secured. If we, for our part, will keep near to that Gospel which brings peace into our hearts, the peace that it brings will make us able to stand and bear unmoved any force that may be hurled against us. If we are to be 'steadfast, unmovable,' we can only be so when our feet are shod with the preparedness of the Gospel of peace.

The most of your temptations, most of the things that would pluck you away from Jesus Christ, and upset you in your standing will come down upon you unexpectedly. Nothing happens in this world except the unexpected; and it is the sudden assaults that we were not looking for that work most disastrously against us. A man may be aware of some special weakness in his character, and have given himself carefully and patiently to try to fortify himself against it, and, lo! all at once a temptation springs up from the opposite side; the enemy was lying in hiding there, and whilst his face was turned to fight with one foe, a foe that he knew nothing about came storming behind him. There is only one way to stand, and that is not merely by cultivating careful watchfulness against our own weaknesses, but by keeping fast hold of Jesus Christ manifested to us in His Gospel. Then the peace that comes from that communion will itself guard us.

You remember what Paul says in one of his other letters, where he has the same beautiful blending together of the two ideas of peace and warfare: 'The peace of God, which passeth all understanding, shall garrison your hearts and minds in Christ Jesus.' It will be, as it were, an armed force within your heart which will repel all antagonism, and will enable you to abide in that Christ, through whom and in whom alone all peace comes. So, because we are thus liable to be overwhelmed by a sudden rush of unexpected temptation, and surprised into a sin before we know where we are, let us keep fast hold by that Gospel which brings peace, which will give us steadfastness, however suddenly the masked battery may begin to play upon us, and the foe may steal out of his ambush and make a rush against our unprotectedness. That is the only way, as I think, by which we can walk scatheless through the world.

Now, dear brethren, remember that this text is part of a commandment. We are to put on the shoes. How is that to be done? By a very simple way: a way which, I am afraid, a great many Christian people do not practise with anything like the constancy that they ought. For it is the Gospel that brings the peace, and if its peace brings the preparedness, then the way to get the preparedness is by soaking our minds and hearts in the Gospel of Jesus Christ.

You hear a good deal nowadays about deepening the spiritual life, and people hold conventions for the purpose. All right; I have not a word to say against that. But, conventions or no conventions, there is only one thing that deepens the spiritual life, and that is keeping near the Christ from whom all the fulness of the spiritual life flows. If we will hold fast by our Gospel, and let its peace lie upon our minds, as the negative of a photograph lies upon the paper that it is to be printed upon, until the image of Jesus Christ Himself is reproduced in us, then we may laugh at temptation. For there will be no temptation when the heart is full of Him, and there will be no sense of surrendering anything that we wish to keep when the superior sweetness of His grace fills our souls. It is empty vessels into which poison can be poured. If the vessel is full there will be no room for it. Get your hearts and minds filled with the wine of the kingdom, and the devil's venom of temptation will have no space to get in. It is well to resist temptation; it is better to be lifted above it, so that it ceases to tempt. And the one way to secure that is to live near Jesus Christ, and let the Gospel of His grace take up more of our thoughts and more of our affections than it has done in the past. Then we shall realise the fulfilment of the promise: 'He will not suffer thy foot to be moved.'

THE SHIELD OF FAITH

Ephesians 6:16

There were two kinds of shields in use in ancient warfare-one smaller, carried upon the arm, and which could be used, by a movement of the arm, for the defence of threatened parts of the body in detail; the other large, planted in front of the soldier, fixed in the ground, and all but covering his whole person. It is the latter which is referred to in the text, as the word which describes it clearly shows. That word is connected with the Greek word meaning 'door,' and gives a rough notion of the look of the instrument of defence-a great rectangular oblong, behind which a man could stand untouched and untouchable. And that is the kind of shield, says Paul, which we are to have-no little defence which may protect some part of the nature, but a great wall, behind which he who crouches is safe.

'Above all' does not mean here, as superficial readers take it to mean, most especially and primarily, as most important, but it simply means in addition to all these other things. Perhaps with some allusion to the fact that the shield protected the breastplate, as well as the breastplate protected the man, there may be a reference to the kind of double defence which comes to him who wears that breastplate and lies behind the shelter of a strong and resolute faith.

I. Now, looking at this metaphor from a practical point of view, the first thing to note is the missiles, 'the fiery darts of the wicked.'

Archaeologists tell us that there were in use in ancient warfare javelins tipped with some kind of combustible, which were set on fire, and flung, so that they had not only the power of wounding but also of burning; and that there were others with a hollow head, which was in like manner filled, kindled, and thrown into the ranks of the enemy. I suppose that the Apostle's reason for specifying these fiery darts was simply that they were the most formidable offensive weapons that he had ever heard of. Probably, if he had lived to-day, he would have spoken of rifle-bullets or explosive shells, instead of fiery darts. But, though probably the Apostle had no further meaning in the metaphor than to suggest that faith was mightier than the mightiest assaults that can be hurled against it, we may venture to draw attention to two particulars in which this figure is specially instructive and warning. The one is the action of certain temptations in setting the soul on fire; the other is the suddenness with which they assail us.

'The fiery darts.' Now, I do not wish to confine that metaphor too narrowly to any one department of human nature, for our whole being is capable of being set on fire, and 'set on fire of hell,' as James says. But there are things in us all to which the fiery darts do especially appeal: desires, appetites, passions; or-to use the word which refined people are so afraid of, although the Bible is not, 'lusts-which war against the soul,' and which need only a touch of fire to flare up like a tar-barrel, in thick foul smoke darkening the heavens. There are fiery darts that strike these animal natures of ours, and set them all aflame.

But, there are other fiery darts than these. There are plenty of other desires in us: wishes, cowardices, weaknesses of all sorts, that, once touched with the devil's dart, will burn fiercely enough. We all know that.

Then there is the other characteristic of suddenness. The dart comes without any warning. The arrow is invisible until it is buried in the man's breast. The pestilence walks in darkness, and the victim does not know until its poison fang is in him. Ah! yes! brethren, the most dangerous of our temptations are those that are sprung upon us unawares. We are going quietly along the course of our daily lives, occupied with quite other thoughts, and all at once, as if a door had opened, not out of heaven but out of hell, we are confronted with some evil thing that, unless we are instantaneously on our guard, will conquer us almost before we know. Evil tempts us because it comes to us, for the most part, without any beat of drum or blast of trumpet to say that it is coming, and to put us upon our guard. The batteries that do most harm to the advancing force are masked until the word of command is given, and then there is a flash from every cannon's throat and a withering hail of shot that confounds by its unexpectedness as well as kills by its blow. The fiery darts that light up the infernal furnace in a man's heart, and that smite him all unawares and unsuspecting, these are the weapons that we have to fear most.

II. Consider next, the defence: 'the shield of faith.'

Now, the Old Testament says things like this: 'Fear not, Abraham; I am thy Shield.' The psalmist invoked God, in a rapturous exuberance of adoring invocations, as his fortress, and his buckler, and the horn of his salvation, and his high tower. The same psalm says, 'The Lord is a shield to all them that put their trust in Him'; and the Book of Proverbs, which is not given to quoting psalms, quotes that verse. Another psalm says, 'The Lord God is a sun and shield.'

And then Paul comes speaking of 'the shield of faith.' What has become of the other one? The answer is plain enough. My faith is nothing except for what it puts in front of me, and it is God who is truly my shield; my faith is only called a shield, because it brings me behind the bosses of the Almighty's buckler, against which no man can run a tilt, or into which no man can strike his lance, nor any devil either. God is a defence; and my trust, which is nothing in itself, is everything because of that with which it brings me into connection. Faith is the condition, and the only condition, of God's power flowing into me, and working in me. And when that power flows into me, and works in me, then I can laugh at the fiery darts, because 'greater is He that is with us than all they that are with them.'

So all the glorification which the New Testament pours out upon the act of faith properly belongs, not to the act itself, but to that with which the act brings us into connection. Wherefore, in the first Epistle of John, the Apostle, who recorded Christ's saying, 'Be of good cheer; I have overcome the world,' translates it into, 'This is the victory that overcometh the world'-not, our Christ, but-'even our faith.' And it overcomes because it binds us in deep, vital union with Him who has overcome; and then all His conquering power comes into us.

That is the explanation and vindication of the turn which Paul gives to the Old Testament metaphor here, when he makes our shield to be faith. Suppose a man was exercising trust in one that was unworthy of it, would that trust defend him from anything? Suppose you were in peril of some great pecuniary loss, and were saying to yourself, 'Oh! I do not care. So-and-so has guaranteed me against any loss, and I trust to him,' and suppose he was a bankrupt, what would be the good of your trust? It would not bring the money back into your pocket. Suppose a man is leaning upon a rotten support; the harder he leans the sooner it will crumble. So there is no defence in the act of trust except what comes into it from the object of trust; and my faith is a shield only because it grasps the God who is the shield.

But, then, there is another side to that thought. My faith will quench, as nothing else will, these sudden impulses of fiery desires, because my faith brings me into the conscious presence of God, and of the unseen realities where He dwells. How can a man sin when God's eye is felt to be upon him? Suppose conspirators plotting some dark deed in a corner, shrouded by the night, as they think; and suppose, all at once, the day were to blaze in upon them, they would scatter, and drop their designs. Faith draws back the curtain which screens off that unseen world from so many of us, and lets in the light that shines down from above and shows us that we are compassed about by a cloud of witnesses, and the Captain of our Salvation in the midst of them. Then the fiery darts fizzle out, and the points drop off them. No temptation continues to flame when we see God.

They have contrivances in mills that they call 'automatic sprinklers.' When the fire touches them it melts away a covering, and a gas is set free that puts the fire out. And if we let in the thought of God, it will extinguish any flame. 'The sun puts out the fire in our grates,' the old women say. Let God's sun shine into your heart, and you will find that the infernal light has gone out. The shield of faith quenches the fiery darts of the 'wicked.'

Yes! and it does it in another way. For, according to the Epistle to the Hebrews, faith realises 'the things hoped for,' as well as 'unseen.' And if a man is walking in the light of the great promises of Heaven, and the great threatenings of a hell, he will not be in much danger of being set on fire, even by 'the fiery darts of the wicked.' He that receives into his heart God's strength; he that by faith is conscious of the divine presence in communion with him; he that by faith walks in the light of eternal retribution, will triumph over the most sudden, the sharpest, and the most fiery of the darts that can be launched against him.

III. The Grasp of the Shield.

'Taking the shield,' then, there is something to be done in order to get the benefit of that defence. Now, there are a great many very good people at present who tell Christian men that they ought to exercise faith for sanctifying, as they exercise it for justifying and acceptance. And some of them-I do not say all-forget that there is effort needed to exercise faith for sanctifying; and that our energy has to be put forth in order that a man may, in spite of all resistance, keep himself in the attitude of dependence. So my text, whilst it proclaims that we are to trust for defence against, and victory over, recurring temptations, just as we trusted for forgiveness and acceptance at the beginning, proclaims also that there must be effort to grasp the shield, and to realise the defence which the shield gives to us.

For to trust is an act of the heart and will far more than of the head, and there are a great many hindrances that rise in the way of it; and to keep behind the shield, and not depend at all upon our own wit, our wisdom, or our strength, but wholly upon the Christ who gives us wit and wisdom, and strengthens our fingers to fight-that will take work! To occupy heart and mind with the object of faith is not an easy thing.

So, brethren, effort to compel the will and the heart to trust; effort to keep the mind in touch with the verities and the Person who are the objects of our faith; and effort to keep ourselves utterly and wholly ensconced behind the Shield, and never to venture out into the open, where our own arm has to keep our own heads, but to hang wholly upon Him-these things go to 'taking' the shield of faith. And it is because we fail in these, and not because there are any holes or weak places in the shield, that so many of the fiery darts find their way through, and set on fire and wound us. The Shield is impregnable, beaten as we have often been. 'This is the victory that overcometh the world'-and the devil and his darts-'even our faith.'

THE HELMET OF SALVATION

Ephesians 6:17

We may, perhaps, trace a certain progress in the enumeration of the various pieces of the Christian armour in this context. Roughly speaking, they are in three divisions. There are first our graces of truth, righteousness, preparedness, which, though they are all conceived as given by God, are yet the exercises of our own powers. There is next, standing alone, as befits its all-comprehensive character, faith which is able to ward against and overcome not merely this and that temptation, but all forms of evil. That faith is the root of the three preceding graces, and makes the transition to the two which follow, because it is the hand by which we lay hold of God's gifts. The two final parts of the Christian armour are God's gifts, pure and simple-salvation and the word of God. So the progress is from circumference to centre, from man to God. From the central faith we have on the one hand that which it produces in us; on the other, that which it lays hold of from God. And these two last pieces of armour, being wholly God's gift, we are bidden with especial emphasis which is shown by a change in construction, to take or receive these.

I. The Salvation.

Once more Old Testament prophecy suggests the words of this exhortation. In Isaiah's grand vision of God, arising to execute judgment which is also redemption, we have a wonderful picture of His arraying Himself in armour. Righteousness is His flashing breastplate: on His head is an helmet of salvation. The gleaming steel is draped by garments of retributive judgment, and over all is cast, like a cloak, the ample folds of that 'zeal' which expresses the inexhaustible energy and intensity of the divine nature and action. Thus arrayed He comes forth to avenge and save. His redeeming work is the manifestation and issue of all these characteristics of His nature. It flames with divine fervour: it manifests the justice which repays, but its inmost character is righteousness, and its chief purpose is to save. His helmet is salvation;

the plain, prose meaning of which would appear to be that His great purpose of saving men is its own guarantee that His purpose should be effected, and is the armour by which His work is defended.

The Apostle uses the old picture with perfect freedom, quoting the words indeed, but employing them quite differently. God's helmet of salvation is His own purpose; man's helmet of salvation is God's gift. He is strong to save because He wills to save; we are strong and safe when we take the salvation which He gives.

It is to be further noticed that the same image appears in Paul's rough draft of the Christian armour in Thessalonians, with the significant difference that there the helmet is 'the hope of salvation,' and here it is the salvation itself. This double representation is in full accord with all Scripture teaching, according to which we both possess and hope for salvation, and our possession determines the measure of our hope. That great word negatively implies deliverance from evil of any kind, and in its lower application, from sickness or peril of any sort. In its higher meaning in Scripture the evil from which we are saved is most frequently left unexpressed, but sometimes a little glimpse is given, as when we read that 'we are saved from wrath through Him' or 'saved from sin.' What Christ saves us from is, first and chiefly, from sin in all aspects, its guilt, its power, and its penalty; but His salvation reaches much further than any mere deliverance from threatening evil, and positively means the communication to our weakness and emptiness of all blessings and graces possible for men. It is inward and properly spiritual, but it is also outward, and it is not fully possessed until we are clothed with 'salvation ready to be revealed in the last time.'

Hence, in Scripture our salvation is presented as past, as present, and as future. As past it is once for all received by initial faith in Christ; and, in view of their faith, Paul has no scruples as to saying to the imperfect Christians whose imperfections he scourges, 'Ye have been saved,' or in building upon that past fact his earnest exhortations and his scathing rebukes. The salvation is present if in any true sense it is past. There will be a daily growing deliverance from evil and a daily growing appropriation and manifestation of the salvation which we have received. And so Paul more than once speaks of Christians as 'being saved.' The process begun in the past is continued throughout the present, and the more a Christian man is conscious of its reality even amidst flaws, failures, stagnation, and lapses, the more assured will be his hope of the perfect salvation in the future, when all that is here, tendency often thwarted, and aspirations often balked, and sometimes sadly contradicted, will be completely, uninterruptedly, and eternally realised. If that hope flickers and is sometimes all but dead, the reason mainly lies in its flame not being fed by present experience.

II. The helmet of salvation.

This salvation in its present form will keep our heads in the day of battle. Its very characteristic is that it delivers us from evil, and all the graces with which Paul equips his ideal warrior are parts of the positive blessings which our salvation brings us. The more assured we are in our own happy consciousness of possessing the salvation of God, the more shall we be defended from all the temptations that seek to stir into action our lower selves. There will be no power in our fears to draw us into sin, and the possible evils that appeal to earthly passions of whatever sort will lose their power to disturb us, in the precise measure in which we know that we are saved in Christ. The consciousness of salvation will tend to damp down the magazine of combustibles that we all carry within us, and the sparks that fall will be as innocuous as those that light on wet gunpowder. If our thoughts are occupied with the blessings which we possess they will be guarded against the assaults of evil. The full cup has no room for poison. The eye that is gazing on the far-off white mountains does not see the filth and frivolities around. If we are living in conscious possession and enjoyment of what God gives us, we shall pass scatheless through the temptations which would otherwise fall on us and rend us. A future eagerly longed for, and already possessed in germ, will kill a present that would otherwise appeal to us with irresistible force.

III. Take the helmet.

We might perhaps more accurately read receive salvation, for that salvation is not won by any efforts of our own, but if we ever possess it, our possession is the result of our accepting it as a gift from God. The first word which the Gospel speaks to men and which makes it a Gospel, is not Do this or that, but Take this from the hands that were nailed to the Cross. The beginning of all true life, of all peace, of all self-control, of all hope, lies in the humble and penitent acceptance by faith of the salvation which Christ brings, and with which we have nothing to do but to accept it.

But Paul is here speaking to those whom he believes to have already exercised the initial faith which united them to Christ, and made His salvation theirs, and to these the exhortation comes with special force. To such it says, 'See to it that your faith ever grasps and feeds upon the great facts on which your salvation reposes-God's changeless love, Christ's all-sufficient sacrifice and ascended life, which He imparts to us if we abide in Him. Hold fast and prolong by continual repetition the initial act by which you received that salvation. It is said that on his death-bed Oliver Cromwell asked the Puritan divine who was standing by it whether a man who had once been in the covenant could be lost, and on being assured that he could not, answered, 'I know that I was once in it'; but such a building on past experiences is a building on sand, and nothing but continuous faith will secure a continuous salvation. A melancholy number of so-called Christians in this day have to travel far back through the years before they reach the period when they took the helmet of salvation. They know that they were far better men, and possessed a far deeper apprehension of Christ and His power in the old days than is theirs now, and they need not wonder if God's great gift has unnoticed slipped from their relaxed grasp. A hand that clings to a rock while a swollen flood rushes past needs to perpetually be tightening its grip, else the man will be swept away; and the present salvation, and, still more, the hope of a future salvation, are not ours on any other terms than a continual repetition of the initial act by which we first received them. But there must also be a continually increased appropriation and manifestation in our lives of a progressive salvation that will come as a result of a constantly renewed faith; but it will not come unless there be continuous effort to work into our characters, and to work out in our lives, the transforming and vitalising power of the life given to us in Jesus Christ. If our present experience yields no sign of growing conformity to the image of our Saviour, there is only too abundant reason for doubting whether we have experienced a past salvation or have any right to anticipate a perfect future salvation.

The last word to be said is, Live in frequent anticipation of that perfect future. If that anticipation is built on memory of the past and experience of the present, it cannot be too confident. That hope maketh not ashamed. In the region of Christian experience alone the weakest of us has a right to reckon on the future, and to be sure that when that great to-morrow dawns for us, it 'shall be as this day and much more abundant.' With this salvation in its imperfect form brightening the present, and in its completeness filling the future with unimaginable glory, we can go into all the conflicts of this fighting world and feel that we are safe because God covers our heads in the day of battle. Unless so defended we shall go into the fight as the naked Indians did with the Spanish invaders, and be defeated as they were. The plumes may be shorn off the helmet, and it may be easily dinted, but the head that wore it will be unharmed. And when the battle and the noise of battle are past, the helmet will be laid aside, and we shall be able to say, 'I have fought a good fight, henceforth there is laid up for me a crown of righteousness.'

THE SWORD OF THE SPIRIT

Ephesians 6:18

We reach here the last and only offensive weapon in the panoply. The 'of' here does not indicate apposition, as in the 'shield of faith,' or 'the helmet of salvation,' nor is it the 'of' of possession, so that the meaning is to be taken as being the sword which the Spirit wields, but it is the 'of' expressing origin, as in the 'armour of God'; it is the sword which the Spirit supplies. The progress noted in the last sermon from subjective graces to objective divine facts, is completed here, for the sword which is put into the Christian soldier's hand is the gift of God, even more markedly than is the helmet which guards his head in the day of battle.

I. Note what the word of God is.

The answer which would most commonly and almost unthinkingly be given is, I suppose, the Scriptures; but while this is on the whole true, it is to be noted that the expression employed here properly means a word spoken, and not the written record. Both in the Old and in the New Testaments the word of God means more than the Bible; it is the authentic utterance of His will in all shapes and applying to all the facts of His creation. In the Old Testament 'God said' is the expression in the first chapter of Genesis for the forthputting of the divine energy in the act of creation, and long ages after that divine poem of creation was written a psalmist re-echoed the thought when he said 'For ever, O Lord, Thy word is settled in the heavens. Thou hast established the earth and it abideth.'

But, further, the expression designates the specific messages which prophets and others received. These are not in the Old Testament spoken of as a unity: they are individual words rather than a word. Each of them is a manifestation of the divine will and purpose; many of them are commandments; some of them are warnings; and all, in some measure, reveal the divine nature.

That self-revelation of God reaches for us in this life its permanent climax, when He who 'at sundry times and in divers manner spake unto the fathers by the prophets, hath in these last days spoken unto us by a Son.' Jesus is the personal 'word of God' though that name by which He is designated in the New Testament is a different expression from that employed in our text, and connotes a whole series of different ideas.

The early Christian teachers and apostles had no hesitation in taking that sacred name-the word of the Lord-to describe the message which they spoke. One of their earliest prayers when they were left alone was, that with all boldness they might speak Thy word; and throughout the whole of the Acts of the Apostles the preached Gospel is designated as the word of God, even as Peter in his epistle quotes one of the noblest of the Old Testament sayings, and declares that the 'word of the Lord' which 'abideth for ever' is 'the word which by the gospel is preached unto you.'

Clearly, then, Paul here is exhorting the Ephesian Christians, most of whom probably were entirely ignorant of the Old Testament, to use the spoken words which they had heard from him and other preachers of the Gospel as the sword of the Spirit. Since he is evidently referring to Christian teaching, it is obvious that he regards the old and the new as one whole, that to him the proclamation of Jesus was the perfection of what had been spoken by prophets and psalmists. He claims for his message and his brethren's the same place and dignity that belonged to the former messengers of the divine will. He asserts, and all the more strongly, because it is an assertion by implication only, that the same Spirit which moved in the prophets and saints of former days is moving in the preachers of the Gospel, and that their message has a wider sweep, a deeper content, and a more radiant light than that which had been delivered in the past. The word of the Lord had of old partially declared God's nature and His will: the word of God which Paul preached was in his judgment the complete revelation of God's loving heart, the complete exhibition to men of God's commandments of old; longing eyes had seen a coming day and been glad and confidently foretold it, now the message was 'the coming one has come.'

It is as the record and vehicle of that spoken Gospel, as well as of its earlier premonitions, that the Bible has come to be called the word of God, and the name is true in that He speaks in this book. But much harm has resulted from the appropriation of the name exclusively to the book, and the forgetfulness that a vehicle is one thing and that which it carries quite another.

II. The purpose and power of the word.

The sword is the only offensive weapon in the list. The spear which played so great a part in ancient warfare is not named. It may well be noted that only a couple of verses before our text we read of the Gospel of peace, and that here with remarkable freedom of use of his metaphors, Paul makes the word of God, which as we have seen is substantially equivalent to the preached Gospel, the one weapon with which Christian men are to cut and thrust. Jesus said 'I come not to send peace, but a sword,' but Paul makes the apparent contradiction still more acute when he makes the very Gospel itself the sword. We may recall as a parallel, and possibly a copy of our text, the great words of the Epistle to the Hebrews which speak of the word of God as 'living and active and sharper than any two-edged sword.' And we cannot forget the magnificent symbolism of the Book of Revelation which saw in the midst of the candlestick one like unto a Son of Man, and 'out of His mouth proceeded a sharp, two-edged sword.' That image is the poetic embodiment of our Lord's own words which we have just quoted, and implies the penetrating power of the word which Christ's gentle lips have uttered. Gracious and healing as it is, a Gospel of peace, it has an edge and a point which cut down through all sophistications of human error, and lay bare the 'thoughts and intents of the heart.' The revelation made by Christ has other purposes which are not less important than its ministering of consolation and hope. It is intended to help us in our fight with evil, and the solemn old utterance, 'with the breath of His mouth He will slay the wicked,' is true in reference to the effect of the word of Christ on moral evil. Such slaying is but the other side of the life-giving power which the word exercises on a heart subject to its influence. For the Christian soldier's conflict with evil as threatening the health of his own Christian life, or as tyrannising over the lives of others, the sword of the Spirit is the best weapon.

We are not to take the rough-and-ready method, which is so common among good people, of identifying this spirit-given sword with the Bible. If for no other reason, yet because it is the Spirit which supplies it to the grasp of the Christian soldier, our possession of it is therefore a result of the action of that Spirit on the individual Christian spirit; and what He gives, and we are to wield, is 'the engrafted word which is able to save our souls.' That word, lodged in our hearts, brings to us a revelation of duty and a chart of life, because it brings a loving recognition of the character of our Father, and a glad obedience to His will. If that word dwell in us richly, in all wisdom, and if we do not dull the edge of the sword by our own unworthy handling of it, we shall find it pierce to the 'dividing asunder of joints and marrow,' and the evil within us will either be cast out from us, or will shrivel itself up, and bury itself deep in dark corners.

Love to Christ will be so strong, and the things that are not seen will so overwhelmingly outweigh the things that are seen, that the solemn majesty of the eternal will make the temporal look to our awed eyes the contemptible unreality which it really is. They who humbly receive and faithfully use that engrafted word, have in it a sure touchstone against which their own sins and errors are shivered. It is for the Christian consciousness the true Ithuriel's spear, at the touch of which 'upstarts in his own shape the fiend' who has been pouring his whispered poison into an unsuspicious ear. The standard weights and measures are kept in government custody, and traders have to send their yard measures and scales thither if they wish them tested; but the engrafted word, faithfully used and submitted to, is always at hand, and ready to pronounce its decrees, and to cut to the quick the evil by which the understanding is darkened and conscience sophisticated.

III. The manner of its use.

Here that is briefly but sufficiently expressed by the one commandment, 'take,' or perhaps more accurately, 'receive.' Of course, properly speaking, that exhortation does not refer to our manner of fighting with the sword, but to the previous act by which our hand grasps it. But it is profoundly true that if we take it in the deepest sense, the possession of it will teach the use of it. No instruction will impart the last, and little instruction is needed for the first. What is needed is the simple act of yielding ourselves to Jesus Christ, and looking to Him only, as our guide and strength. Before all Christian warfare must come the possession of the Christian armour, and the commandment that here lies at the beginning of all Paul's description of it is 'Take.' Our fitness for the conflict all depends on our receiving God's gift, and that reception is no mere passive thing, as if God's grace could be poured into a human spirit as water is into a bucket. Hence, the translation of this commandment of Paul's by 'take' is better than that by 'receive,' inasmuch as it brings into prominence man's activity, though it gives too exclusive importance to that, to the detriment of the far deeper and more essential element of the divine action. The two words are, in fact, both needed to cover the whole ground of what takes place when the giving God and the taking man concur in the great act by which the Spirit of God takes up its abode in a human spirit. God's gift is to be received as purely His gift, undeserved, unearned by us. But undeserved and unearned as it is, and given 'without money and without price,' it is not ours unless our hand is stretched out to take, and our fingers closed tightly over the free gift of God. There is a dead lift of effort in the reception; there is a still greater effort needed for the continued possession, and there is a life-long discipline and effort needed for the effective use in the struggle of daily life of the sword of the Spirit.

If that engrafted word is ever to become sovereign in our lives, there must be a life-long attempt to bring the tremendous truths as to God's will for human conduct which it plants in our minds into practice, and to bring all our practice under their influence. The motives which it brings to bear on our evils will be powerless to smite them, unless these motives are made sovereign in us by many an hour of patient meditation and of submission to their sweet and strong constraint. One sometimes sees on a wild briar a graft which has been carefully inserted and bandaged up, but which has failed to strike, and so the strain of the briar goes on and no rosebuds come. Are there not some of us who profess to have received the engrafted word and whose daily experience has proved, by our own continual sinfulness, that it is unable to 'save our souls'?

There are in the Christian ranks some soldiers whose hands are too nerveless or too full of worldly trash to grasp the sword which they have received, much less to strike home with it at any of the evils that are devastating their own lives or darkening the world. The feebleness of the Christian conflict with evil, in all its forms, whether individual or social, whether intellectual or moral, whether heretical or grossly and frankly sensual, is mainly due to the feebleness with which the average professing Christians grasp the sword of the Spirit. When David asked the priests for weapons, and they told him that Goliath's sword was lying wrapt in a cloth behind the ephod, and that they had none other, he said, 'There is none like that, give it me.' If we are wise, we will take the sword that lies in the secret place, and, armed with it, we shall not need to fear in any day of battle.

We do well that we take heed to the word of God, 'as unto a lamp shining in a dark place until the day dawn,' when swords will be no more needed, and the Word will no longer shine in darkness but be the Light that makes the Sun needless for the brightness of the New Jerusalem.

PEACE, LOVE, AND FAITH

Ephesians 6:23

The numerous personal greetings usually found at the close of Paul's letters are entirely absent from this Epistle. All which we have in their place is this entirely general good wish, and the still more general and wider one in the subsequent verse.

There is but one other of the Apostle's letters similarly devoid of personal messages, viz. the Epistle to the Galatians, and their absence there is sufficiently accounted for by the severe and stern tone of that letter. But it is very difficult to understand how they should not appear in a letter to a church with which the Apostle had such prolonged and cordial relations as he had with the church at Ephesus. And hence the absence of these personal greetings is a strong confirmation of the opinion that this Epistle was not originally addressed to the church at Ephesus, but was a kind of circular intended to go round the various churches in Asia Minor, and only sent first to that at Ephesus. That opinion is further confirmed by the fact known to many of you that in some good ancient manuscripts the words 'at Ephesus' are omitted from the first verse of the letter; which thus stands without any specific address.

Be that as it may, this trinity of inward graces is Paul's highest and best wish for his friends. He has no earthly prosperity to wish for them. His ambition soars higher than that; he desires for them peace, love, faith.

Now, will you take the lesson? There is no better test of a man than the things that he wishes for the people that he loves most. He desires for them, of course, his own ideal of happiness. What do you desire most for those that are dearest to you? You parents, do you train up your children, for instance, so as to secure, or to do your best to secure, not outward prosperity, but these loftier gifts; and for yourselves, when you are forming your wishes, are these the things that you want most? 'Set your affections on things above,' and remember that whoso has that trinity of graces, peace, love, faith, is rich and blessed, whatsoever else he has or needs. And whoso has them not is miserable and poor.

But I wish especially to look a little more closely at these three things in themselves and in their relation to one another. I take it that the Apostle is here tracking the stream to its fountain; that he is beginning with effects and working backwards and downwards to causes; so that to get the order of nature and of time we must reverse the order here, and begin where he ends and end where he begins. The Christian life in its higher vigour and excellence is rooted in faith. That faith associates to itself, and is inseparably connected with love, and the faith and love together issue in a deep restful tranquillity which nothing can break.

Now, let us look at these three things as the three greatest blessings that any can bear in their hearts, and wring out of time, sorrow, and change.

I. First, the root of everything is a continuous and growing trust.

Remember that this prayer or wish of my text was spoken in reference to brethren; that is to say, to those who, by the hypothesis, already possessed Christian faith. And Paul wishes for them, and can wish for them, nothing better and more than the increase and continuousness of that which they already possess. The highest blessing that the brethren can receive is the enlargement and the strengthening of their faith.

Now we talk so much in Christian teaching about this 'faith' that, I fancy, like a worn sixpence in a man's pocket, its very circulation from hand to hand has worn off the lettering. And many of us, from the very familiarity of the word, have only a dim conception of what it means. It may not be profitless, then, to remind you, first of all, that this faith is neither more nor less than a very familiar thing which you are constantly exercising in reference to one another-that is to say, simple confidence. You trust your husband, your wife, your child, your parent, your friend, your guide, your lawyer, your doctor, your banker. Take that very same emotion and attitude of the mind by which you put your well-being, in different aspects and provinces, into the hands of men and women round about you; lift the trailing flowers that go all straggling along the ground, and twine them round the pillars of God's throne, and you get the confidence, the trust, of the praises and glories of which the New Testament is full. There is nothing mysterious in it, it is simply the exercise of confidence, the familiar cement that binds all human relationship together, and makes men brotherly and kindred with their kind. Faith is trust, and trust saves a man's soul.

Then, remember further that the faith which is the foundation of everything is essentially personal trust reposing upon a person, upon Jesus Christ. You cannot get hold of a man in any other way than by that. The only real bond that binds people together is the personal bond of confidence, manifesting itself in love. And it is no mere doctrine that we present for a man's faith, but it is the person about whom the doctrine speaks. We say, indeed, that we can only know the person on whom we must trust by the revelation of the truths concerning Him which make the Christian doctrines; but a man may believe the whole of them, and have no faith. And what is the step in advance which is needed in order to turn credence into faith-belief in a doctrine into trust? In one view it is the step from the doctrine to the person. When you grasp Christ, the living Christ, and not merely the doctrine, for yours, then you have faith.

Only remember, my brother, if you say you trust Christ, the question has immediately to be asked: What Christ is it that you are trusting? Is it the Christ that died for your sins on the Cross, or is it a Christ that taught you some great moral truths and set you a lovely example of life and conduct? Which of the two is it? for these two Christs are very different, and the faith that grasps the one is extremely unlike the faith that grasps the other. And so I press upon you this question: What Christ is it to Whom your confidence turns, and for what is it that you are looking to Him? Is it for help and guidance of some vague kind; is it for pattern or example, or is it for the salvation of your sinful souls, by the might of His great sacrifice?

Then, remember still further, that this personal outgoing of confidence, which is the action both of a man's will and of a man's intellect, to the person revealed to us in the great doctrines of the Gospel-that this faith, if it is to be worth anything, must be continuous. Paul could desire nothing better for his Ephesian friends than that they should have that which they had-faith; that they should continue to have it, and that it should be perennial and increasing all through their lives. You can no more get present good from past faith than the breath you drew yesterday into your lungs will be sufficient to oxygenate your blood at this moment. As soon as you break the electric contact, the electric light goes out, and no matter how long a man has been living a life of faith, that past life will not in the smallest degree help him at the present moment unless the faith is continuous. Remember this, then, a broken faith is a broken peace; a broken faith is a broken salvation; and so long, and only so long, as you are knit to Jesus Christ by the conscious exercise of a faith realised at the moment, are you in the reception of blessing from Him at the moment.

And, still further, this faith ought to be progressive. So Paul desired it to be with these people. If there is no growth, do you think there is much life? I know I am speaking to plenty of people who call themselves Christians, whose faith is not one inch better to-day than it was when it was born-perhaps a little less rather than more. Oh! the hundreds and thousands of professing Christians, average Christians, that clog and weaken all churches, whose faith has no progressive element in it, and is not a bit stronger by all the discipline of life and by their experience of its power. Brethren! is it so with us? Let us ask ourselves that; and let us ask very solemnly this other question: If my faith has no growth, how do I know that it has got any life?

And so let me remind you further that this faith, the personal outgoing of a man's intellect and will to the personal Saviour revealed in the Scriptures as the sacrifice for our sins, and the life of our spirits, which ought to be continuous and progressive, is the foundation of all strength, blessedness, goodness, in a human character; and if we have it we have the germ of all possible excellence and growth, not because of what it is in itself, for in itself it is nothing more than the opening of the heart to the reception of the celestial influences of grace and righteousness that He pours down. And, therefore, this is the thing that a wise man will most desire for himself, and for those that are dearest to him.

Depend upon it, whether it is what we want most or not, it is what God wants most for us. He does not care nearly so much that our lives should be joyful as that they should be righteous and full of faith; and He subjects us to many a sorrow and loss and disappointment in order that the life of nature may be broken and the life of faith may be strong. If we rightly understand the relative value of outward and of inward things, we shall be thankful for the storms that drive us nearer to Him; for the darkening earth that may make the pillar of cloud glow at the heart into a pillar of fire, and for all the discipline, painful though it may be, with which God answers the prayer, 'Lord, increase our faith.'

II. And now, next, notice how inseparably associated with a true faith is love.

The one is effect that never is found without its cause; the other is cause which never but produces its effect. These two are braided together by the Apostle as inseparable in reality and inseparable in thought. And that it is so is plain enough, and there follow from it some practical lessons that I desire to lay upon your hearts and my own.

There are, then, here two principles, or rather two sides of one thought; no faith without love, no love without faith.

No faith is genuine and deep which does not at once produce in the heart where it is lodged an answering love to God. That is clear enough. Faith is, as I have said, the recognition and the reception of the divine love into the heart; and we are so constituted as that if a man once knows and believes in any real sense the love that God has to him, he answers it back again with his love as certainly as an echo which gives back the sound that reaches it.

Our faith is, if I may so say, like a burning-glass, which concentrates the rays of the divine love upon our hearts, and focuses them into a point that kindles our hearts into flame. If we have the confidence that God loves us, in any real depth, we shall answer by the gush of our love to Him.

And so here is a test for men's faith. You call yourselves Christians. If I were to come to you and ask you, 'Do you believe in the Lord Jesus Christ?' most of you would say, 'Yes!' Try your faith, my friend, by this test: Does it make you love Him at all? If it does not, it is more words than anything else; and it needs a wonderful deepening before it can have any real power in your hearts. There is no faith worthy the name unless its child, all but as old as itself, be the answer of the heart to Him, pouring itself out in thankful gratitude.

No love without faith; 'we love Him because He first loved us.' God must begin, we can only come second. Man's natural selfishness is only overcome by the clearest demonstration of the love of God to him; and until that love, in its superbest because its lowliest form, the form of the sacrifice on the Cross, has penetrated into a man's heart through his faith, there will be no love.

So then, dear friends, there is a test for your love. We hear a great deal said nowadays, as there has always been a great deal said, about the essence of all religion consisting in love to God; and about men 'rejecting the cumbrous dogmas of the New Testament, and falling back upon the great and simple truths, Thou shalt love the Lord thy God with all thy heart, and with all thy soul, and with all thy mind, and with all thy strength; and thy neighbour as thyself,' and saying 'that is their religion.' Well, I venture to say that without the faith of the heart in, not the cumbrous dogmas, but the central fact of the New Testament, that Christ died on the Cross for me, you will never get the old commandment of love to God with heart and soul and strength and mind really kept and carried out; and that if you want men to have their hearts and wills bound into loving fellowship with God, it is only by the path of faith in Him who is the sacrifice for sin that such fellowship is reached. Hence there follows a very plain, practical advice. Do you want your heart's love to be increased? Learn the way to do it. You cannot work yourselves into a fervour of religious emotion of any valuable kind. A man cannot get to love more by saying, 'I am determined I will.' We have no direct control over our affections in that fashion. You cannot make water boil except by one way, and that is by putting plenty of fire under it; and you cannot make your affections melt and flow except by heating them by the contemplation of the truth which is intended to bring them out. That is to say, the more we exercise our minds on the contemplation of Christ's great love to us, and the more we put forth the energies of our souls in the act of simple self-distrust and reliance upon Him, the more will our love be fervent and strong. You can only increase love by increasing the faith from which it comes. So do you see to it, if you call yourselves Christians, that you try to deepen all your Christian affections by an honest, meditative, prayerful contemplation and grasp of the great love of God in Jesus Christ. And do not wonder if your Christian life be, as it is in so many of us, stunted, not progressive, bringing no blessing to ourselves and little good to anybody else. The explanation is easy enough. You do not look at the Cross of Christ, nor live in the contemplation and reception of His great grace.

III. And now, lastly, these two inseparably associated graces of faith and love bring with them, and lead to, the third-peace.

It seems to be but a very modest, sober-tinted wish which the Apostle here has for his brethren that the highest and best thing he can ask for them is only quiet. Very modest by the side of joy and excitement, in their coats of many colours, and yet the deepest and truest blessing that any of us can have-peace. It comes to us by one path, and that is by the path of faith and love.

These two bring peace with God, peace in our inmost spirits, the peace of self-annihilation and submission, the peace of obedience, the peace of ceasing from our own works, and entering, therefore, into the rest of God. Trust is peace. There is no tranquillity like that of feeling 'I am not responsible for this: He is; and I rest myself on Him.'

Love is peace. There is no rest for our hearts but on the bosom of some one that is dear to us, and in whom we can confide. But ah, brother! every tree in which the dove nestles is felled down sooner or later, and the nest torn to pieces, and the bird flies away. But if we turn ourselves to the undying Christ, the perpetual revelation of the eternal God, then, then our love and our faith will bring us rest. There will be peace in trusting Him whom we never can trust and be put to shame. There will be peace in loving Him who is more than worthy of and able to repay the deep and perennial love of all hearts.

Self-surrender is peace. It is our wills that trouble us. Disturbance comes, not from without, but from within. When the will bows, when I say, 'Be it then as Thou wilt,' when in faith and love I cease to strive, to murmur, to rebel, to repine, and enter into His loving purposes, then there is peace.

Obedience is peace. To recognise a great will that is sovereign, and to bow myself to it, not because it is sovereign, but because it is sweet, and sweet because I love it, and love Him whose it is-that is peace. And then, whatever may be outward circumstances, there shall be 'peace subsisting at the heart of endless agitation'; and deep in my soul I may be tranquil, though all about me may be the hurly-burly of the storm.

The Christian peace is an armed peace, paradoxical as it appears; and according to the great word of the Apostle, is a sentry which garrisons the beleaguered heart and mind, surrounded by many foes, and keeps them in Christ Jesus.

'There is no peace, saith my God, to the wicked,' he is 'as a troubled sea which cannot rest, whose waters cast up mire and dirt'; but over the wildest commotion one Voice, low, gentle, omnipotent, says: 'Peace! be still!' and the heart quiets itself, though there may be a ground swell, and the weather clears. He is your peace, trust Him, love Him, and you cannot but possess the 'peace of God which passeth understanding.'

THE WIDE RANGE OF GOD'S GRACE

Ephesians 6:24

In turning to the great words which I have read as a text, I ask you to mark their width and their simplicity. They are wide; they follow a very comprehensive benediction, with which, so to speak, they are concentric. But they sweep a wider circle. The former verse says, 'Peace be to the brethren.' But beyond the brethren in these Asiatic churches {as a kind of circular letter to whom this epistle was probably sent} there rises before the mind of the Apostle a great multitude, in every nation, and they share in his love, and in the promise and the prayer of my text. Mark its simplicity: everything is brought down to its most general expression. All the qualifications for receiving the divine gift are gathered up in one-love. All the variety of the divine gifts is summed up in that one comprehensive expression-'grace.'

I. So then, note, first, the comprehensive designation of the recipients of grace.

They are 'all who love our Lord Jesus Christ in incorruption.' Little need be said explanatory of the force of this general expression. We usually find that where Scripture reduces the whole qualification for the reception of the divine gift, and the conditions which unite to Jesus Christ, to one, it is faith, not love, that is chosen. But here the Apostle takes the process at the second stage, and instead of emphasising the faith which is the first step, he dwells upon the love which is its uniform consequence. This love rests upon the faith in Jesus Christ our Lord.

Then note the solemn fulness of the designations of the object of this faith-born love. 'Jesus Christ our Lord'-the name of His humanity; the name of His office; the designation of His dominion. He is Jesus the Man. Jesus is the Christ, the Fulfiller of all prophecy; the flower of all previous revelation; the Anointed of God with the fulness of His Divine Spirit as Prophet, Priest, and King. Jesus Christ is the Lord-which, at the lowest, expresses sovereignty, and if regard be had to the Apostolic

314

usage, expresses something more, even participation in Deity. And it is this whole Christ, the Jesus, the Christ, the Lord; the love to whom, built upon the faith in Him in all these aspects and characteristics, constitutes the true unity of the true Church.

That Church is not built upon a creed, but it is built upon a whole Christ, and not a maimed one. And so we must have a love which answers to all those sides of that great revealed character, and is warm with human love to Jesus; and is trustful with confiding love to the Christ; and is lowly with obedient love to the Lord. And I venture to go a step further, and say,-and is devout with adoring love to the eternal Son of the Father. This is the Apostle's definition of what makes a Christian: Faith that grasps the whole Christ and love that therefore flows to Him. It binds all who possess it into one great unity. As against a spurious liberalism which calls them Christians who lay hold of a fragment of the one entire and perfect chrysolite, we must insist that a Christian is one who knows Jesus, who knows Christ, who knows the Lord, and who loves Him in all these aspects. Only we must remember, too, that many a time a man's heart outruns his creed, and that many a soul glows with truer, deeper, more saving devotion and trust to a Christ whom the intellect imperfectly apprehends, than are realised by unloving hearts that are associated with clearer heads. Orchids grow in rich men's greenhouses, fastened to a bit of stick, and they spread a fairer blossom that lasts longer than many a plant that is rooted in a more fertile soil. Let us be thankful for the blessed inconsistencies which knit some to the Christ who is more to them than they know.

There is also here laid down for us the great principle, as against all narrowness and all externalism, and all so-called ecclesiasticism, that to be joined to Jesus Christ is the one condition which brings a man into the blessed unity of the Church. Now it seems to me that, however they may be to be lamented on other grounds, and they are to be lamented on many, the existence of diverse Churches does not necessarily interfere with this deep-seated and central unity. There is a great deal said to-day about the reunion of Christendom, by which is meant the destruction of existing communions and the formation of a wider one. I do not believe, and I suppose you do not, that our existing ecclesiastical organisations are the final form of the Church of the living God. But let us remember that the two things are by no means contradictory, the belief in, and the realising of, the essential unity of the Church, and the existence of diverse communions. You will see on the side of many a Cumberland hill a great stretch of limestone with clefts a foot or two deep in it-there are flowers in the clefts, by the bye-but go down a couple of yards and the divisions have all disappeared, and the base-rock stretches continuously. The separations are superficial; the unity is fundamental. Do not let us play into the hands of people whose only notion of unity is that of a mechanical juxtaposition held together by some formula or orders; but let us recognise that the true unity is in the presence of Jesus Christ in the midst, and in the common grasp of Him by us all.

There is a well-known hymn which was originally intended as a High Church manifesto, which thrusts at us Nonconformists when it sings:

'We are not divided,
All one body we.'

And oddly enough, but significantly too, it has found its way into all our Nonconformist hymn-books, and we, 'the sects,' are singing it, with perhaps a nobler conception of what the oneness of the body, and the unity of the Church is, than the writer of the words had. 'We are not divided,' though we be organised apart. 'All one body we,' for we all partake of that one bread, and the unifying principle is a common love to the one Jesus Christ our Lord.

II. Mark the impartial sweep of the divine gifts.

My text is a benediction, or a prayer; but it is also a prophecy, or a statement, of the inevitable and uniform results of love to Jesus Christ. The grace will follow that love, necessarily and certainly, and the lovers will get the gift of God because their love has brought them into living contact with Jesus Christ; and His life will flow over into theirs. I need not remind you that the word 'grace' in Scripture means, first of all, the condescending love of God to inferiors, to sinners, to those who deserved something else; and, secondly, the whole fulness of blessing and gift that follow upon that love. And, says Paul, these great gifts from heaven, the one gift in which all are comprised, will surely follow the opening of the heart in love to Jesus Christ.

Ah, brethren! God's grace makes uncommonly short work of ecclesiastical distinctions. The great river flows through territories that upon men's maps are painted in different colours, and of which the inhabitants speak in different tongues. The Rhine laves the pine-trees of Switzerland, and the vines of Germany, and the willows of Holland; and God's grace flows through all places where the men that love Him do dwell. It rises, as it were, right over the barriers that they have built between each other. The little pools on the sea-shore are separate when the tide is out, but when it comes up it fills all the pot-holes that the pebbles have made, and unifies them in one great flashing, dancing mass; and so God's grace comes to all that love Him, and confirms their unity.

Surely that is the true test of a living Church. 'When Barnabas came, and saw the grace of God, he was glad.' It was not what he had expected, but he was open to conviction. The Church where he saw it had been very irregularly constituted; it had no orders and no sacraments, and had been set a-going by the spontaneous efforts of private Christians, and he came to look into the facts. He asked for nothing more when he saw that the converts had the life within them. And so we, with all our faults-and God forbid that I should seem to minimise these-with all our faults, we poor Nonconformists, left to the uncovenanted mercies, have our share of that gift of grace as truly, and, if our love be deeper, more abundantly, than the Churches that are blessed with orders and sacraments, and an 'unbroken historical continuity.' And when we are unchurched for our lack of these, let us fall back upon St. Augustine's 'Where Christ is, there the Church is'; and believe that to us, even to us also, the promise is fulfilled, 'Lo! I am with you always, even to the end of the world.'

III. Lastly, note the width to which our sympathies should go.

The Apostle sends out his desires and prayers so as to encircle the same area as the grace of God covers and as His love enfolds. And we are bound to do the same.

I am not going to talk about organic unity. The age for making new denominations is, I suppose, about over. I do not think that any sane man would contemplate starting a new Church nowadays. The rebound from the iron rigidity of a mechanical unity that took place at the Reformation naturally led to the multiplication of communities, each of which laid hold of something that to it seemed important. The folly of ecclesiastical rulers who insisted upon non-essentials lays the guilt of the schism at their doors, and not at the doors of the minority who could not, in conscience, accept that which never should have been insisted upon as a condition. But whilst we must all feel that power is lost, and much evil ensues from the isolation, such as it is, of the various Churches, yet we must remember that re-union is a slow process; that an atmosphere springs up round each body which is a very subtle, but none the less a very powerful, force, and that it will take a very, very long time to overcome the difficulties and to bring about any reconstruction on a large scale. But why should there be three Presbyterian Churches in Scotland, with the same creed, confessions of faith, and ecclesiastical constitution? Why should there be half a dozen Methodist bodies in England, of whom substantially the same thing may be said? Will it always pass the wit of man for Congregationalists and Baptists to be one body, without the sacrifice of conviction upon either side? Surely no! You young men may see these fair days; men like me can only hope that they will come and do a little, such as may be possible in a brief space, to help them on.

Putting aside, then, all these larger questions, I want, in a sentence or two, to insist with you upon the duty that lies on us all, and which every one of us may bear a share in discharging. There ought to be a far deeper consciousness of our fundamental unity. They talk a great deal about 'the rivalries of jarring sects.' I believe that is such an enormous exaggeration that it is an untruth. There is rivalry, but you know as well as I do that, shabby and shameful as it is, it is a kind of commercial rivalry between contiguous places of worship, be they chapels or churches, be they buildings belonging to the same or to different denominations. I, for my part, after a pretty long experience now, have seen so little of that said bitter rivalry between the Nonconformist sects, as sects, that to me it is all but non-existent. And I believe the most of us ministers, going about amongst the various communities, could say the same thing. But in the face of a cultivated England laughing at your creed of Jesus, the Christ, the Lord; and in the face of a strange and puerile recrudescence of sacerdotalism and sacramentarianism, which shoves a priest and a rite into the place where Christ should stand, it becomes us Nonconformists who believe that we know a more excellent way to stand shoulder to shoulder, and show that the unities that bind us are far more than the diversities that separate.

It becomes us, too, to further conjoint action in social matters. Thank God we are beginning to stir in that direction in Manchester-not before it was time. And I beseech you professing Christians, of all Evangelical communions, to help in bringing Christian motives and principles to bear on the discussion of social and municipal and economical conditions in this great city of ours.

And there surely ought to be more concert than we have had in aggressive work; that we should a little more take account of each other's action in regulating our own; and that we should not have the scandal, which we too often have allowed to exist, of overlapping one another in such a fashion as that rivalry and mere trade competition is almost inevitable.

These are very humble, prosaic suggestions, but they would go a long way, if they were observed, to sweeten our own tempers, and to make visible to the world our true unity. Let us all seek to widen our sympathies as widely as Christ's grace flows; to count none strangers whom He counts friends; to discipline ourselves to feel that we are girded with that electric chain which makes all who grasp it one, and sends the same keen thrill through them all. If a circle were a mile in diameter, and its circumference were dotted with many separate points, how much nearer each of these would be if it were moved inwards, on a straight line, closer to the centre, so as to make a circle a foot across. The nearer we come to the One Lord, in love, communion, and likeness, the nearer shall we be to one another.

Thank you for purchasing this kindle book. We truly value your custom. This book was put together to provide you with a collection of good commentary resources on the books of the Bible. It is our prayerful hope that God might use this work for His own glory and sovereign will.

We would be delighted to hear from you and received any messages, suggestions or corrections. You can contact us at:

expansivecommentarycollection@gmail.com

It is our promise that you email address will not be added to any mailing list or used for any purpose other than to communicate regarding this commentary series.

We trust that the Lord will continue to bless you as you live for Him.